REVISED and UPDATED

knitting
ganseys

Techniques and Patterns For
Traditional Sweaters

BETH BROWN-REINSEL

Interweave

www.fwcommunity.com

Interweave®
www.interweave.com

22 21 20 19 18   5 4 3 2 1
SRN: 18KN01
ISBN-13: 978-1-63250-616-0

EDITORIAL DIRECTOR
Kerry Bogert

EDITOR
Maya Elson

TECHNICAL EDITOR
Therese Chynoweth

ART DIRECTOR & COVER DESIGNER
Ashlee Wadeson

INTERIOR DESIGNER
Julie Levesque

ILLUSTRATOR
Therese Chynoweth

PHOTOGRAPHER
David Baum; George Boe

STYLIST
Grace Brumley

HAIR AND MAKEUP
Kalyn Slaughter

Let us knit A Great Peace together,

Each loving stitch filled with kindness and respect,

For the many colors and textures of all living beings.

contents

preface

Twenty-five years. How could that much time have passed since the first edition of this book was published? It almost seems like last week that I sat huddled next to the space heater in a cold, dark, windowless room, punching out chapter after chapter on my Apple IIe, my first computer. (Every four pages, I would have to save the document to the floppy disk because the computer only had 128kb of memory. That seems so laughable now, when my current Mac, which is getting on in years, has one terabyte of storage!)

As I look back on that time, I realize that this book was a door that I stepped through into a new life. Of course I didn't know that then. But this book paved the way for me to travel, to create and teach workshops, to design more garments . . . and my wandering, eager mind went from the British gansey to the Irish Aran, the Scottish Fair Isle jumper, and on to Scandinavia. I gathered the courage to travel to Sweden, Denmark, and Norway, and later many other countries, searching through museums, because I had lost my heart to traditional knitting.

The further I travel on this knitting road, the more I want to know about all traditional knitting and those who practice it. The best part is meeting so many knitters, from all walks of life around the world, who share my passion. I have been invited to teach all over the United States and Canada and in England, Scotland, New Zealand, Iceland, and Sweden, on cruises, and via the Internet. I am still amazed!

The gansey tradition encompasses so many aspects of life: the practicality of clothing your family, the financial aspects of knitting for pay, the broader economic context of supporting fishing industry workers, the social history of knitters who relied on knitting for comfort and pleasure in the off hours after a hard day's work. That era has passed, and yet, every day I teach I see aspects of this tradition continuing: the bonding between knitters and the creative passion to knit something warm and beautiful for oneself or a loved one.

And now, full circle, here is my updated gansey book. It is bigger and brighter than before, but still full of reverence for the tradition of clothing those you love. That there is still interest in my book is a testament to the enduring qualities of the humble gansey sweater itself.

I have been privileged to meet thousands of knitters on this path. My students inspire me with their enthusiasm and determination. They, along with my many talented colleagues, have enriched my life immeasurably. The first edition of this book started it all for me. I am so blessed to have experienced this and so much more. I wish the same for you, dear knitter—a passionate experience between you, your yarn, and your needles.

The Wool-life is good.

— *Beth*

introduction

Gansey sweaters, also known as guernseys, developed in nineteenth-century England as hard-wearing garments for hardworking fishermen. Characterized by dense, dark yarns; rich knit/purl patterns; dropped shoulders; and underarm gussets that allow the wearer additional freedom of movement, these simple square garments provide the modern knitter with a template for a wide variety of classic, comfortable designs.

Several books have been written about the history of ganseys, but while many of the construction techniques are mentioned or illustrated, they are not always presented in enough detail for knitters to reproduce. This book is my attempt to explain how to accomplish these techniques successfully and create a variety of gansey garments.

The structure of this book is based on my knitting workshops, in which I teach knitters step-by-step how to create a gansey sweater in miniature. I have always found projects less intimidating if I make them on a small scale first, and this sampler is the perfect tool for learning. It contains many of the traditional gansey techniques, such as the Channel Island Cast-on and the neck and underarm gussets. As my students knit, they learn the principles of gansey construction and quickly see these principles in practice before tackling a full-size garment.

Each chapter presents the step-by-step particulars of constructing the sampler, offers ideas for design and technique variations, and explains the calculations and considerations to be made when working full-size. Throughout, step-by-step photographs, sidebars, and formulas help you carefully and systematically build a solid foundation of skills. In Chapter 11, you'll find guidelines for designing your own gansey sweaters along with blank design worksheets. I also included charts and pattern instructions for nine of my own designs that you can try yourself or borrow ideas from.

I've written this book assuming that you have a basic knowledge of knitting in the round. This includes casting onto a circular needle, joining stitches into a round, and working stockinette stitch, garter stitch, and ribbing in the round, as well as working these stitch patterns flat (back and forth).

I have taught knitting classes and workshops for many years. If I've learned anything from all that experience, it is that my way is one way, not the only way. I encourage you to use what you learn here as a springboard for your own creativity. My hope is that these techniques will find their way into your own garments and that you'll be encouraged to experiment with them and improve upon them. Even within its traditional framework, the gansey is a fluid style, flexible and adaptable. I hope you will develop your own interpretation of this wonderful form. The possibilities are infinite!

CHAPTER ONE
what is a gansey?

Ganseys are wonderfully varied and thoughtfully constructed sweaters that originated in the fishing villages along the coasts of England, Scotland, and Cornwall in the nineteenth century. Designed as a working garment for fishermen, ganseys were traditionally seamless and knitted in the round with an overall simple square shape and dropped shoulders. Their most distinctive feature was the gusset that eliminated stress in the underarm area, giving the wearer freedom of movement and prolonging the life of the garment. Fishermen's wives, mothers, sisters, and daughters most often knit them (although some men knitted them as well), using a highly twisted five-ply dark navy blue yarn, known as "seaman's iron." (This yarn was about the weight of American sport weight and is still available today.) With a typical gauge of 7 to 9 stitches per inch (2.5 cm), the resulting dense fabric was impervious to wind and cold and sharply defined the rich knit/purl pattern combinations that usually adorned the chest and upper arms. Hard-wearing, warm even when wet, and a comfortable fit (by virtue of underarm gussets and the give of the knitted fabric), ganseys were perfectly suited to the fishermen's lifestyle.

Although the gansey's first appearance cannot be dated precisely, Bishop Richard Rutt notes in A *History of Hand Knitting* (1987) that the earliest printed reference to a "guernsey frock" occurred in 1832. Ganseys (or guernseys) took their name from the knitted fabric that has been called guernsey or jersey since the sixteenth century, when Queen Elizabeth I set up knitting guilds on the Channel Islands for the production of hosiery. The stockinette stocking fabric gradually became synonymous with the areas in which it was produced—the islands of Guernsey and Jersey. As Rutt notes, "Seaman's guernseys and jerseys were not so called because they came from the Channel

Islands, but because their fabric had long been called guernsey or jersey before seamen took to wearing them." Rae Compton, author of *The Compete Book of Traditional Guernsey and Jersey Knitting* (1985), writes that "throughout the British Isles the fisherman's garment is known in some places as a guernsey, in others as a gansey, and in others it has always been and still is a jersey." The garments have also been known as knit-frocks, fisher shirts, and fisher-ganseys.

b

a. In *Traditional Knitting* (1984) Michael Pearson observed, "Many of the old pictures ... of women standing knitting as they wait at the port for their husbands and brothers—may look quite charming; in reality, however, they are classic documents to the exploitation of people desperate to increase inadequate and irregular incomes." (Photo courtesy of the Sutcliffe Gallery; B16)

b. Several men at the pier wearing ganseys: "Whitby Fisher People." (Photo courtesy of the Sutcliffe Gallery; 17-32)

c. In the mid- to late-nineteenth century, gansey sweater shapes and styles spread throughout Great Britain and the Netherlands. Specific gansey textural patterns were found by researchers in the areas noted here.

GANSEY OR GUERNSEY?

In recent years some authors have made distinctions between ganseys and guernseys. Ganseys, it seems, were tight-fitting patterned garments that reached to the waist and were worn in the northern areas of the United Kingdom, while guernseys were long, looser, and plain, hailing from the southern parts, such as the Channel Islands. For the purposes of this book, I will make no distinctions between the two, using "gansey" and "guernsey" interchangeably, as my focus is garment construction. Both types had underarm gussets and many other shared attributes, according to the ninteenth-century photographs I have seen from different areas of Scotland, Cornwall, and England.

The finest ganseys were worn as Sunday best or for special occasions such as being photographed.
(Photo courtesy of Wick Society, Johnston Collection)

The early ganseys were most likely undergarments. Bishop Rutt suggests that as men worked, they would remove their outer clothing, revealing their undergarments, and so knitters took more care in constructing these garments. As patterning crept in and construction techniques became more sophisticated, these undershirts became handsome outershirts, worn with pride. The finest ganseys were worn as Sunday best and to weddings and other important occasions, including the event of being photographed.

As the fishing boats traveled from port to port, the gansey style spread. According to Bishop Rutt, "From the Hebrides clockwise round Scotland, past Northumbria and East Anglia to Cornwall, British seamen's jerseys are essentially the same." Even Holland was influenced by these practical, durable garments, as explained in Henriette van der Klift-Tellegen's *Knitting from the Netherlands* (1985). The fisherman sweaters first appeared in Holland in the 1860s, when trade routes were reestablished with Britain and other countries after an economic boycott of France earlier in the nineteenth century.

In fact, many people, not just fishermen, wore ganseys. Even the fisher-lassies who followed the boats to clean the fish, and who knitted the sweaters during their off-time, would knit variations for themselves.

Indeed it is fortunate that many old photographs of ganseys still exist. From 1850 to 1860, the photographer Lewis Harding documented the faces and the garments of many of the fishermen of Polperro, Cornwall. Frank M. Sutcliffe, a renowned nineteenth-century photographer, documented the fisher way of life in the area of Whitby in England. Researchers have carefully studied these photographs to record the construction techniques and chart the wide variety of sweater patterning. As Elizabeth Lovick writes in *A Gansey Workbook* (2009) "Although it is not true that each village had its own designs, certain types of stitch pattern are found in certain areas of the coast. The ways of placing pattern can also be indicative of different parts of the UK."

the yarns

Guernsey yarns developed at the end of the Industrial Revolution and were manufactured as "worsted" yarns, a term that refers to the way in which the fibers are prepared prior to spinning as well as the way in which the yarns are spun. This type of yarn is less common today.

To begin the yarn-making process, first the wool is scoured (washed and fluff-dried) to remove the oily lanolin that occurs naturally in sheep's wool. Wool with lanolin in it does not always dye evenly, so "oiled yarns" are usually not dyed and remain their natural shade. The wool then either goes through the carder (similar to using a brush on your hair) or is combed (just like using a comb on your hair). These processes align the fibers and remove some of the vegetation that may be in the wool; they are essential to creating smooth, consistent yarn. Ultimately, the wool is spun into a single-ply yarn, either perpendicular to the alignment of the fibers (woolen-spun) or parallel to the alignment of the fibers (worsted-spun).

Perhaps you can imagine how fibers drawn into a spinning machine at a perpendicular angle to their alignment fold on themselves. This folding creates air pockets among the fibers, which trap heat and make woolen-spun yarn warm and lofty. Now, think of fibers that are aligned and drawn out in a parallel direction to each other. The result is a very strong, dense worsted-spun yarn.

The manufacture of Guernsey yarns includes more steps. The individual yarns are highly twisted, then five single yarns are plied together in the opposite direction, again in a high twist. It is this final twist, and the number of plies, that makes the yarns so durable and the patterns show up so well, for the light bounces off the yarn at more angles (due to more plies), creating complex highlights, midtones, and shadows.

a

a. Worsted-spun yarns (left), well suited for ganseys, are dense and smooth, while woolen-spun yarns (right) are lofty.

b. Knitting wires: The gansey knitters sometimes used curved needles such as these. *(Photo courtesy of Dales Countryside Museum)*

c. A knitting belt, also known as a whisk, or whiska. *(Photo courtesy of the Moray Firth Gansey Project)*

d. These tools, some quite elaborately carved, aided the knitters by stabilizing the needles. This is a beautiful example of the goose-wing style of knitting stick. It was tucked into the knitter's waistband or held at the waist by a tape. *(Photo courtesy of Dales Countryside Museum)*

e. In Scotland, the use of the knitting belt was well established for knitting ganseys as well as other items, while in the Dales and other areas of England, the use of the knitting stick was more prevalent. *(Photo courtesy of Dales Countryside Museum)*

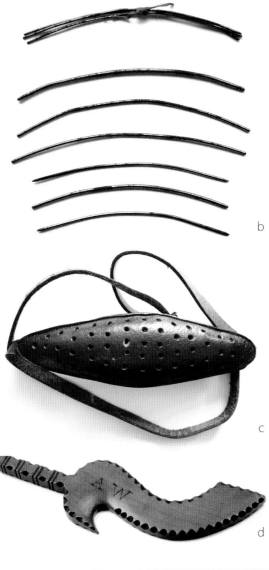

b

c

d

e

tools of the trade

The women who knitted the ganseys used "wires," lengths of steel wire whose ends had been ground to points on a stone or doorstep. Even bicycle spokes were used for needles at times. Some used four or more double-pointed needles comparable in size to US 1 and 2 (2.25 and 2.75 mm). To increase knitting speed, many used wooden knitting sticks, sometimes elaborately carved, which were secured to a belt or a skirt waistband or tied with a woven tape. With one needle held stationary in the knitting stick, the weight of the knitting was supported and the knitter's hands were free to work more quickly. (Some production knitters were purportedly clocked at 200 stitches per minute and could knit a gansey in less than a week.)

GANSEY KNITTERS

During the mid-nineteenth century, production knitting offered employment to women whose husbands had gone to sea, leaving them with the family's financial burdens for extended periods. Many women worked through an agent who visited them regularly to pick up the finished goods, pay them for their work, and deliver more yarn. Others organized among themselves, making trips on foot to deliver their ganseys to shops several miles away. The production of hand-knit ganseys appears to have ended in the 1930s, although machine-knitted ganseys are still produced by Le Tricoteur on the Isle of Guernsey (see Sources and Supplies, page 186).

Few knitters still invest their time and talents to create authentic ganseys by hand. Fortunately, well-worn garments that had been lovingly packed away in trunks are now finding their way to museums. These beautifully knitted garments not only present rich history and tradition, but also provide a standard of excellence and source of inspiration for modern knitters.

form and construction

Ganseys are close-fitted, squarish garments with dropped shoulders. The bottom edge of earlier ganseys hung straight but later versions were knitted with ribbing. The neckline traditionally was unshaped, but shaping (or rounding of the neck by binding off and decreasing) appeared on some sweaters.

These sweaters are knitted in the round from the bottom edge up to the armholes and have no seams. After the gussets are knitted to their midpoints, the body is then split in two, and the front and back are worked separately back and forth to the shoulders. The front and back shoulders are then joined, sometimes bridged by an extra piece of fabric. The sleeve stitches are picked up around the armhole and knitted down to the cuff. The gussets are completed as the sleeves are knitted. Stitches for the neck are then picked up and finished in the chosen neckband style.

Within the prescribed parameters of gansey form and construction, many different techniques were used to create one-of-a-kind garments. For example, there are both utilitarian and decorative cast-ons, one using multiple strands of yarn for added strength and another using several strands for embellishment. Welting (garter-stitch bands) at the bottom edge was common in earlier ganseys, but later gave way to ribbing, which yields a snugger fit. The welts were either knitted as a continuous band or split at the sides.

Seam stitches—a column of purls or a decorative pattern—give the sweater the appearance of having been knitted in pieces and sewn together. The seam stitches also serve as markers for the beginning and midpoint of each round. These seams grow out of the bottom ribbing, continue up the side, flow around each side of the underarm gusset, come together again at the sleeve, and continue out the sleeve to the cuff.

Above the welt is the plain area. Plain knitting, in British terminology, refers to stockinette stitch, or an all-knit surface. The length of this section might vary from 1–12" (2.5–30.5 cm), ending at or before the armhole. Plain knitting helps balance the design and can help to evenly arrange repeating pattern motifs.

The initials of the intended wearer were often worked in a garter stitch or purl pattern in the lower part of the plain area near one of the seam stitches. At the top of the plain area, a ridge of texture, usually about 1" (2.5 cm) long, is worked in either garter or seed stitch, or a contrasting pattern. I call this the definition ridge because it defines where the patterning begins.

The patterning, richly varied combinations of knit and purl stitches, begins above the definition ridge. Sometimes the pattern incorporates a few simple cables.

The diamond-shaped underarm gusset allows freedom of movement by adding extra fabric to the underarm area. The underarm in any fitted garment is a point of great stress. Expanding that area by knitting in a gusset reduces the stress, thereby increasing the life of the garment.

When half the gusset has been worked, the armhole begins, and the knitting no longer continues in the round. The front stitches are placed on a holder and the back is worked flat (back and forth) to the shoulder.

The shoulders are joined in a variety of ways. Grafting and the knitted bind-off were often used traditionally, but the most spectacular technique is the perpendicular shoulder join, in which a shoulder strap is worked from the neck to the armhole along the shoulder line and simultaneously joins the front to the back.

After the body is completed, stitches are picked up around the armhole for the sleeve, which is worked in the round. The gusset is decreased as the sleeve is knitted, shaped to the cuff, and bound off. The amount of patterning on the sleeve varies.

The neck stitches are picked up, knitted to the desired length, and bound off. Neckband styles varied from locale to locale. They included ribbing, turtlenecks with buttons and buttonholes, rolled neckbands, and stockinette-stitch bands that ended in welting. Neckline gussets were sometimes worked within the shoulder strap or on the shoulder line to widen the neck or in the neckband to narrow it to keep out the cold.

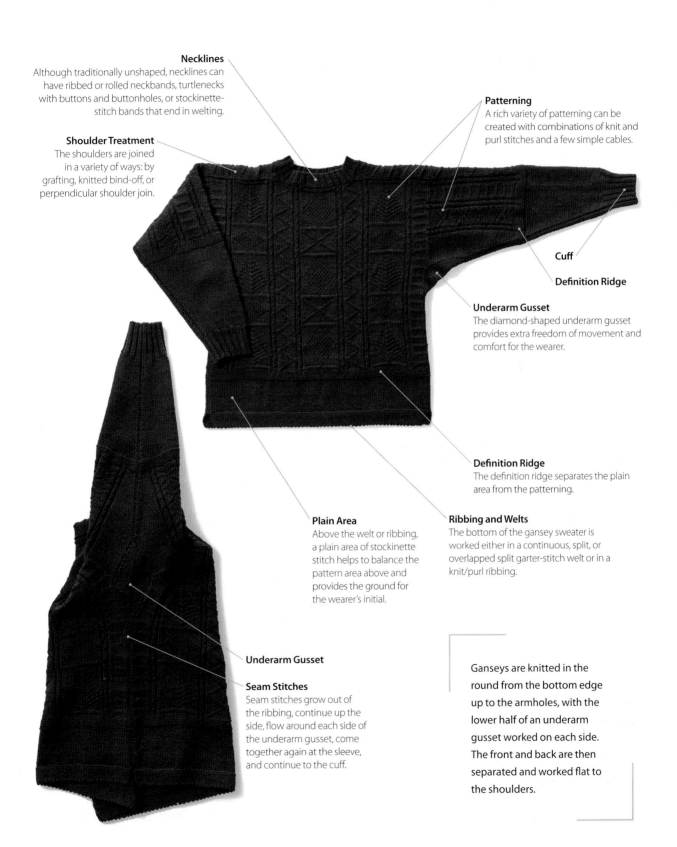

Necklines
Although traditionally unshaped, necklines can have ribbed or rolled neckbands, turtlenecks with buttons and buttonholes, or stockinette-stitch bands that end in welting.

Patterning
A rich variety of patterning can be created with combinations of knit and purl stitches and a few simple cables.

Shoulder Treatment
The shoulders are joined in a variety of ways: by grafting, knitted bind-off, or perpendicular shoulder join.

Cuff

Definition Ridge

Underarm Gusset
The diamond-shaped underarm gusset provides extra freedom of movement and comfort for the wearer.

Definition Ridge
The definition ridge separates the plain area from the patterning.

Plain Area
Above the welt or ribbing, a plain area of stockinette stitch helps to balance the pattern area above and provides the ground for the wearer's initial.

Ribbing and Welts
The bottom of the gansey sweater is worked either in a continuous, split, or overlapped split garter-stitch welt or in a knit/purl ribbing.

Underarm Gusset

Seam Stitches
Seam stitches grow out of the ribbing, continue up the side, flow around each side of the underarm gusset, come together again at the sleeve, and continue to the cuff.

Ganseys are knitted in the round from the bottom edge up to the armholes, with the lower half of an underarm gusset worked on each side. The front and back are then separated and worked flat to the shoulders.

CHAPTER 2
getting started and casting on

As explained in the Introduction, the chapters in this book are arranged in the logical sequence of knitting a sample garment:

- casting on
- working the welt or ribbing
- increasing for the body
- knitting the plain area
- adding the initials
- planning and working patterning
- shaping the gusset
- dividing body to work front and back flat
- joining the shoulders
- knitting the sleeves
- finishing the neckline

Each step of traditional gansey construction offers several options. (Knitters then, as now, didn't like to be tied down to a set formula.) In each chapter, I first introduce the principles of a technique, then present directions for knitting that technique on the sampler. I also discuss options and variations of those techniques that you can use for your own designs, as well as adjustments needed for working full-size. (The project instructions in Chapter 12 include additional design-variation explanations.)

Sampler instructions throughout are for a miniature gansey 8" (20.5 cm) long that incorporates a number of traditional techniques:

- the Channel Island Cast-on
- split and overlapped garter welts
- mock seams of two purl stitches
- an initial in the plain area
- a garter-stitch definition ridge
- vertical patterning
- underarm gussets
- an unshaped neckline
- the perpendicular shoulder join
- neck gussets
- a stockinette-stitch neckband that ends in welting

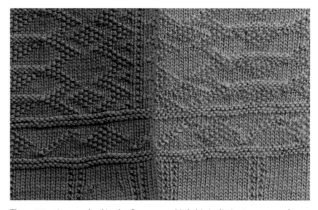

The patterning worked in the fuzzy yarn (right) is indistinct compared to the crisp knits and purls of the knitted fabric on the left.

YARN

You may use sport-, DK- or worsted-weight yarn for your gansey sweaters. A smooth solid-colored yarn will ensure that your patterning stands out.

The traditional gansey yarns, produced in commercial spinning mills, were highly twisted five-ply yarns that made the garment's patterning very visible despite the dark navy blue color. One of the original manufacturers of this yarn was Richard Poppleton of Yorkshire, whose label once stated that his yarn had been "used by Guernsey knitters since 1847." Though the label has changed to "Wendy Guernsey yarn," the yarn is still spun in the same mill (see Sources and Supplies, page 186). Knitting with traditional yarns can be a joy and a challenge,

Each of the traditional gansey cast-ons yields a different finished effect. From top to bottom: Multi-Strand Cast-on, Knotted Cast-on, Long-Tail Cast-on, Channel Island Cast-on.

although some find it difficult to work with and maintain a gauge of 7 to 9 stitches per inch (2.5 cm).

THE GANSEY CAST-ONS

Ganseys are worked from the bottom up, so the first consideration is which cast-on method to use. The bottom edge of any garment is subject to abrasion and wear, and special cast-ons were devised to prevent the gansey from fraying, thus prolonging its life.

There are three traditional gansey cast-ons. The Knotted Cast-on shown on page 20, is a blend of function and embellishment.

The Multi-Strand Cast-on (page 22) is purely utilitarian; strength and durability are its key characteristics. The Channel Island Cast-on (page 19) is durable, elastic, and decorative and is the one you'll use for the sampler.

The Channel Island Cast-on is made up of pairs of stitches with a bead of doubled yarn between them. It's lovely with either a welt or ribbing, though it is very subtle in the latter case. The beads along the bottom edge of the garment accentuate, by contrast, the horizontal lines of a garter welt. If you use this cast-on with ribbing, however, take care to center the knit stitches over the bead, or the bead will recede into the fabric along with the purl stitches.

the sampler

YARN

About 4 oz (113.4 g) of worsted-weight wool yarn. (We used Brown Sheep Nature Spun [100% wool; 224 yds (244 m)/3½ oz (100 g)]: Natural.)

NEEDLES

US 5 (3.75 mm) and US 7 (4.5 mm) double-pointed (dpn)

US 7 (4.5 mm) 16" (40.5 cm) circular (cir)

Adjust needle size to achieve approximate gauge.

GAUGE

About 4½ to 5 sts per inch (2.5 cm).
Gauge is not critical for the sampler.

NOTIONS

Stitch markers; stitch holders; a tape measure; scrap pieces of a contrasting color of yarn.

CAST ON

Begin by breaking off two 24" (61 cm) pieces of yarn from your ball. These yarns will form the bead at the bottom of the CO. (In a full-size garment, you would use the ends from 3 different balls of yarn.)

Joining your 2 pieces of yarn with 1 end from your ball, make a slipknot with all 3 strands as one. (The yarn from the ball will create the sts on your needle.) The slipknot is very bulky and will not be counted as a st. Once the welts are knitted, you can pull out the slipknot.

CO 34 sts using the Channel Island Cast-on method. This CO makes 2 sts on the needle at a time, so you will work the CO 17 times to create 34 sts. You can use either the Continental or English method.

The sampler instructions continue on page 25.

By knitting the sampler gansey, shown here, you'll learn many of the traditional techniques and will be ready to design and knit full-size garments.

channel island cast-on

Note: This cast-on creates two stitches at a time. **To begin either method,** first make a slipknot with three strands of yarn held together, with the tail ends about 4" (10 cm) long. Place the loop on a double-pointed needle.

CONTINENTAL METHOD

*Wrap the 2 lengths of yarn around your left thumb counter-clockwise so that they lie in front of your thumb as they connect to the needle (opposite of the way the yarn is held for the Long-Tail Cast-on, page 21). Hold the single strand that is connected to the ball over your left index finger. Hold the needle in your right hand (fig. 1).

Bring the needle over, behind, and under the single strand that is on your left index finger, as you would for a yo. This will form the first st.

Insert the needle kwise into the 2 double loops on the thumb to form the bead (fig. 2).

Pick up the single strand again, like a yo, for the second st (fig. 3) and pull the new stitch through the loops on the thumb (fig. 4). Tighten all 3 yarns evenly. Rep from *.

ENGLISH METHOD

*Wrap the 2 lengths of yarn around your left thumb counterclockwise so that they lie in front of your thumb as they connect to the needle (opposite of the way the yarn is held for the Long-Tail Cast-on, page 21).

Holding the single strand that is connected to the ball in your right hand, along with the needle, bring it in front of and over the needle as for a yo. This will form the first st after the slipknot (fig. 1).

Insert the needle kwise into the 2 loops on the thumb to form the bead (fig. 2).

Throw the single yarn over as for a yo (this is the second stitch) (fig. 3), pull the new stitch through theloops on the thumb, tighten all 3 yarns evenly (fig. 4). Rep from *.

figure 1

figure 2

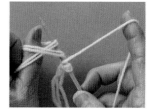

figure 1

figure 2

figure 3

figure 4

figure 3

figure 4

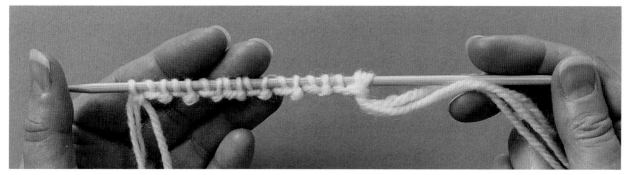

The completed cast-on.

design variations

THE KNOTTED CAST-ON

This cast-on is decorative as well as functional; it looks great with a garter welt, but is poorly suited to ribbing. It comprises little knots along the base of the cast-on and is formed by casting on two stitches, then binding off one stitch. The bound off stitches add extra bulk that make this cast-on extra durable. Using needles as many as three to four sizes smaller than the body needle size will ensure the best result with this cast-on. It is essential to tighten the knot firmly to avoid a wavy edge with poorly-defined knots.

This cast-on begins with either a Long-Tail Cast-on or a Knitted Cast-on (below), but the technique you choose will affect the shape of the resulting knot. The knot is more prominent if you begin with the Knitted Cast-on and more compact if you use the Long-Tail Cast-on.

*Using either the Knitted Cast-on or the Long-Tail Cast-on, CO 2 sts (fig. 1). Pass the first st over the second, as you would for binding off (fig. 2). Repeat from * until you have the desired number of sts. Pull both yarns firmly after each bind-off to tension the knot—it will slip forward into place.

figure 1

figure 2

TIP

Even tensioning is tricky and comes with practice. Be patient.

knitted cast-on

Create a slipknot. *Insert your right-hand needle kwise into the st (fig. 1). Throw (English) or pick (Continental) the yarn as you would to form a knit st, but leave the old st on the left-hand needle (fig. 2). Sl the new st on your right-hand needle back onto your left-hand needle pwise (fig. 3). Repeat from * for the desired number of st.

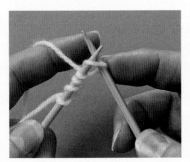

figure 1

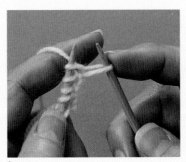

figure 2

figure 3

long-tail cast-on: two methods

CONTINENTAL METHOD

Make a slipknot, allowing 1" (2.5 cm) length of the tail per cast-on st, and place it on your needle. Hold the needle in your right hand.

With your left hand, hold one tail over your thumb and the working yarn (the strand connected to the ball) over your index finger, so that both yarns are on the outsides of your fingers. Use your other three fingers to hold the 2 strands under tension (fig. 1).

*Insert your needle knitwise into the loop wrapped around your thumb (fig. 2). Reach with your needle back to the yarn held by your index finger and go over, behind, and under the yarn (fig. 3).

Bring the yarn forward through the loop on your thumb (fig. 4).

Drop the loop off the thumb, pull both yarns taut (fig. 5). Insert your thumb and index finger in between the 2 yarns as before, and repeat from * for the desired number of sts.

ENGLISH METHOD

Make a slipknot, allowing 1" (2.5 cm) length of the tail per cast-on st, and place it on your needle. Hold the needle in your right hand along with the strand of yarn coming from the ball (fig. 1).

With your left hand and the other strand of yarn, *form a loop with your thumb by placing your thumb on top of the yarn and bringing your thumb down, then forward toward your body. Insert the needle into the loop knit-wise without removing your thumb (fig. 2).

Throw the right-hand yarn (fig. 3) and pull the loop on your thumb up over the top of the needle (fig. 4).

Withdraw your thumb and adjust the tension on the yarns (fig. 5). Repeat from * for the desired number of sts.

figure 1

figure 1

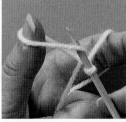

figure 2

figure 3

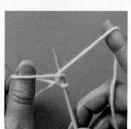

figure 2

figure 3

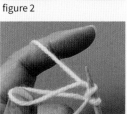

figure 4

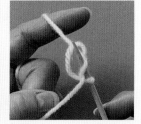

figure 5

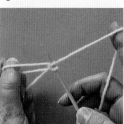

figure 4

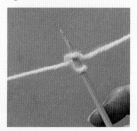

figure 5

THE MULTISTRAND CAST-ON

In reading old gansey patterns, I found that many would instruct the knitter to "cast on in double yarn." This was a straightforward method for strengthening the lower garment edge by forming a prominent bottom ridge. The knitter would use two strands of yarn as one to cast on the stitches with the long-tail method (essentially using four strands), then work the first several rows or rounds of the ribbing with two strands. As a result the garment edge is very strong and durable, yet elastic. I have had the best results using this cast-on with traditional gansey yarn.

The Multistrand Cast-on was created specifically for ribbing, rather than garter-stitch welts. It can be worked on needles three to four

sizes smaller than those used for the body for the first part of the ribbing to keep the resulting stitches in scale. Use needles two sizes smaller for the rest of the ribbing, then change to the size needed for the body. However, some knitters used only one size needle for this technique.

Cast on using the Long-Tail method (see page 21) with 2 strands of yarn doubled. Join circularly and drop 2 strands to work 4–6 rounds with the other 2 yarns. Then drop 1 strand and work the remainder of the ribbing and garment with 1 strand. If you have a lot of stitches to cast on, make a slipknot of the ends of 4 balls allowing for short tails. (See Jorn's Gansey, page 130.)

MULTISTRAND RIBBED EDGE

With doubled yarn, make a slipknot. Holding 2 strands over your thumb and 2 over your index finger, CO with all 4 strands (fig. 1). Drop 2 strands and work 4–6 rows of ribbing with the remaining 2 strands (fig. 2). Drop 1 strand and work the remainder of ribbing and garment with 1 strand (fig. 3).

figure 1

figure 2

figure 3

working full-size

Before you begin a full-size sweater, you must knit a test swatch to determine your stitch and row gauge, so the final sweater will match the desired dimensions of the pattern. If you are designing a garment, the gauge will tell you how many stitches to cast on (and much more). At a minimum you will need to knit a 4" × 4" (10 × 10 cm) swatch to gather the measurements you need, although the larger the swatch, the more accurate the measurements. For traditional ganseys without cable patterning, a stockinette swatch will do. If the fabric seems too stiff, knit another swatch on larger needles. If it's too loose or limp, drop down a needle size or two.

Traditional gansey yarn relaxes and becomes a great deal more supple after blocking. All knitting benefits from being blocked once it is finished. Therefore, I suggest that you measure your chosen swatch before and after you block it. You will use the measurements

taken from the unblocked fabric to check your gauge while knitting your garment. The gauge of the blocked swatch will reveal the dimensions of the finished garment and is the one you need to match to the gauge given on whatever pattern you are knitting. In addition, a blocked swatch gives you a better idea of the hand and drape of the fabric that your chosen yarn will create.

I try to be as precise as I can about fractions of stitches, but at a tight gauge such as 9 stitches per inch (2.5 cm), ¼ stitch is less significant than at 4 stitches per inch (2.5 cm). I work with gauges in whole numbers whenever possible and check the gauge every 2" (5 cm) as I am knitting. My goal is consistency, and I don't hesitate to change needle sizes while knitting, or to rip back if needed, to keep in gauge.

THE PERCENTAGE METHOD

The percentage method, originated by Elizabeth Zimmermann and further explored by Priscilla Gibson-Roberts, is a helpful tool for determining a gansey's dimensions. All calculations are based on one measurement: the chest plus ease. (Ease is the extra amount of fabric created to make the garment fit comfortably, usually 2–4" [5–10 cm]).

Let's suppose your stitch gauge is 4 stitches per inch (2.5 cm) and you want to knit a sweater measuring 42" (106.5 cm) around the fullest part of the chest, including ease. Multiply the chest measurement including the ease by the number of stitches per inch to get the number of body stitches:

42" × 4 sts/in. = 168 sts

This measurement, which is the circumference of the sweater, can be expressed as 100 percent. From this calculation, you can determine the number of stitches you need to cast on. Ribbings that hug the body use 90 percent of the total body stitches:

168 × .90 = 151.2 sts

Round this figure to the nearest whole number, according to the repeat of your ribbing pattern.

The old ganseys varied greatly in the ratio of ribbing stitches to body stitches. Whereas in some modern garments, the ratio of ribbing to body stitches is 90 percent, many old gansey ribbings had the same number of stitches as the body (100 percent). In these cases, only the fabric structure of the ribbing served to pull the garment bottom in. Working on a smaller needle would also have pulled the ribbing in, but often only one size of needle was used for the entire garment. At the other end of the spectrum, some ganseys had as much as a 22 percent increase from the ribbing stitches to the body. The knitters wisely spread out this substantial increase over six to eight rounds, rather than increasing all at once in the first round above the ribbing.

Many knitters today prefer ribbing that does not pull in. In that case, drop down one needle size for the ribbing and cast on the same number of stitches as the body; no increasing is necessary once the ribbing is done. For a sharply pulled-in ribbing, drop down two to three needle sizes for the ribbing and cast on 90 percent of the total body stitches.

CHAPTER 3
ribbing and welts

According to *Mary Thomas's Knitting Book* (1972), ribs are "made by alternating the two stitches, knit and purl, keeping each vertically above its kind," whereas welts "consist of horizontal ridges running across the width of the fabric, and are formed by alternating knit and purl rows, either singly or in groups." While this is the technical distinction, the word "welt" has come to mean the part at the bottom of the gansey, whether ribbed or welted. I use the terms "ribbing" or "garter welts."

The bottom edges of the old ganseys were quite varied. Ribbings of 1 × 1 (knit 1, purl 1) or 2 × 2 (knit 2, purl 2) range from 2–4½" (5 to 11.5 cm) long, and garter welts might be as long as 2½" (6.5 cm).

GARTER WELTS

Garter welts cause the garment to hang straight down rather than hug the body, which decreases the stress and wear at the bottom of the sweater. They may be continuous, split, or overlapped. (The sampler has a split and overlapped garter welt.) Garter stitch tends to spread out more than stockinette stitch, whereas ribbing pulls in, so fewer stitches can be cast on than are needed for the main body. Don't be alarmed if the welts flip up while knitting a gansey. This is common and once blocked, the welts will behave and hang straight.

To knit a continuous (circular) garter welt, simply cast on 90 to 96 percent of the total number of body stitches, join them (being careful not to twist them), and alternate rounds of knit and purl for the desired length.

You can alternatively knit two garter welts flat (one for the front and one for the back) and then join them, leaving a "split" at the sides of the garment where the joining occurred. This treatment allows more give at the bottom of the sweater and therefore more freedom of movement. To take the split style a step further, the welts are overlapped a few stitches to reinforce the stress point where they are joined, as in the sampler. (The sampler overlap is only two stitches wide, whereas in a full-size garment, a three-stitch overlap looks more substantial.) Split garter welts are knitted on every row.

Sample of finished overlapped split garter welts on a full-sized gansey.

the sampler

GARTER WELTS

Continued from page 18.

Row 1: K3, k2tog, knit to end of row—33 sts.

From the CO sts, continue to work back and forth on 2 dpns in garter st (knit every row) for 8 more rows. Break the yarn and set the welt aside. Knit a second welt in the same manner, but do not break the yarn when finished.

Lay the 2 completed welts on a flat surface in front of you. Place the second welt, still connected to the ball of yarn, on the left, with the yarn coming off the right-hand side of the welt. The RS of the welts (the side with 5 purl ridges) should be facing up and needles oriented point to point (fig. 1). (The welts have an odd number of rows, so that it is easy to identify the RS of the work and the cast-on.)

With a third dpn, sl the 2 end sts on the left side of the right-hand welt to a third dpn (fig. 2). Hold this third needle behind the 2 end sts on the right-hand side of the left-hand welt.

Overlap the end sts (with the left-hand welt in front) by using your cir needle to p2tog (one from each needle) twice (fig. 3). (*Note: When p2tog from two needles, insert your right needle tip into the st purlwise on the back needle first, then into the st on the front needle.*)

K29. Overlapping again (but this time with the needle holding 2 sts on it in front), p2tog twice (fig. 4).

K29, pm. The front and back of the sweater are now joined with the front welt overlapping the back at the side "seams." The 2 purl sts created at each side when the welts were overlapped become the seam sts and are maintained throughout the rest of the garment—62 sts.

The sampler instructions continue on page 30.

figure 1

figure 2

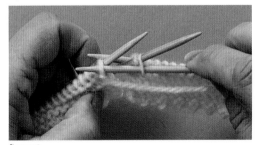

figure 3

figure 4

design variations

When creating a garter welt, you don't need to be limited to the American definition of garter stitch (knitting every row if working flat, alternating single rounds of stockinette [knitting] and reverse stockinette [purling] when working in the round). Try working two rounds each of stockinette and reverse stockinette or experiment with an uneven garter stitch: two stockinette, three reverse stockinette; or four stockinette, two reverse stockinette. A welt can even be worked in seed stitch.

The bottom edges of ganseys are treated as either ribbing or welts. From top to bottom: 2 × 2 ribbing, overlapped split garter welt with margin rib, split garter welt, and 2 × 2 ribbing with Multi-Strand Cast-on.

working full-size

Note: From this point on I use the Chapter 11 garment as an example in the Working Full-Size sections. Refer to it as needed to help visualize the process. On page 31, you can see the beginning stages of the charting process.

If you plan to use a garter welt on a full-size garment, work a sample welt on the end of your final test swatch. Use the length and pattern you have chosen for your garment. See how the stockinette and garter fabrics behave with one another, but keep in mind that you are looking at only a 4" (10 cm) swatch.

Garter stitch has a tendency to spread horizontally as it is knitted, depending on your yarn and needle size. If the number of stitches in the welt is 90 percent of the total number of body stitches, you shouldn't have any problems, but if the welt in your swatch begins to flare, you may want to cast on fewer stitches. After knitting the welt, you will increase the number of stitches evenly to 100 percent.

For example, if the garment requires 168 stitches for the total body circumference (chest plus ease), multiply 168 by .90. For a continuous welt, cast on a total of 152 stitches (151.2 rounded to the nearest even whole number), and join your knitting. After knitting the welt to the desired length, increase 16 stitches evenly in the next round to attain the 168 total body stitches. The intention here is to avoid a flared welt, not to create a welt that hugs the body like ribbing.

To make a split garter welt, you will work flat. Cast on 45 percent of the total number of body stitches for each welt, depending on the amount of flare in your test swatch. (If the gansey requires 168

stitches at full circumference and the test swatch shows little flare, each welt will have 76 cast-on stitches.)

Knit both of the welts to the desired length—usually 1" (2.5 cm) for a child's garment and 1½–2½" (3.8–6.5 cm) for an adult's. (Make certain that they are the same length by counting the number of rows in each. As with any knitted fabric, use measurements only to approximate.) To join them, knit across one welt with a circular needle, then pick up the other welt and knit across it. When you come to the end of the second welt, knit into the first stitch of the first welt, taking care not to twist the knitting. Continue working in the round. (If you wish, join the split welts with an overlap, as on page 24.)

RIBBING

For ribbing, you can use 90 percent of the total body stitches. The total number of cast-on stitches must be evenly divisible by the multiple of the ribbing pattern. Add or subtract a few stitches to accomplish this.

For example, if you choose a 2 × 2 rib, one repeat (or multiple) is 4 stitches. Cast on the number of stitches divisible by 4 that is closest to your value of 90 percent.

If 100 percent body stitches = 168, ribbing stitches = 168 × .90 = 151.2, rounded to 152.

Cast-on stitches = 152 / 4 = 38 repeats of the 2 × 2 rib pattern.

Always round fractions to the nearest number evenly divisible by your pattern multiple, so that the ribbing will flow continuously without leftover stitches.

CHAPTER 4
the lower body
the plain area, seam stitches, and definition ridge

After you've completed the welts or ribbing, you'll begin the plain area, a field of stockinette stitch, in which the wearer's initials can be worked in a decorative pattern. Above the plain area are several rows of garter stitch for the definition ridge. The definition ridge marks the end of the plain area and the beginning of the garment's body patterning. Seam stitches are added where seams would be sewn were the garment knitted flat.

THE PLAIN AREA

Plain knitting, in British terminology, refers to a stockinette-stitch fabric as well as to the knit stitch itself. The plain area was traditionally from one to several inches long, sometimes continuing up the garment to the beginning of the underarm gusset, and it served three functions. It enabled the knitter to replace worn welts or ribbing simply by ripping out the garment bottom, pick up the stitches, and knit down. It also helped to balance the design motifs visually by being flexible in height to accommodate the most attractive pattern layout. Last, it provided a clear background for the initials so they were easy to read.

Garter welt with plain area featuring garter-stitch initials.

The L made entirely of purls (right) is not as readable as the Ls made of garter stitch (left) and seed stitch (middle), as the vertical portion of the letter recedes, while the horizontal base comes forward.

INITIALS

The sweater owner's initials were often worked just above the front welt next to a side seam. The tighter your knitting gauge, the more detailed the initials can be. Seed-stitch or garter-stitch letters, rather than purl, are the easiest to read, because these two fabrics lie flat. For stitches arranged vertically, such as ribbing, the knits protrude, while the purls recede. Arranged horizontally, the purls come forward, while the knits recede. Depending on the chosen letter, one made entirely of purl stitches could be quite unreadable.

SEAM STITCHES

Seam stitches were common in ganseys. These were often single or double purl stitches that marked the beginning and halfway points of the round. The seam stitches took the place of stitch markers and defined the side "seams." They continued from the welt or ribbing up the garment sides, around the underarm gusset, and down the sleeve into the cuff.

Seam stitches should flow logically out of ribbing—for example, a two-purl seam from a 2 × 2 rib or a one-purl seam from a 1 × 1 rib. With an overlapped split welt, as on the sampler, the two-purl seam works well. As I join the two flat welts into a circular welt, I purl the two joining stitches together to create a logical base for the two-purl seam.

DEFINITION RIDGE

This detail is a line of knitting, a few rounds of either garter or seed stitch, usually no more than 1–1½" (2.5–3.8 cm) long. It clearly defines the end of the plain area and the beginning of the patterned area on both the garment body and the sleeves.

Sometimes the definition ridge can expand, since garter stitch is wider than stockinette stitch. If this occurs, you can remedy this effect by dropping down one needle size for the duration of knitting the garter stitch. Some yarns readily respond to just knitting a bit tighter in this area to keep the garter stitch under control, and blocking will help as well. Remember to return to the original needle size after this section is complete.

the sampler

LOWER BODY

Continued from page 25.

For the lower body of the sampler—the area between the welt and the midpoint of the gusset—you will be knitting in the round. The instructions start with Rnd 11; you completed Rnd 10 of the chart when you joined the welts.

Rnds 11 and 12: P2, k29, pm for midpoint of rnd, p2, k29.

INITIAL PLACEMENT

Take a moment to design your initial for your sampler. On page 31, at the bottom of the main body chart is a placeholder box for the initial. Your chosen initial may exceed the left boundary, but start from the right boundary of the box for proper placement.

Draw your chosen initial into the initial chart.

Rnd 13: P2, k2, work the initial, knit to midpoint marker, p2, knit to end of round.

Rnds 14–22: Continue to work in St st, purling the 2 seam sts at either side, working the initial for a total of 10 rnds.

Rnds 23–25: Rep Rnd 11 three times.

DEFINITION RIDGE

Rnds 26, 28, and 30: Purl, maintaining the p2 seams.

Rnds 27 and 29: Knit, maintaining p2 seams.

The sampler instructions continue on page 40.

The sampler initial (an uppercase B) is worked in seed stitch within the plain area. The definition ridge is made of five rounds of garter stitch.

gansey sampler chart

This is the entire sampler chart. Sections of it will be repeated in later chapters for you to refer to as you knit.

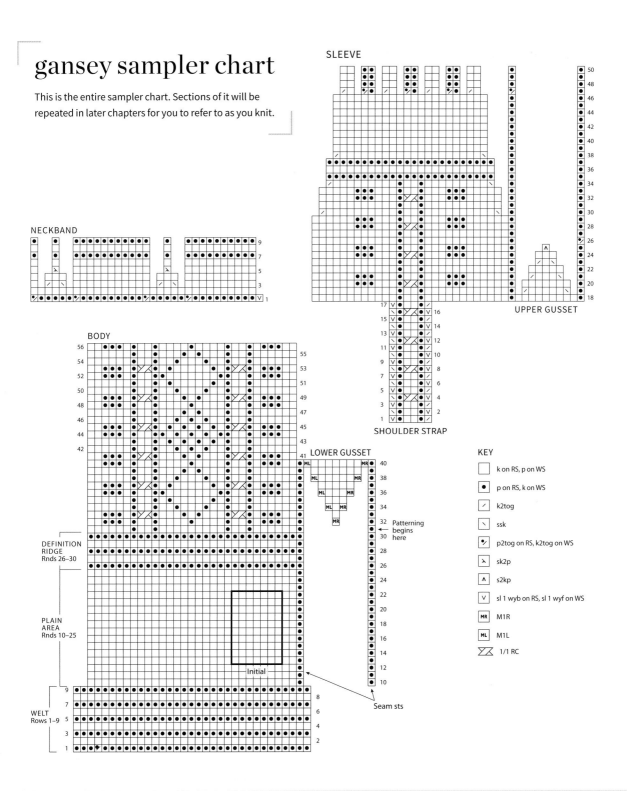

SLEEVE

UPPER GUSSET

NECKBAND

SHOULDER STRAP

BODY

LOWER GUSSET

DEFINITION
RIDGE
Rnds 26–30

PLAIN
AREA
Rnds 10–25

Initial

Patterning
begins
here

Seam sts

WELT
Rows 1–9

KEY

☐	k on RS, p on WS
●	p on RS, k on WS
╱	k2tog
╲	ssk
●	p2tog on RS, k2tog on WS
⅄	sk2p
∧	s2kp
V	sl 1 wyb on RS, sl 1 wyf on WS
MR	M1R
ML	M1L
⟩⟨	1/1 RC

reading a chart

Charts are a handy way to visualize what a garment will look like before you make it. Because both sides of most ganseys are the same (except for the initial, which is just on the front), I only chart the front of the garment. For a garment with a shaped neckline, I also chart the stitches at the back of the neckline, outlining the neckline with a bold line. Each square on the chart represents a stitch on your needle. In this book, squares filled with a dark circle represent purl stitches on the right side, and empty ones represent knit stitches on the right side of the work. These same symbols, when worked on the wrong side, represent knit and purl, respectively. Other authors and designers may use different symbols for those stitches, but there's usually a key to explain what's what.

When knitting flat, as you will for the upper body, read the chart back and forth. When knitting in the round, as you will for the lower body, read the chart from right to left—each line twice (once for the front and once for the back).

Just as you knit a gansey from the bottom up, you read the chart from the bottom to the top. Because you'll knit the sleeves from the shoulder to the cuff (see Chapter 9), the sleeve chart has the shoulder at the bottom.

Imagine that you are knitting in the round on the right side of your work, as for the lower body of the sampler. You begin at the right-hand side, knitting across to the left-hand side. At the beginning of each new round, move your eye up one line and again read from the right-hand side of the chart to the left-hand side (twice). When knitting in the round, the right side of the garment always faces you. This makes it easy to keep track of the patterning because what you see on the chart will match what you see on the work in front of you.

When knitting flat, as you will be for the upper body of the sampler, read the chart back and forth, just as you knit. For example, for the first row, begin at the row above the top of the gusset (where the work is split) on the right-hand side and work across to the left-hand side. The second row of the upper body is a wrong-side row, so you begin reading the chart at the left-hand side and move to the right, working the stitches according to their corresponding symbol's meaning on the wrong side.

The gusset is depicted in a triangular shape on the chart, just as it looks when knitted. The stitches in a straight line below the gusset represent the seam stitches. When knitting, begin at the outermost seam stitch, skip across the open area to the corresponding line within the body chart, and continue to work across. The open area between the two rows of seam stitches exists to allow for the eventual gusset increases. It also helps depict a three-dimensional shape on the two-dimensional surface of the paper.

Many ganseys are made with both garment halves the same, so you only need one chart. The shaping for a neckline occurs only on the garment front and can be indicated like this.

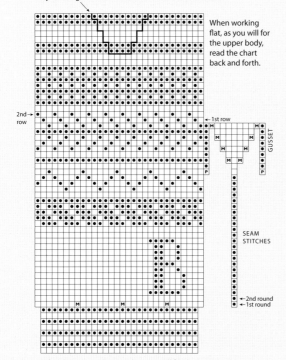

When working flat, as you will for the upper body, read the chart back and forth.

2nd row →   ← 1st row

GUSSET

SEAM STITCHES

←2nd round
←1st round

When knitting in the round, as you will for the lower body, read the chart from right to left—each line twice.

Seam stitches are both functional and decorative. They mark the beginning and the midpoint of each round and fall where seams would be if the garment had been knitted flat. From left to right: four-stitch seam, three-stitch seam, cabled seven-stitch seam, two-stitch garter seam, one-stitch purled seam, and two-stitch seed-stitch seam. The sampler has a two-stitch purled seam.

design variations

Gansey knitters sometimes added decorative seam stitches. For example, a two-stitch seam that alternates knits and purls creates a seed-stitch effect. A one-stitch seam that alternates knits and purls creates a garter effect. A variation on this is a three-stitch seam with a purl flanking each side of the one-stitch seam. For this seam, you'd overlap the garter welts three stitches. A 1 × 1 ribbing works well with a three-stitch seam, but be sure to center the middle stitch (in garter or plain knit) over a knit rib so that the purl stitches flow out of the purl ribs.

In some ganseys, a decorative margin ribbing was worked to mark the beginning of the plain area. This was simply a 1 × 1 or 2 × 2 ribbing worked immediately after a garter welt for about 1" (2.5 cm).

The 2 × 2 margin ribbing after the welt on this garment marks the beginning of the plain area.

working full-size

INITIALS

For an adult sweater, the initials can be 1–2" (2.5–5 cm) high. This gives you lots of room to play. (For a worsted-weight yarn, use an alphabet with fewer rounds than you would use for a sportweight or gansey yarn.) These pages include three versions of the alphabet. Use these as a jumping-off point to design your own letters!

THE PLAIN AREA

The length of the plain area can also vary. This flexibility allows you to adjust the garment's length, if necessary, or to visually balance the design of the patterning. When designing, gansey pattern motifs are laid out from the shoulder down to the definition ridge (see Chapters 5 and 11). To ensure you start and end with full repeats of your chosen motif, simply increase or decrease the number of rows in the plain area.

CUSTOM SHAPING USING SHORT-ROWS

Another alteration can be made to avoid the "hiking-up" of the back of the garment. This happens primarily when the back neck of the garment has not been shaped, but it can also occur in garments worn by a person with a large bust or stomach, which also causes the garment to shift.

To compensate, "short-rows" can be knitted into the plain area along the back or the front, depending on where more fabric is needed. Short-rows are rows that don't go from edge to edge (in flat knitting) or from side seam to side seam (in circular knitting). You stop knitting just before the seam stitches, then turn the work to the wrong side and purl to a few stitches before the other set of seam stitches.

When knitting is turned and worked in the other direction, a hole will develop in the knitting. There are several different short-row methods—the traditional short-row with wrap and turn, German short-rows, and Japanese short-rows—and they each remedy this issue in different ways. (For more information, see Jennifer Dassau's book *Knitting Short Rows*, Interweave, 2016.)

Traditional Short-rows with Wrap and Turn

Knit across the front, then knit the back to 3 sts before the seam sts.

Wrap and turn: Bring the yarn forward, slip the next st, take the yarn to the back and return the slipped stitch to the left needle, then turn the work so the WS is facing you. Purl across to 3 sts before the seam sts, wrap and turn again. Now, knit to the first wrap, knitting the wrap tog with the stitch it encircles as follows:

On RS rows: When you come to the wrap on a knit row, use the tip of your right needle, lift up under the wrap, then into the next stitch, knitting them together.

On WS rows: When you come across a wrap as you are purling, peer over the edge of your work to find it on the knit side. From the back pick up under it with the tip of your right needle and place it on the left needle. Now, purl those 2 sts tog. The wrap should no longer be visible on the knit side.

Two extra rows have been added in the back. You can work the other wrap together with the adjacent st when you pass it on the next rnd. This short-row shaping can be worked one or two times more if desired.

Japanese Short-rows

Knit across the back to 3 sts before the seam sts. Turn the work to the WS and place a removable marker on the working yarn, close to the fabric. Purl to 3 sts before the seam sts on the other side of the back. Turn the work to the RS and place a removable marker on the working yarn, close to the fabric. Knit up to the first marker. Pull the marker up and place that loop of yarn onto the left needle, so that the right leg of the loop is in front of the needle. Knit the loop and the next stitch together. Remove the marker.

Two extra rows have been added in the back. When you come to the other marker in the next round, pull the marker up and place that loop of yarn onto the left needle. Knit the loop and the next stitch together. Remove the marker. This short-row shaping can be worked one or two times more if you desire.

German Short-rows

Knit across the back to 2 sts before the seam sts. Turn the work to the WS, slip the first stitch on the left needle purlwise to the right needle. Bring the yarn to the front and pull the yarn upward and toward the back so that the stitch appears to be 2 stitches. Take the yarn to the back and forward between the 2 needles. Begin purling.

Purl across to 2 sts before the seam sts. Turn to the RS, bring the yarn to the front between the 2 needles, then slip the first stitch on the left needle purlwise to the right needle. Pull the yarn upward and toward the back so that the stitch appears to be 2 stitches. Begin knitting.

Now, knit across the entire back, and when the first double-stitch is reached, knit the 2 loops together. Continue working in the round.

Two extra rows have been added in the back. You can work the other double-stitch when you pass it on the next rnd. This short-row shaping can be worked one or two times more if you desire.

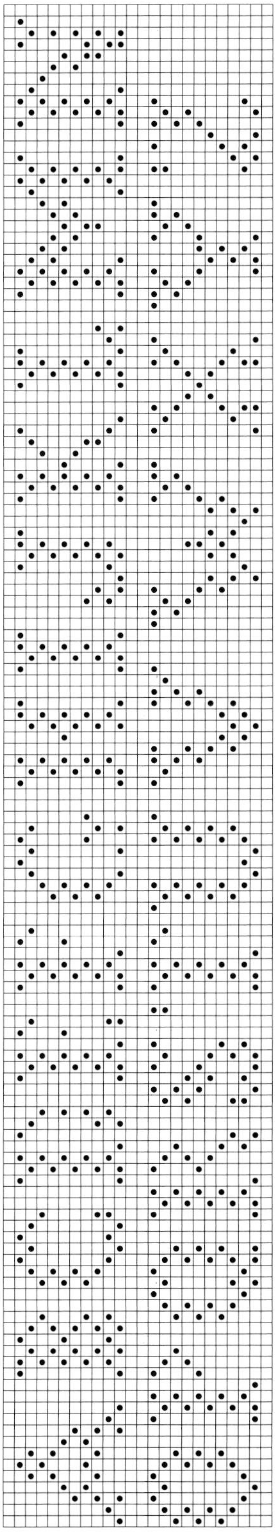

SEED-STITCH ALPHABET

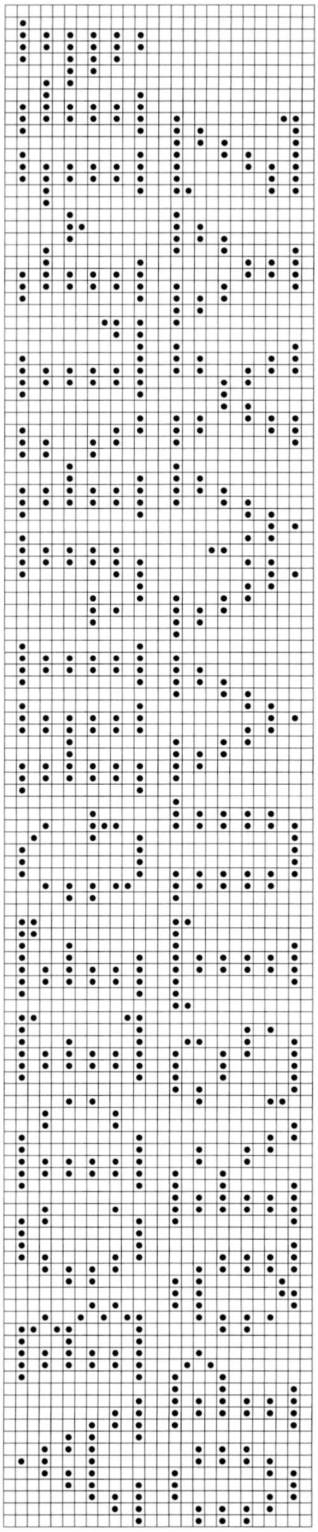

GARTER-STITCH ALPHABET

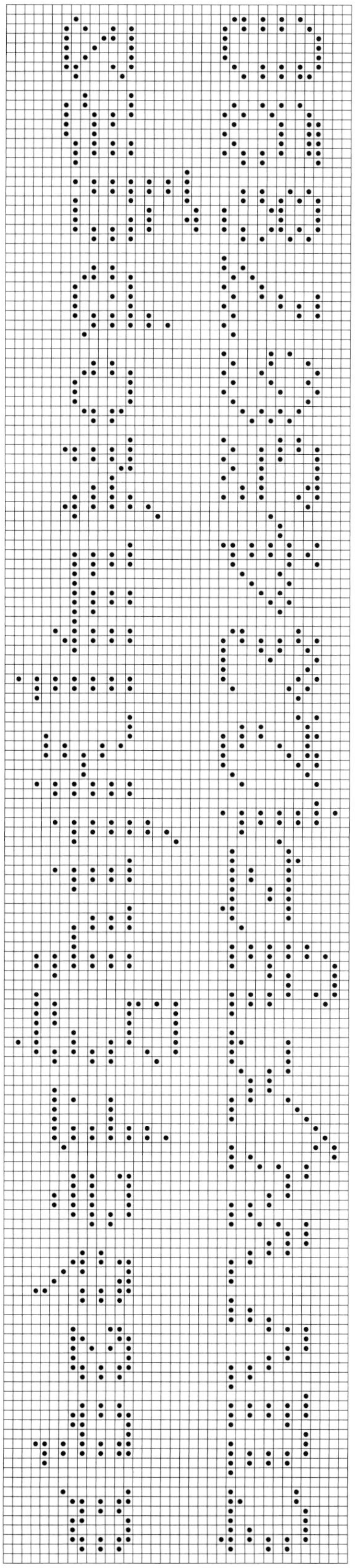

EIGHTH-CENTURY HALF-UNCIAL ALPHABET

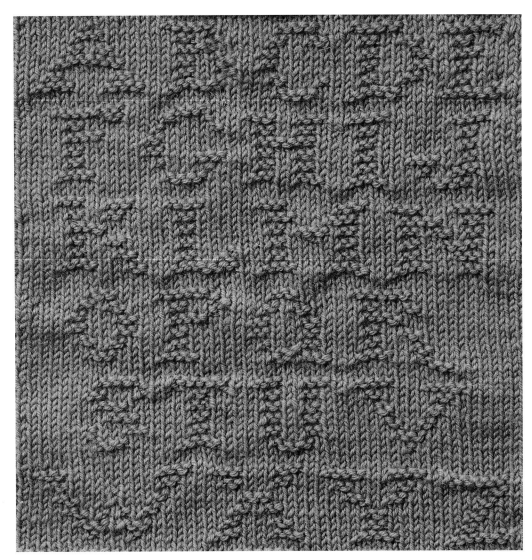

Garter Stitch Alphabet Sample Swatch

BLANK INITIAL CHART

Use this blank chart to chart initals for your gansey.

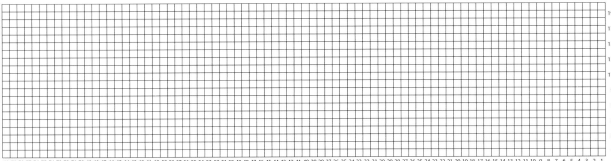

the fishing industry and the fisher-girls

In the ninteenth century, a bustling fishing industry grew around the Moray Firth in Scotland. It boasts 500 miles of coastline and was fished for salmon, whitefish, shellfish, mackerel, and herring. The herring industry in particular saw enormous expansion in the early 1800s, which greatly increased employment opportunities and caused ports like Wick, base population 1,500 people, to experience tremendous seasonal growth by 1820. The population of Wick grew to over 5,000 during herring season as tradesmen (coopers, curers, gutters, and others) streamed into town for work.

A mobile workforce made up of thousands of women of all ages followed the fishing fleet and the seasonal shoals of herring along the UK coasts from early summer until late autumn. The herring-girls (or fisher-girls or fisher-lassies) would come to work in groups of three, two to gut and one to pack the fish, and would knit during their off-times.

Wherever the fisher-girls traveled with the herring industry, they gathered and shared new gansey patterns, greatly contributing to widespread distribution of these motifs in the UK. Many pattern motifs were named after the town or location where they were found by researchers such as Gladys Thompson and Michael Pearson. But thanks to the hardworking fisher-girls, these patterns were seen beyond those locations around the UK—then and now.

a. In the 1800s, Wick was a busy, industrious town during herring season. The harbor was expanded to accommodate over 600 boats. (Photo courtesy Wick Society, Johnston Collection)

b. The herring-girls: gutters and packers in Wick. (Photo courtesy Wick Society, Johnston Collection)

c. On their off-time, the herring-girls knitted, outside their accommodation hut. (Photo courtesy of Norman Kennedy)

CHAPTER FIVE

pattern motifs

By studying antique garments and old photographs, researchers such as Michael Pearson and Rae Compton have found an endless and rich variety of gansey pattern motifs (see Sources and Supplies, page 186). Gladys Thompson, author of *Patterns for Guernseys, Jerseys, and Arans* (1971), began her work around World War II and was lucky enough to interview several traditional gansey knitters. She charted many of the pattern motifs that until then had only been part of an oral tradition.

Most of the gansey motifs consisted of simple knit/purl combinations, sometimes with a few cables added. The common orientation of the patterns was vertical, with the motifs beginning at the definition ridge and continuing to the shoulders. However, some beautiful old ganseys had horizontal, or side-to-side, patterns. Others had allover patterning—one motif repeated across the entire sweater surface.

TYPES OF PATTERN MOTIFS

In most of the literature about gansey knitting, the pattern motifs are organized by place of origin. While this system may have merit historically, it is frustrating from a designer's point of view. I find it helpful to have all the motifs in front of me so that I may compare and contrast as I choose what to knit. So I have organized them into the following groups based on their shared uses and characteristics.

BACKGROUND PATTERNS

These small motifs (among them, seed, moss, and double moss stitch) can be used around and between motifs or as panes within a horizontal or vertical repeat. Seed stitch consists of alternating knit and purl stitches. A variant, moss stitch, has double rows of alternating knit and purl stitches. Double moss is made of alternating blocks of knit and purl stitches, each block two or more stitches wide or high.

DIAGONAL PATTERNS

Most historical examples made use of diagonal patterns: marriage lines, chevrons, zigzag, herringbone, and unadorned diagonal purl lines. These motifs were used both as side panels and as the primary focus of a garment. They work well either in a vertical or horizontal orientation.

DIAMOND PATTERNS

Diamonds were very popular in the traditional ganseys and were often filled with moss or seed stitch or the two alternately. (The sampler's center panel has two diamond outlines and a center diamond filled in with seed stitch.)

PICTURE PATTERNS

Anchors, flags, trees, hearts, stars, and starfish can all be created with knit and purl stitches. In the traditional garments, these images were placed in a prominent, highly visible position on the garment, usually in the vertical center panel.

VERTICAL AND HORIZONTAL PATTERNS

This group comprises a large variety of simple motifs and cables, as well as combinations of motifs that borrow from all the pattern

By combining traditional motifs in horizontal and vertical orientations, you can create a variety of gansey surface patterning. Most of the motifs consist of simple knit/purl combinations, occasionally with cables added.

groupings. The vertical patterns repeat along the length of the garment from the definition ridge to the shoulders. The horizontal patterns repeat across the width of the garment.

NAMED PATTERNS

In some villages, popular motifs would be named for the inventor of that motif or for the name of the area. Michael Pearson found that by identifying connections between locations and frequency of motifs appearing on ganseys, he was able to determine the provenance of many gansey motifs. For example, knitters in Filey often used Betty Martin on the sleeves. The Humber Star motif was on many ganseys worn by inland watermen who built and worked canals in the nineteenth century. The Humber is a large tidal estuary in eastern England, which feeds into many of the canals that were built.

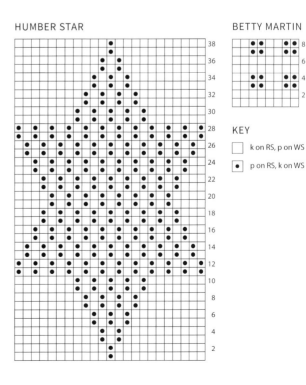

HUMBER STAR

BETTY MARTIN

KEY

| | k on RS, p on WS |
| • | p on RS, k on WS |

the sampler

THE BODY

Continued from page 30.

The sampler body, shown in chart below, incorporates diamond outlines, filled-in diamonds, two-stitch cables, and a simple background pattern at the sides. The pattern orientation is vertical.

You have already worked the nine rows of the welt (Rows 1–9), the plain area (Rnds 10–25), and the definition ridge (Rnds 26–30).

To begin the patterning, work Rnd 31. To work the round, knit each line of the chart twice—once for the front and once for the back—with the two-purl-st seam at each side.

Rnd 31: *P2, k6, p1, k2, p1, k9, p1, k2, p1, k6; repeat from *.

At Rnd 32, you'll begin creating the gusset with increases.

The sampler instructions continue on page 58.

BODY CHART

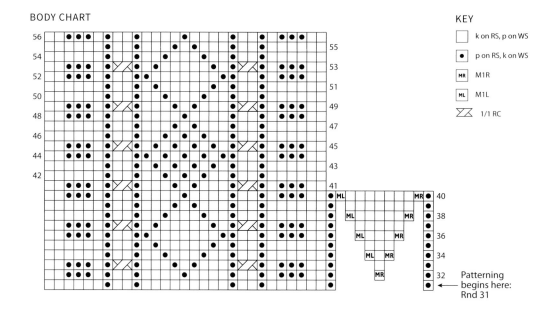

KEY

☐ k on RS, p on WS

● p on RS, k on WS

MR M1R

ML M1L

⧖ 1/1 RC

Patterning begins here: Rnd 31

drowning at sea

A tale exists—and fervently persists—that ganseys (and/or the Irish Arans) were patterned to include motifs that represented each fisherman's village or family. The supposed purpose of this was to be able to identify the hapless sailor if he drowned and later washed up onshore.

This cannot be true for several reasons:

1. Tides being what they are, a body could wash up hundreds of miles away, where that village might not be aware of the meaning of that particular patterning.

2. Grisly though it is, many drowned men lost at sea never made it to shore, and instead became some underwater creature's lunch.

3. Knitters knitted motifs "out of their head" and did not write them down. (Many people of that time period did not know how to read and would not have known how to express their knitting in written form.)

4. People of the nineteenth century tended to be quite superstitious, and to knit something with a connection to the possible death of the wearer could not have been conceivable.

5. And last, what knitter would commit to knitting the same pattern over and over again?

Instead, I believe that knitters then were like knitters today—creative, engaged in the intricacies of patterns, a bit competitive. Even within families, as some of the old photos clearly illustrate, each man might have a different pattern on his gansey. I can imagine a knitter checking out the sweaters of fishermen who might have landed for the night from elsewhere, a quick glance to study a new and different motif to file away in her mind for the next gansey she would knit.

arans vs ganseys

There is great confusion as to the dissimilarity between these two very unique traditional garments. This chart contrasts some of these variances.

	THE ARAN	THE GANSEY
Provenance	1900s Ireland	1800s England, Cornwall, Scotland, Netherlands
Style	Pullovers, vests, cardigans	Drop-shoulder pullovers
Construction	Varied: top down, bottom up, flat or circular	Lower body & sleeves circular/ upper body flat
Gauge	4 to 5 stitches per inch	7+ stitches per inch
Spin of yarn	Woolen-spun	Worsted-spun
Ply of yarn	3-ply	5-ply
Color of yarn	Undyed (cream colored)	Dark navy blue
Surface Design	Complex cables, highly textured	Knit/purl combinations, simple cables
Special Features	Deep skirt (ribbing), saddle shoulders (sometimes)	Underarm gussets, shoulder straps (sometimes)
Purpose	For the tourist trade ultimately	The original fisherman's sweater

design variations

From here through page 53, you'll find a selection of gansey pattern motifs that can be used individually or combined to create a variety of textural designs. These charts indicate how the motif is worked and how it will appear on the right side of the fabric. The unit repeat is indicated with red lines, where appropriate.

BACKGROUND PATTERNS

SEED STITCH

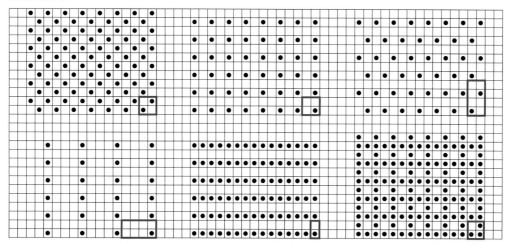

MOSS STITCH

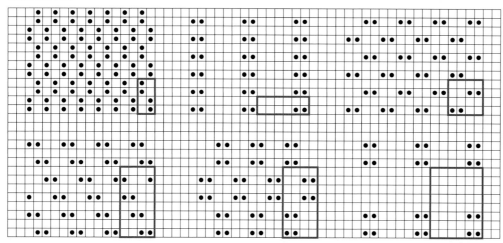

DOUBLE MOSS STITCH

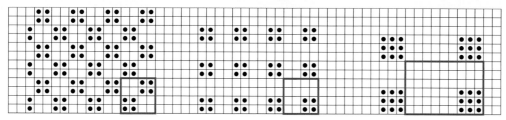

BACKGROUND PATTERNS, CONTINUED

OTHER BACKGROUND PATTERNS

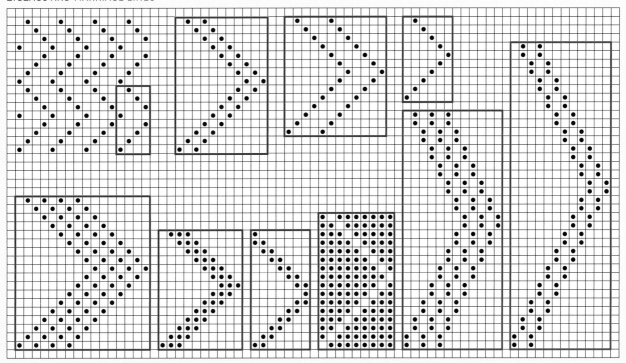

DIAGONAL PATTERNS

ZIGZAGS AND MARRIAGE LINES

DIAGONAL PATTERNS, CONTINUED

DIAGONAL PURL LINES

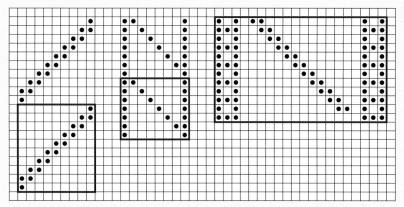

VERTICAL HERRINGBONE

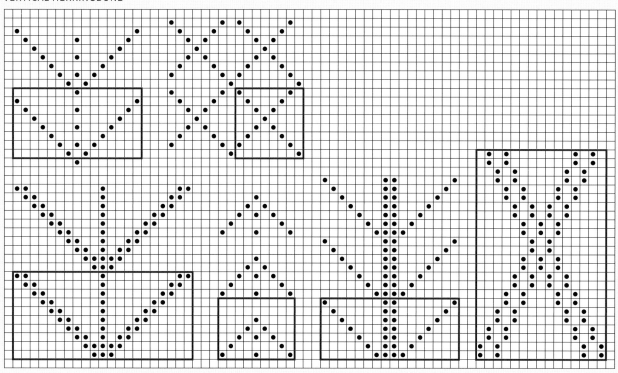

CHEVRONS

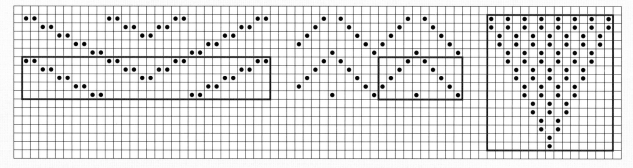

DIAGONAL PATTERNS, CONTINUED

CHEVRONS, CONTINUED

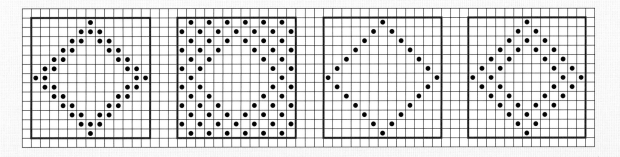

DIAMOND PATTERNS

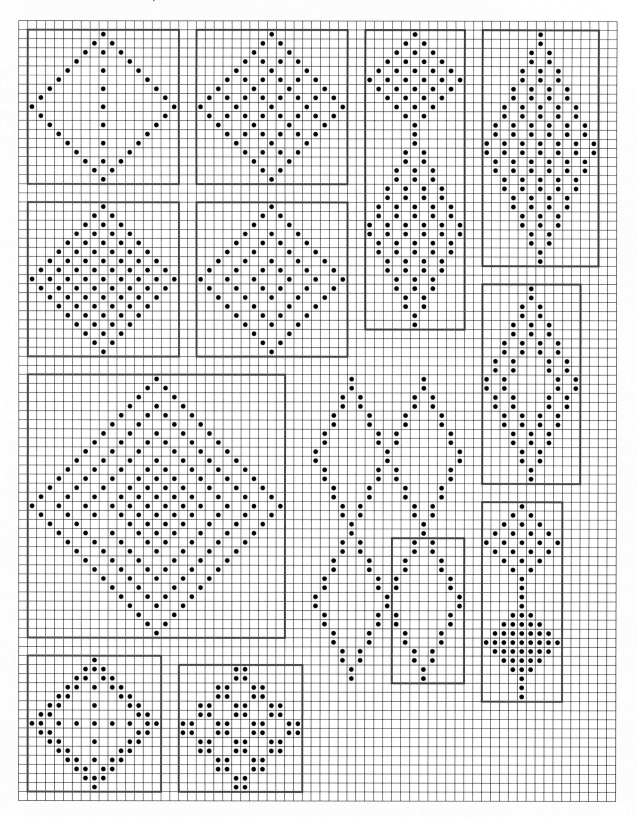

DIAMOND PATTERNS, CONTINUED

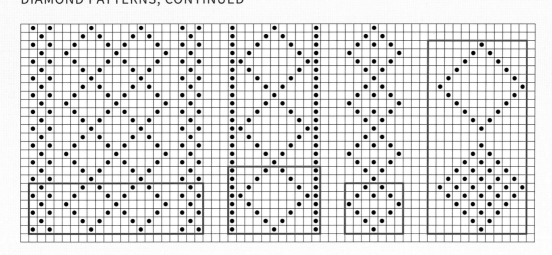

PICTURE MOTIFS

HEARTS

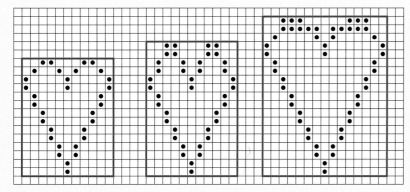

STARFISH

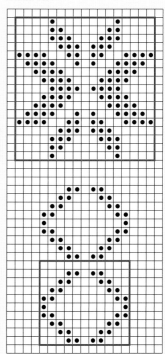

ANCHORS

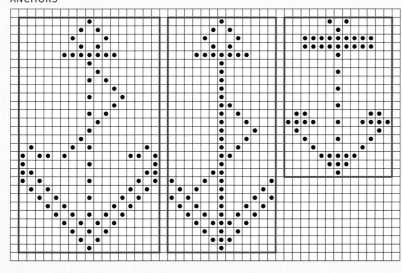

FLAGS

TREES

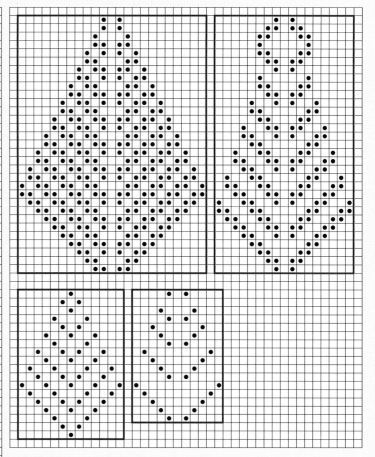

VERTICAL MOTIFS

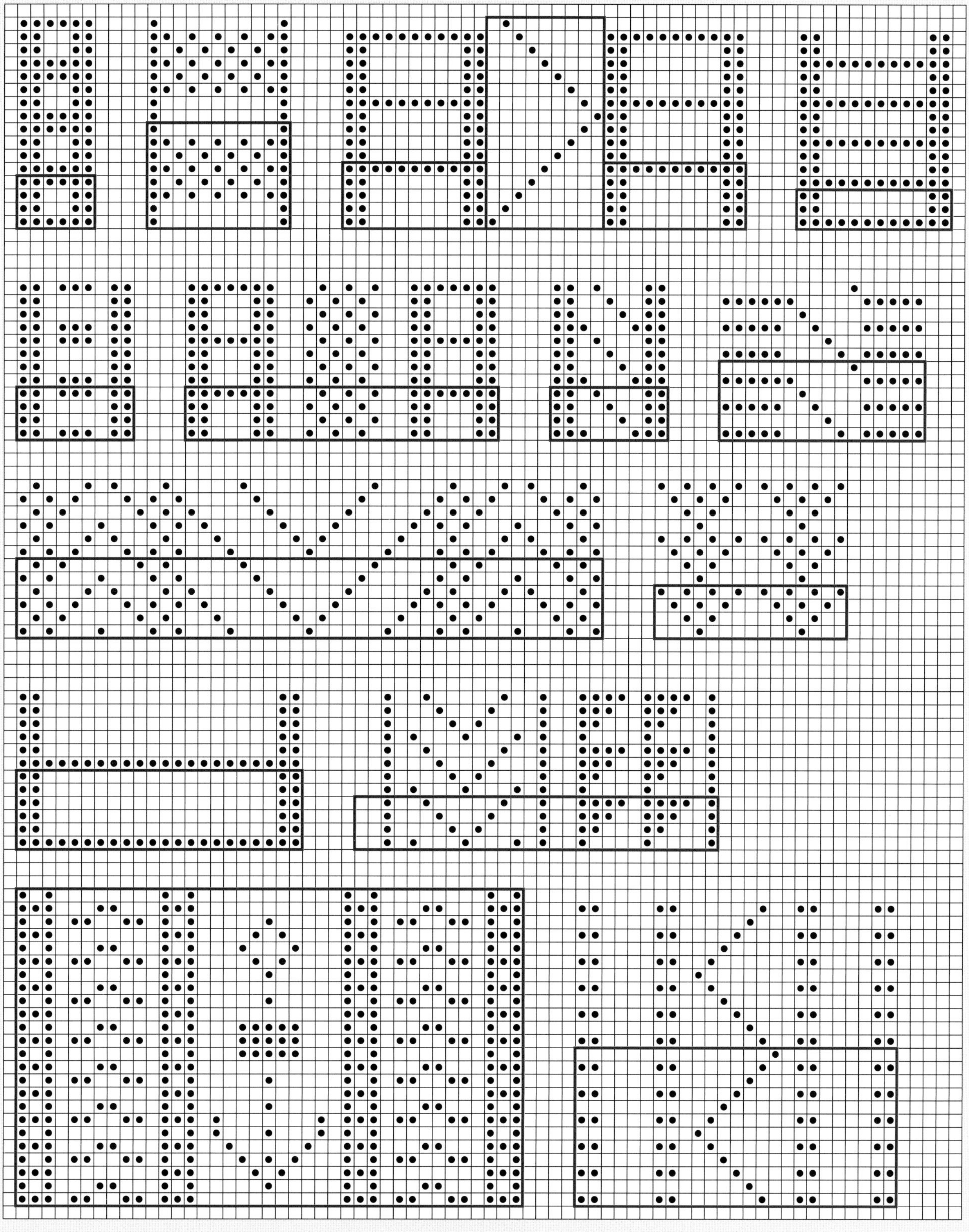

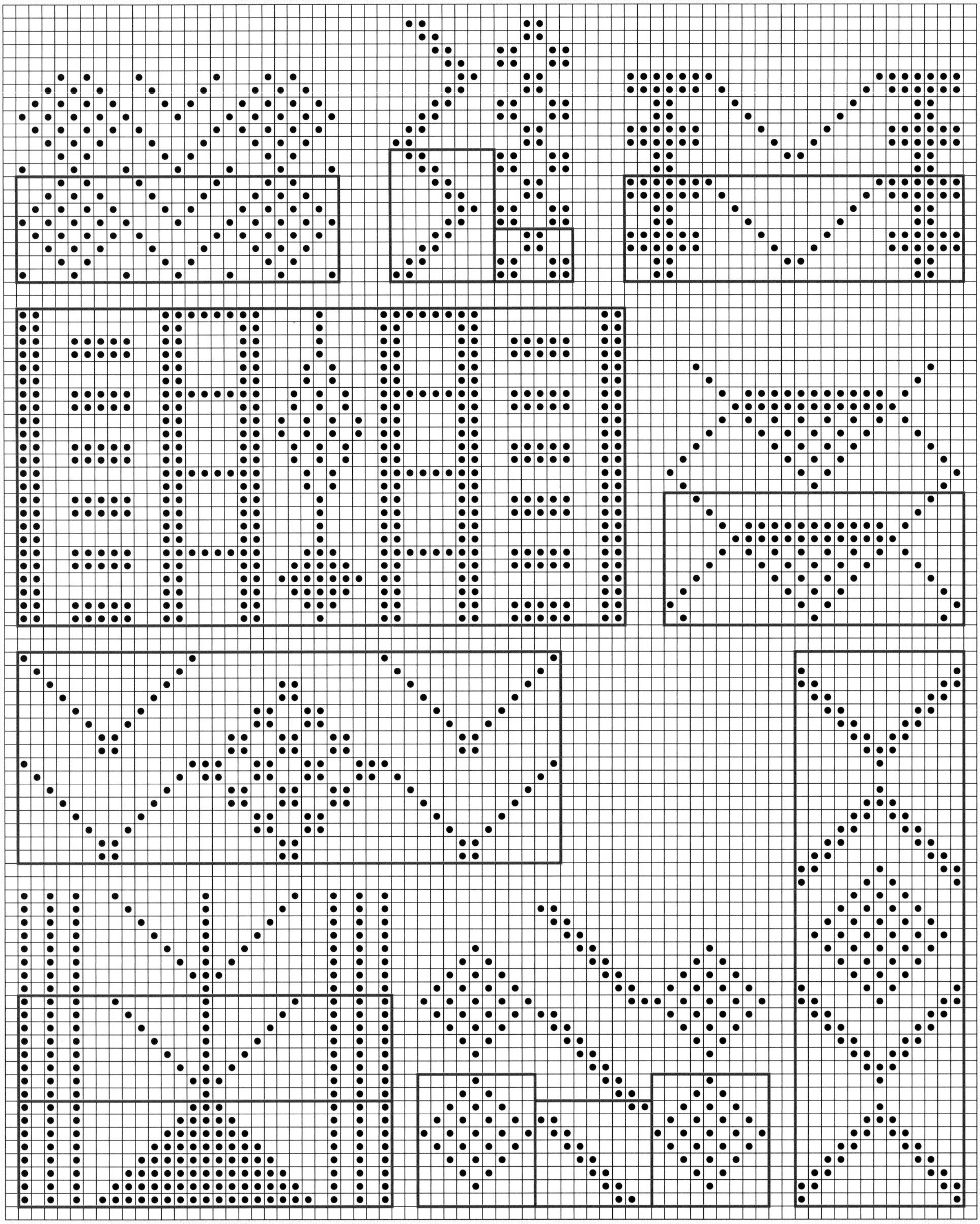

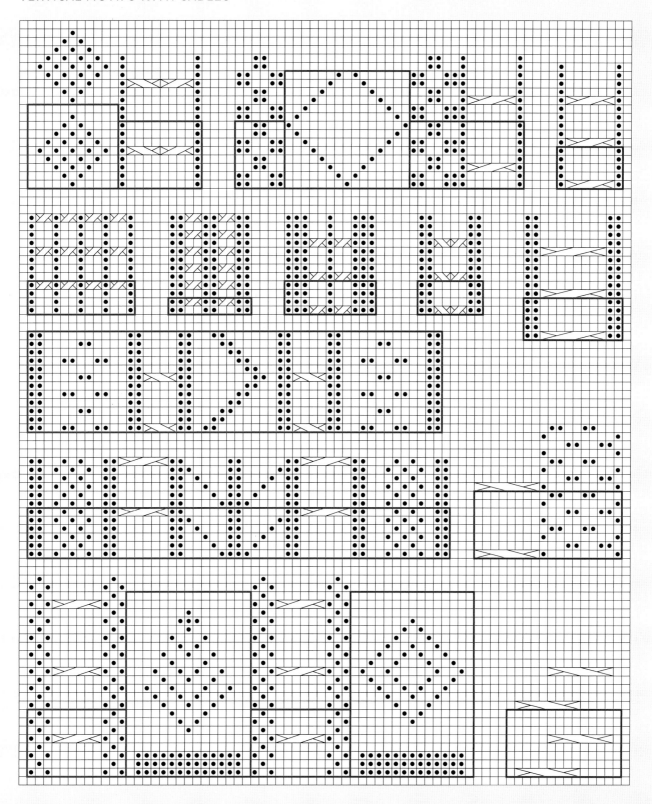

VERTICAL MOTIFS WITH CABLES, CONTINUED

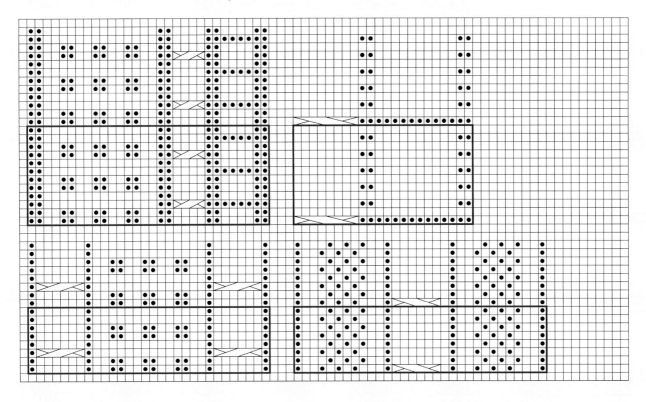

HORIZONTAL MOTIFS

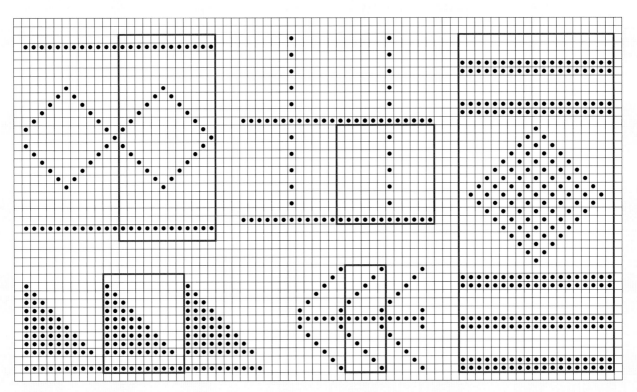

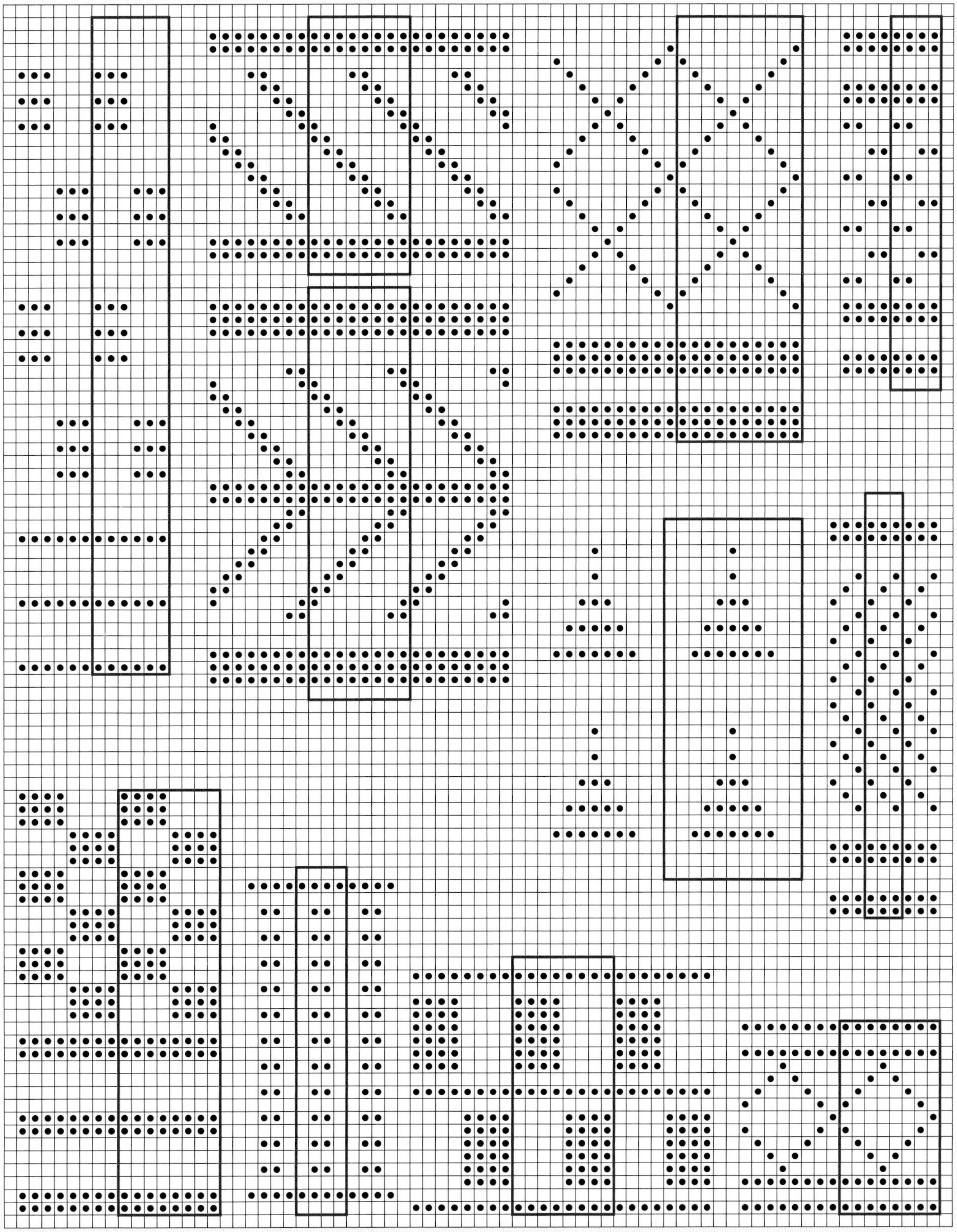

working full-size

Before knitting a full-size gansey, plan the layout and chart the garment body to be certain all the pattern motifs will begin and end attractively. By doing this you're less likely to find yourself wishing, halfway through knitting your sweater, that you had done something differently.

To see a sample chart for the full-size gansey, see page 108.

GAUGE AND STITCH COUNT

Before you begin, you'll need to make a swatch to determine your gauge and calculate your stitch count based on your desired chest circumference, including ease. Refer to the table on page 106 or take this measurement from a favorite sweater that fits well. Multiply the chest measurement by your stitch gauge.

For example, If your gauge is 4 stitches and 6 rounds per inch and your chest measurement is 42" (106.5 cm):

$$42" \times 4 \text{ sts/in.} = 168 \text{ total body stitches}$$

Remember, because the front and the back of the sweater are the same, your motif layout need only represent one side, which is 50 percent of the sweater's circumference:

$$168 \text{ sts} \times .50 = 84 \text{ sts}$$

Next, you'll need to determine the length of your sweater above the ribbing. Again refer to the table on page 106 or measure a favorite garment.

Measurement from bottom edge of garment to underarm – Length of ribbing + Armhole depth = Total garment length from shoulder, not including ribbing

$$15" – 3" + 8" = 20"$$

Multiply that figure by your row gauge to determine the total number of rows in your sweater body:

$$20" \times 6 \text{ rounds/in.} = 120 \text{ rounds, or } 120 \text{ vertical squares on the chart}$$

Note: The ribbing is not included in the calculation because it is often worked on smaller-size needles and therefore not the same gauge as the rest of the sweater. It can be added to your plans later.

PLANNING THE PATTERNING

Think about whether you want a vertical or horizontal orientation for your patterning and decide which pattern motifs you'd like to use. (For more information on pattern layout, see Chapter 11.) If your patterning has a vertical orientation, like the sampler, an uneven number of panels will look more attractive. Horizontal patterning can be easier to design and knit since you only need to remember one motif across the body, rather than multiple columns of different motifs. Traditionally, the horizontal bands were of equal height and repeated as many times as would fit.

Choose one or more background patterns to separate your motifs. The motifs within the columns or bands may be the same or different.

Lay out all your horizontal motifs so that they are symmetrical along the length and across the width of the garment. Vertical panels across the width of a garment should have varying widths to avoid too precise and stiff an appearance.

Even though you knit from the bottom up, it is important to lay out the pattern motifs from the shoulder down to the definition ridge. This way you can make sure there is enough room on the sweater body for a full repeat of each motif. Start with entire motifs at the shoulder (which is at the viewer's eye level and therefore highly visible) and end with whole ones at the definition ridge. As discussed in Chapter 4, the length of the plain area can vary to accommodate the number of full repeats you can fit on the garment body.

CREATING A CHART

After you have worked out your stitch count and motifs, it's time to create a chart.

A chart is a visual and practical guide to knitting your garment's patterning, stitch by stitch. You can create it using a pencil and graph paper or one of the many available computer programs designed specifically for creating knitting charts. While some of these have a steep learning curve, others are more intuitive, and I find them invaluable. Most offer free demos so you can try them out before you buy. See the list of recommended charting programs in Sources and Supplies, page 186.

Note: If you use regular graph paper, be aware that your chart will be elongated and your knitting a bit squat in comparison. However, if you use knitters' graph paper, it will be more visually accurate. Knitters' graph paper has squares that are wider than they are high, proportional to actual knit stitches. There are many online resources for knittter's graph paper. You may need to tape pieces of graph paper together to chart the entire sweater front.

To make a chart on graph paper, count out one square per stitch and mark the garment's width in pencil, leaving room at the right-hand side for the eventual gusset.

Plot the length on the graph paper, leaving room at the bottom for the welt or ribbing.

Once you plot out the vertical and horizontal measurements, you'll have a rectangle that contains squares representing each stitch of your sweater where you can design your gansey patterning.

For a vertically patterned gansey, first chart the main center motif, working from the neckline down to where you want the patterning to end. Finish with a full motif (not one-third of a diamond, for example). Now, draw the other motifs in on each side. Add the definition ridge (usually 1" [2.5 cm]) and the plain area, including an initial if you wish.

If you are including cables, add the increases at the base of the cables and the decreases at the ends to account for cable splay. Chart the seam stitches only up to the point where the armholes begin. The number of squares between the body chart and the gusset and seam stitches depends on the full width of the gusset (see Chapter 6).

Your chart is an important source of information. As long as you keep good records, if you are interrupted while making your sweater, you can go back to it months later and know where to pick up your work. On the front of the chart, I write down my gauge, yarn, and needle sizes. On the back, I list the features in my sweater such as cast-on, ribbing, seam stitch, definition ridge pattern, neck shaping, shoulder bind-off, and neck gusset. I also work out and label my calculations on the back so it's clear which set of numbers is for what part of the garment.

cable splay

Cable splay is an important aspect to address when working with cables. It is an unsightly gathering up or bowing out at the edges of the fabric around a cable, caused by the crossing stitches. By increasing at the base of a cable you can add extra stitches where they are needed to help prevent splay. By the same token, decreasing an equal number of stitches at the top of the cable restores the fabric to its stockinette-stitch width before joining the shoulders.

Many patterns are not written to accommodate cable splay, but you can make adjustments for it in any pattern. Use a swatch of the cable in question to measure the width and count the stitches of the cable. Next, multiply the width of the cable in inches by the stockinette-stitch gauge. The difference in stitches between the cable and a piece of stockinette stitch of the same width is the number of stitches needed to offset cable splay.

For example, the gauge of a stockinette-stitch swatch is 4 stitches per inch. The cable swatch shows the cable is one inch wide, made of 6 stitches. The difference between the stockinette gauge and the cable is 2 stitches. Your chart for the lower body (before the cable begins) should reflect the number of stitches needed based on your desired measurements. Those 2 extra stitches are increased at the cable's base and decreased at the end for the shoulder.

The splay along the bottom edge is apparent. This is due to casting on the total number of stitches that will be needed for the cable—too numerous to get a straight edge. The top edge is a clean line because three decreases were worked at the terminus of the cable.

Full cable splay (left) and cable splay resolved (right).

CHAPTER 6
the underarm gusset

If you have ever knitted a pair of mittens or gloves, you have most likely worked a gusset, an expanded section of knitting that helps a garment fit better over a bent or protruding area of the body such as a heel or the base of a thumb. Ganseys feature diamond-shaped gussets that create extra ease under the arms. The lower half of each gusset, one under each armhole, is worked in the round as part of the gansey body and resembles the thumb gusset of a mitten. The gusset begins as one increase worked in the horizontal bar between two seam stitches. Next, after every few rounds you'll work paired increases in between the seam stitches until the gusset is at full width.

Paired increases, worked within the same round, create two shaping lines that move in opposite directions. Increases that lean in the same direction as the shaping lines, such as the Make 1 increase (see page 57), give the finished gusset a neater look.

Once you knit the lower half of each gusset to its full width, you'll put the stitches on a stitch holder. Here, you'll start knitting the front and back pieces separately, back and forth, to the shoulder. After joining the shoulders, you will pick up the sleeve and gusset stitches. While working the sleeve in the round, you'll complete the upper half of the gusset, decreasing to merge back into the seam stitches.

Historically gussets were worked in stockinette stitch, but when worked in reverse stockinette (purl stitches on the right side), they seem to recede into the body of the garment and are less noticeable.

A diamond-shaped underarm gusset, the gansey's most distinctive feature. Shown: a garter-stitch two-stitch seam that splits to surround the gusset on each side by one seam stitch.

the make 1 increase

I have experimented with many types of increases, but I like the Make 1 increase best. By pairing Make 1 right (M1R) and Make 1 left (M1L) increases for underarm gussets, you can make the increases lean in the same direction as the lines of the diamond shape, which gives the gusset a neater appearance.

MAKE 1 LEFT-LEANING

To work a Make 1 increase that leans to the left (M1L), pick up the horizontal bar between the 2 sts nearest the ends of the needles by inserting your left needle tip from front to back, creating a loop (fig. 1) and knit into the back of the loop (fig. 2). The completed increase is shown in fig. 3.

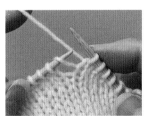

figure 1

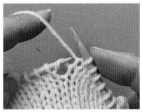

figure 2

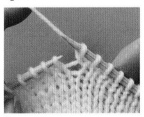

figure 3

MAKE 1 RIGHT-LEANING

To work a Make 1 increase that leans to the right (M1R), pick up the horizontal bar between the 2 sts by inserting your left needle tip from back to front, creating a loop (fig. 1) and knit into the front of the loop (fig. 2). The completed increase is shown in fig. 3.

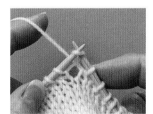

figure 1

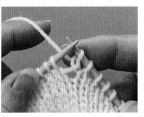

figure 2

figure 3

the sampler

THE GUSSET

Continued from page 40.

The directions are for a true cable (see page 60 for variations).

Rnd 32: *P1, M1R, p1, k2, p3, k1, p1, k2, p1, k4, p1, k4, p1, k2, p1, k1, p3, k2; repeat from *.

Rnd 33: *P1, k1, p1, k2, p3, k1, p1, 1/1RC (put next st on cn and hold at back of work, k1, k1 from cn), p1, k3, p1, k1, p1, k3, p1, 1/1RC, p1, k1, p3, k2; repeat from *.

Rnd 34: *P1, M1R, k1, M1L, p1, work patt across 29 sts; repeat from *.

Rnd 35: Work even.

Increase 1 st every other rnd at each side of both gussets 3 more times—9 sts each gusset.

Break yarn. Put seam and gusset sts of the left side on a st holder, garment back on a second holder, and other gusset and seam sts on a third holder.

The sampler instructions continue on page 68.

PARTIAL BODY CHART (ROUNDS 32–40)

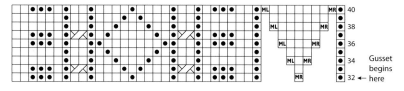

KEY

☐	k on RS, p on WS
●	p on RS, k on WS
MR	M1R
ML	M1L
⤫	1/1 RC

The gusset begins as one increase—either left or right leaning—worked between two seam stitches. After making the first increase, you'll work paired increases every few rounds, just inside the seam stitches until the gusset is at full width (nine stitches for the sampler).

When the lower half of the gusset has been knitted to the full desired width, put the stitches on a stitch holder. The gussets will be completed while knitting the sleeves.

cabling without a cable needle

The patterened area of the sampler features a two-stitch cable (1/1 RC) on the front and back that also repeats on the shoulder straps (see Chapter 8). You can easily work these cables without a cable needle using one of these three methods, each of which involves slightly different stitch movements that result in slightly different looks:

From left to right: True cables, mock cables, Barbara Walker's baby cables

TRUE CABLE

Although a bit awkward to execute, this method produces nice-looking cables that are exactly the same as those you would get with a cable needle.

Knit into second st with the right needle in front of the work (do not go through the st to the back as for the mock cable) (fig. 1). Knit the first st (fig. 2) and then sl both sts off together (fig. 3).

figure 1

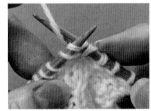

figure 2

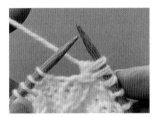

figure 3

MOCK CABLE

In this method, the yarn travels farther, which uses more yarn and results in an enlarged stitch.

Insert the right needle into the second st, to the back of the work, and knit this st (fig. 1). Knit the first st (fig. 2) and sl both sts off together (fig. 3).

figure 1

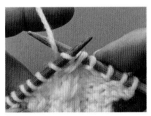

figure 2

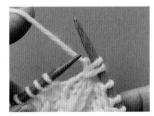

figure 3

BABY CABLE

This method, from Barbara Walker's *A Treasury of Knitting Patterns* (1998), is the easiest to execute and looks nice, too. Unlike some cables, these cabled stitches do not pull at all and are as uniform in shape and size as the stitches in the other rows of the cable.

Knit 2 sts together, but do not slip them off the left needle (fig. 1). Knit the first st again (fig. 2), then sl both sts off the left needle (fig. 3).

figure 1

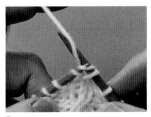

figure 2

figure 3

design variations

The underarm gusset offers numerous possibilities for adding unique touches to your gansey. You can create different visual effects by using different methods of increasing to shape the edge of the gusset. Some increases are more noticeable than others, and it's possible to make many types of increases lean to the right or left.

Gusset shaping can also take place in the center of the gusset, or one stitch in from the edge of the gusset. If you shape the lower half of the gusset this way, it results in a single-stitch outline on either side because the increases stand out from the surrounding stitches. (This same outlining effect naturally occurs in the upper half of the gusset—where you will decrease—without moving the shaping stitches because of the nature of the decreases themselves.)

GUSSETS AND SEAM-STITCH VARIATIONS

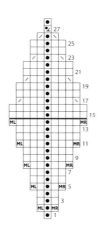

ONE-STITCH SEAM

A one-purl-stitch seam bisected gusset. Without surrounding seam stitches, the gusset is less noticeable.

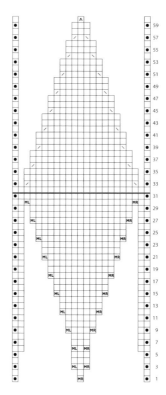

TWO-STITCH SEAM

A two-stitch seam logically splits at the beginning of the gusset. Each line of stitches travels along one side of gusset, and the two lines come together again at end of the gusset. This type of seam can also be effective emerging from 2 × 2 ribbing, bisecting the gusset, and continuing down the the cuff, uninterrupted from start to finish.

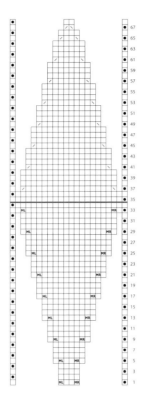

FOUR-STITCH SEAM

Here, a four-stitch seam divides into two seam stitches surrounding the gusset—one to each side—while the interior two seam stitches become part of the gusset.

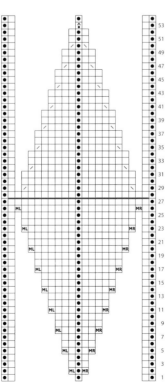

FIVE-STITCH SEAM

A five-stitch seam can also surround the gusset and bisect it. Or, the center stitch can become the first stitch of the gusset while the two seam stitches to either side surround the gusset.

KEY

☐	knit	╱	k2tog
●	purl	╲	ssk
MR	M1R	✖	p3tog
ML	M1L	⬆	s2kp
⬆	s2pp	—	gusset separation

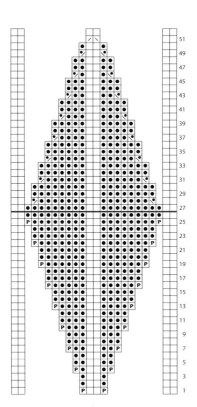

SIX-STITCH SEAM

A six-stitch seam of knitted stitches breaks up into two stitches to each side surrounding the reverse stockinette gusset, while two seam stitches bisect it.

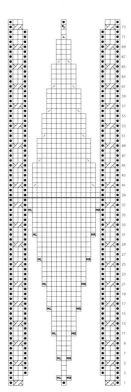

SEVEN-STITCH SEAM WITH CABLES

This seven-stitch seam includes two baby cables that split up, surround the gusset, and then join again to travel down the sleeve and integrate into the cabled cuff. Note natural outlining of upper half caused by decreases. Because increases were worked at the very edge of the lower half of gusset, there is no corresponding outline stitch there.

GUSSET-SHAPING VARIATIONS

Alternative placements for gusset shaping is another way to achieve unusal effects.

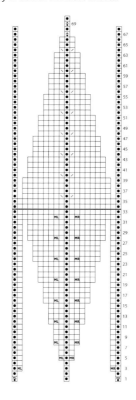

INTERNAL SHAPING

You can move the shaping of the gusset to the inside of the garment to create a more rounded edge. This internally shaped gusset has the shaping placed along the midline, with a one-stitch seam that surrounds and bisects the gusset. This type of gusset can be bisected with seam stitches or just surrounded by them.

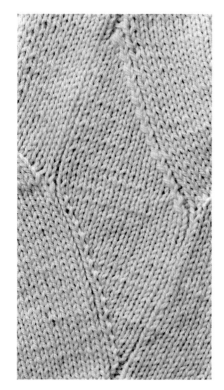

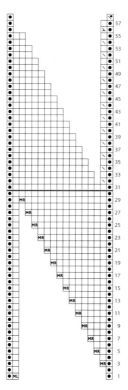

OPPOSING SHAPING

This unusual gusset with opposing shaping was increased on the left in the lower half and decreased on the right in the upper half.

KEY

knit		P	M1P
•	purl	•/	p2tog
MR	M1R	•\	ssp
ML	M1L	•⅄	p3tog
MR•	M1RP	⅄	sk2p
ML•	M1LP	⋏	s2kp
/	k2tog	⬆	s2pp
\	ssk	⨉⨉	1/1 RC
—	gusset separation		

working full-size

To begin, first determine how long your gusset should be. For an adult, the gusset can be up to 8" (20.5 cm) long and 3–4" (7.5–10 cm) wide. For children, gussets should be scaled down to 3–4" (7.5–10 cm) long and 1½–2" (3.8–5 cm) wide. Armholes don't require as much depth when using underarm gussets, but in oversized garments, gussets add too much fabric under the arm.

Since half of the gusset is knit in the body and half is knit in the sleeve, you'll need to divide the total length of the gusset in half to determine where to begin the increases below the armhole division.

Begin by working a Make 1 increase and then make paired increases until you have enough stitches for the total desired width. To determine the frequency of increasing (i.e., the number of plain rounds you should work between increase rounds), use the following formula:

In our example, the gusset is 6" (15 cm) long and 3" (7.5 cm) wide, with a gauge of 4 stitches and 6 rounds per inch (2.5 cm).

Round gauge × gusset length ÷ 2 = Y

Example: *6 rounds/in. × 6" ÷ 2 =*
18 rounds in lower half of gusset.

Next, determine number of paired increases needed to shape gusset:

Stitch gauge × Gusset width ÷ 2 = Z

Example: *4 sts/in. × 3" ÷ 2 =*
6 paired increases in lower half of gusset.

Number of rounds to work from one increase
(or decrease) round to the next = Y÷ Z

Example: *18 rounds ÷ 6 paired increases = 3 rounds per increase.*

Note: If the total is a fraction, round up to the next whole number.

In this example, you would work 3 rounds from 1 increase (or decrease) to the next—count the increase round as the first round and work the second and third rounds even.

(In the Example Body Chart on page 112, I actually charted 19 rounds for the lower half of the gusset for visual balance and added an additional pair of increases to create seam stitches. When designing, you often have to make slight adjustments in the calculations to accommodate the actual garment.)

CHAPTER 7

the upper body and neckline

With the lower half of the sampler's gussets finished and the patterning well under way, now it's time to make the openings for the armholes, finish the upper body, and create the neckline.

Up to this point you've worked the gansey in the round. Now, you'll split the work into two parts—the front and back—and work flat, back and forth, developing the armhole depth. The patterning continues in the same way, but you'll read the chart differently.

READING CHARTS WHEN KNITTING FLAT

A chart shows only the right side of the garment. That's why when you're knitting in the round you ususally read a chart from right to left—the right side is always facing you. But when you knit flat, on every other row the right side is facing away from you. Therefore, when you're working the wrong side, you read the chart left to right. To visualize why it works this way, think of how your knitting looks when you are working the wrong side—if viewed from the right side, you would appear to be working from left to right.

I sometimes write little arrows on the chart to keep track of what row I'm on and which direction to work in. Round and row numbers on the sampler chart help with this—a number on the right-hand side signals a right-side row; a number on the left-hand side signals a wrong-side row.

Keep in mind that the meaning of some symbols change when you are working the wrong side. This is ususally accounted for in the key,

but if it isn't, remember that when working on the wrong side you'll purl where you see the symbol for knit and knit where you see the symbol for purl.

Before you begin knitting flat, it's also important to check the sequence of any cables. It's best to perform stitch crosses on the right side of the work. However, if the sequence is such that you will be on the wrong side when they need to cross, don't panic. You can work a simple cable on the wrong side by twisting the stitches as you would for the right side, but purl them. If you're not up to that, break the yarn at the end of the last complete row, slide your stitches to the other end of your needle, and join the yarn again at that end to work the cable-crossing row on the right side.

NECKLINES

A shaped neckline is simply a curved opening at the top of the garment front, and it can be created in a variety of styles. You're probably familiar with this type of neckline since it is the most common neckline style in modern sweaters.

To create a shaped neckline, you'll either place the center stitches of the garment front on a stitch holder or bind them off. Binding off the neck stitches helps keep the shape of the neckline, whereas putting them on a stitch holder can contribute to the neck eventually stretching out. I have found that children's ganseys will keep their shape either way, but some adult ganseys, which are heavier since they are larger, benefit from bound-off necklines.

Next, you'll decrease on either side of the center stitches every other row (while also working the shoulders) to create a gently sloping, rounded neckline. There is a formula for determining a well-proportioned shape on pages 70-71, but this is by no means the only way to plan a neckline. Sometimes eyeballing works just as well.

Although many of the traditional ganseys had shaped necklines, older examples had unshaped necklines, as does the sampler. One advantage to this style is that you don't have to knit any decreases in the pattern area, which can disrupt the flow of the motifs. Without neckline decreases, the front and back of the garment are simple rectangles. However, joining them together at the shoulder produces a boatneck style, which is not the most comfortable style to wear.

The gansey knitters were most ingenious in solving this problem. They used a variety of shoulder straps, shoulder extensions, and neck gussets to improve the fit and appearance of unshaped necklines (see Chapters 8 and 10). The sampler is worked with shoulder straps, commonly known as saddle shoulders in the Aran tradition, which form a bridge between the back and front of the garment.

the sampler

UPPER BODY AND NECKLINE

Continued from page 58.

At this stage, you should have 29 sts for both your front and back. With the RS of the fabric facing you, attach the yarn to the right-hand side of the garment front and work flat according to the chart, beginning on Row 41. You can switch to US 7 (4.5mm) dpns now, if you wish, or continue with the circular needle. When the front is complete, break the yarn and put the sts on a holder.

Next, slip back sts to a larger-sized dpn. Attach yarn to the right-hand side of the garment back and work according to the chart. Once complete, put the back sts on a holder as well and break the yarn.

The sampler instructions continue on page 75.

PARTIAL BODY CHART (ROUNDS 41–56)

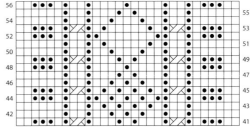

KEY

☐ k on RS, p on WS   ☒• p on RS, k on WS   ⧖ 1/1 RC

Sampler with front and back complete and stitches on holders.

From the bottom: An unshaped neck with shoulder straps and strap gussets; a shaped neckline; an unshaped neck with shoulder extensions; an unshaped neck with inverted triangular neck gussets.

design variations

One way to add more depth to the neckline is to add an extra main pattern repeat to the back. This also moves the shoulder strap forward a bit, making it a more noticeable design element. If you decide to try this, chart the front and back patterns beforehand to make sure the additional back pattern repeat isn't so long it will make the neckline too deep. (See Working Full-Size on the next page for more on neckline depth.) Alternatively, you could knit the back before the front and measure the length of the last motif on the back to determine how deep the neckline will be if you omit this one repeat from the front of the garment. Then make adjustments accordingly.

working full-size

UNSHAPED NECKLINES

To create an unshaped neckline, the gansey knitters divided both the front and back pieces vertically into thirds: one-third for each shoulder and one-third for the neck. With no shaping in the neck area, you can easily accommodate different patterns and knitting strategies, such as placing cables anywhere on the front. However, for child-sized garments up to size 12, you must make allowance for the fact that children's heads are larger in proportion to their bodies than adults. Divide for the neck allowing one-fourth of the stitches for each shoulder and one-half of the stitches for the neck.

Unshaped necklines are very straightforward. Just work the upper front and back to the full garment length, usually determined by the armhole depth. If you're adding shoulder straps, you'll need to determine their width (usually 5 to 10 percent of the total body stitches). Divide the width of the shoulder strap in half. Subtract this amount from the length of the garment (from cast-on edge to shoulder) and knit the front and back to that length. When you add the shoulder straps, the garment will be the correct length.

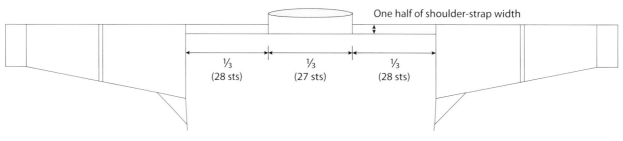

One half of shoulder-strap width

⅓ (28 sts)   ⅓ (27 sts)   ⅓ (28 sts)

Example gansey unshaped-neckline schematic

SHAPED NECKLINES

For an adult-sized gansey, a shaped neckline should be about 2–3" (5–7.5 cm) deep—in other words, begin the decreases when the gansey is 2–3" (5–7.5 cm) less than the desired total length. For a child-sized gansey, begin the neck shaping when the gansey measures 1–2" (2.5–5 cm) less than the finished length. Avoid cable placement in the area where neck shaping will occur.

The neck opening requires 20 percent of the total number of body stitches.

Example: *Total body stitches = 168*

Neck opening = 168 × .20 = 33.6 sts

We'll round the neck opening stitches down to 33 so that we'll be working with whole numbers in the next step (although you could also round up to 34 and make the one-stitch adjustment later).

Now, you'll determine the number of stitches in each shoulder. Each garment half has 50 percent of the total number of body stitches (84). However, the seam stitches, which were part of the original body stitch count, are now on holders with the gusset stitches, so each garment half is now at 83 stitches.

The front stitches that are not used for the neck opening are for the shoulders; divide that figure in half to determine the number of stitches for each shoulder (this is an approximate number):

[Total body stitches × .50] – [Total body stitches × .20] ÷ 2 = Stitches for each shoulder

Example: *[83 sts – 33 sts] ÷ 2 = 25 sts for each shoulder*

In the first row of shaping, 15 percent of the total body stitches are bound off, leaving 5 percent on the needle—half on one side of the bound-off stitches and half on the other side.

[Total body stitches × .20] – [Total body stitches × .15] = Total body stitches to be decreased for shaping

Example: *33 sts – 25 sts = 8 sts*

In this example, you'd evenly decrease a total of 8 stitches in the neck opening, or 4 on each side of the neck. (To vary the slope of the neckline, you can decrease the neck-opening stitches and increase the number of stitches at each side to be done away with, or vice versa. Or, by beginning the neckline sooner, the same number of decreases can be worked less often, such as every fourth row, to create a deeper neckline.)

Decrease 1 stitch at each side of the neckline every other row. After all the neck stitches have been decreased away, work even on the two shoulders until the front is the same length as the back. Put the shoulder stitches on holders.

An alternative way to compute the neckline shaping is to determine the number of shoulder stitches (as above) and simply plan to

decrease 1" (2.5 cm) worth of stitches on either side of the neckline, 1 stitch at a time, every other row. In the first row of shaping, you'll bind off the stitches that remain after calculating the decreases on the sides of the neck. After decreasing away the rest of the neck-opening stitches, work both shoulders even until the front is as long as the back and put the shoulder stitches on holders.

Example Gansey chart is on page 31.

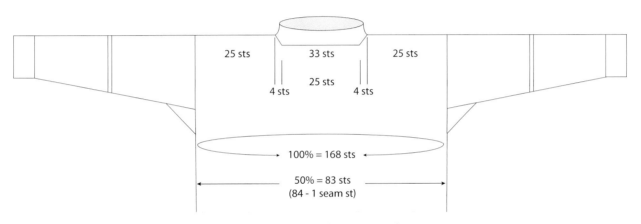

Example gansey shaped-neckline schematic

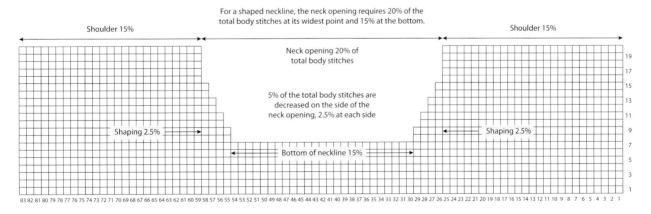

(All percentages are based the total number of body sts; this example has 168 sts.)

CHAPTER 8
shoulder straps and joins

After you've completed the gansey front and back and put the stitches on holders, the next step is to join the shoulders. Typically, the method you use to do this will depend on whether the garment has a shaped or unshaped neckline.

If you're planning a shaped neckline, you'll join the shoulders with the Three-Needle Bind-off (page 79) or by simply grafting. Because the neckline curves gradually on both sides as a result of decreasing, you can add a neckband with no further adjustments.

An unshaped neckline can require shoulder straps and often neckline gussets to create depth and contour. Shoulder straps can be worked either vertically as shoulder extensions (in the established direction of the knitting) or horizontally (perpendicular to the knitting; page 76). Shoulder extensions can be joined either by grafting or with Three-Needle Bind-off. Perpendicular straps, however, such as those in the sampler, are joined with the perpendicular shoulder join, which creates the shoulder strap and joins the garment at the same time.

PERPENDICULAR STRAP AND JOIN

The perpendicular shoulder join, a term coined by Priscilla Gibson-Roberts in *Knitting in the Old Way* (1985), refers to the process of knitting the shoulder strap while joining the garment front and back to that strap at right angles. Perpendicular joining is basically a short-row method of shaping, whereby extra rows are formed within the fabric. It is similar to turning a sock heel in that you decrease at the end of each row.

Cast-on stitches bridge the gap between the front and back of the garment while providing the base for the perpendicular shoulder strap at the neck edge (see page 74). The strap is worked to the armhole edge, at which point the sleeve stitches are picked up and the sleeve is knitted.

Two aspects of working the strap require your careful attention to achieve a satisfying end result: joining stitches and working the decreases. To ensure that the joining stitches at either edge of the strap are an attractive size, you must slip the stitch at the beginning of each row. If worked every row, the edge stitches would be very small and the join would look cramped. So, when working a right-side row, slip the first stitch as if to purl with the working yarn in back (wyb); when working a wrong-side row, slip as if to purl with the working yarn in front (wyf). After slipping the stitch, pull your working yarn and wiggle the slipped stitch around a little bit to cinch it down as much as possible. Slipped stitches tend to grow, and this is a way of keeping them under control.

The second consideration is the type of decrease used. On the wrong side, you should purl together the last stitch of the shoulder strap with the next shoulder stitch. On the right side, work an ssk.

When you knit the perpendicular shoulder join, you work two rows for every stitch in the shoulder, so the strap is a bit longer than the shoulder, and it may puff a little where the additional length has been eased in. The knit stitch is wider than it is tall so the shoulder stitches will somewhat compensate, and the shaping curves around the shoulders, minimize the puffiness. If this bothers you, you can block it out or work the strap on smaller needles than those you used for the body. Alternatively, you can occasionally work double decreases to distribute the ease along the strap.

This may seem like a lot of discussion over joining stitches and which type of decrease is best, but the strap is very noticeable sitting up on one's shoulders at everyone's eye level. A shoulder strap can make or break the look of a gansey.

PROVISIONAL CAST-ONS

Provisional cast-ons often use a length of contrasting-color yarn. This yarn is later removed to reveal stitches, and the contrasting color helps to identify and remove the correct yarn.

INVISIBLE CAST-ON

Note: This method of casting on creates two stitches at a time.

Make a slipknot with 2 strands (your working yarn and a contrasting-color yarn), leaving a short tail 3½–4" (7–10 cm) long. Hold the needle in your right hand and in your left, hold the 2 strands at right angles to each other, with the contrasting yarn in front (fig. 1). *Take the needle over and behind the working yarn (fig. 2), over and in front of the contrasting yarn (fig. 3), over and behind the working yarn again (fig. 4), then under and in front of the contrasting yarn (fig. 5). The waste yarn slips off the needle at this point, but is holding the 2 cast-on sts in place on the needle. Repeat from * until you have cast on all the sts you need. These sts are not yet stable. Turn the work without letting go of the yarns and knit them with your working yarn.

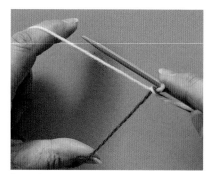

figure 1

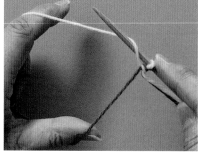

figure 2

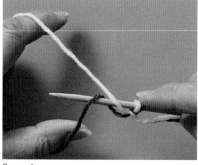

figure 3

figure 4

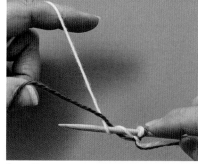

figure 5

ALTERNATE PROVISIONAL CAST-ON

An alternate method of the Invisible Cast-on is to cast on in any method using a contrasting yarn. (I prefer long-tail.) Change to your main color, knitting a row, and work as needed from there. When you are ready to work stitches in the opposite direction, remove the contrasting yarn and pick up the resulting loops of the main color.

the sampler

SHOULDER STRAPS

Continued from page 68.

In order to have live stitches available to pick up for the neckband, you need to use a provisional cast-on for your shoulder straps, which allows your knitting to continue in two directions (down the shoulder strap and up the neckband). There are many types of provisional cast-ons, any of which will work, but I share two in this book: the Invisible Cast-on and the Alternate Provisional Cast-on (see page 74).

If using the Invisible Cast-on method, CO 6 sts, turn the work without letting go of the yarns, and k6 with

your working yarn to make the sts stable. Make sure the contrasting yarn is under your needle, holding the working yarn sts in place. (If it ends up over your needle like a st, start again.) Put these cast-on sts aside for the moment.

Note: When you return to these sts later for the neckband, after removing the contrasting yarn you'll notice that every other st is twisted on the needle. Be sure to turn them so that all sts face the same direction, with right leg of the st in front.

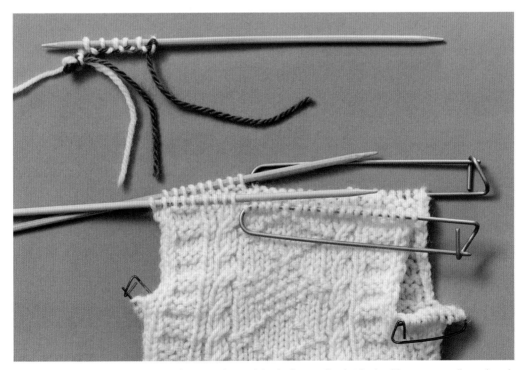

With nine stitches each for the front and back right shoulder on two needles and newly cast-on stitches on a third needle, you are ready to begin the perpendicular shoulder join.

PERPENDICULAR SHOULDER JOIN

The sampler's shoulder strap is 6 sts wide and will join the front and back shoulders on the right and left sides of the sampler. In addition, a 2-st cable, one of the three described on page 59, is worked the length of the strap.

RIGHT SHOULDER

Put 9 sts from the front right shoulder and 9 sts from the back right shoulder onto 2 needles. (To distinguish which shoulder is which, remember that the initial is on the front left of the garment, and pretend you are wearing the little gansey.)

Hold the front right shoulder needle in your left hand and the newly cast-on sts in your right hand. Drop the back right shoulder needle for now (fig. 1).

**With the RS of the sweater facing you, k1 from the neck edge (not the armhole edge) of the left needle, pass the last (adjacent) cast-on st over (fig. 2). Turn the work.

Note: Row 1 is a wrong-side row, read chart from left to right.

Row 1: Sl 1 purlwise with yarn in front (wyf) (fig. 3), k1, p2, k1, p1 tog with 1 st from neck edge of back right shoulder needle.

When purling 2 sts together from 2 needles, insert your right needle tip into the st on the back needle first, then into the st on the front needle. Be careful not to twist shoulder. Make sure the wrong side of back right shoulder is facing you (fig. 4). Turn work. You have connected the front and back shoulders. This creates the neck edge of the shoulder strap (fig. 5).

Note: You will now knit 16 more short-rows, working 2 sts tog (one from the strap and one from a shoulder) at the end of every row until no more shoulder sts remain.

Row 2: (RS) Sl 1 pwise with yarn in back (wyb), p1, k2, p1, ssk, turn.

Row 3: (WS) Sl 1 pwise wyf, k1, p2, k1 p2tog, turn.

Row 4: (RS) Sl 1 pwise wyb, p1, 1/1RC, p1, ssk, turn.

Row 5: (WS) Sl 1 pwise wyf, k1, p2, k1, p2tog, turn.

Repeat Rows 2–5 three more times. Break yarn and slip rem 6 sts to a stitch holder.

LEFT SHOULDER

Cast on 6 provisional sts as for right shoulder. Put 9 sts from the front left shoulder and 9 sts from the back left shoulder onto 2 needles. Hold the needle for the back left shoulder in your left hand with the RS (the outside) of the sweater facing you and the needle with the newly cast-on sts in your right hand. (Drop the other needle for the moment.) Repeat the instructions for the right shoulder from ** (fig. 2) to complete the strap.

The sampler instructions continue on page 84.

SHOULDER STRAP CHART

KEY

- ☐ k on RS, p on WS
- ● p on RS, k on WS
- ＼ ssk
- ／ k2tog on RS, p2tog on WS
- ∨ sl 1wyb on RS, sl 1 wyf on WS
- ⧖ 1/1 RC

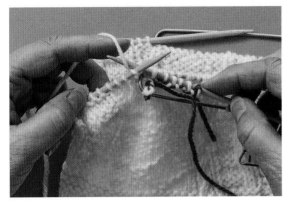

figure 1

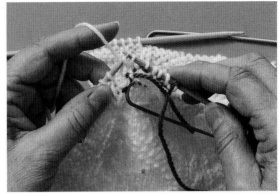

figure 2

figure 3

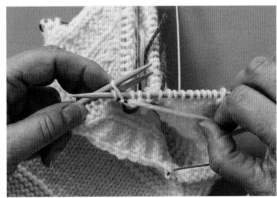

figure 4

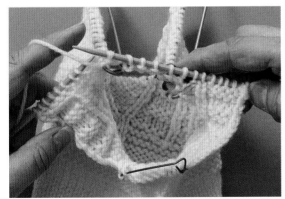

figure 5

The two-stitch cable adds a decorative element to the strap and mirrors the cables on the garment body. Choose whatever style of cable you prefer (see page 59).

three-needle bind-off

Whether the neckline is shaped or unshaped, the simplest method for joining a gansey's shoulders is the Three-Needle Bind-off. This technique requires that the front and back shoulders have the same number of stitches. It can be worked with right sides together for a clean, crisp-looking seam or with wrong sides together for a distinctive ridge along the seam. Early gansey knitters commonly used both methods.

Note: This bind-off creates a ridge along the shoulder that has a distinctive front and back. To ensure the same side of the ridge appears on the front of both shoulders, work one shoulder from shoulder edge to neck edge and the other from neck edge to shoulder edge.

Put the front and back sts of one shoulder on separate needles and hold them together in your left hand as one.

*Take a third needle and insert the right needle kwise into the first st of both needles, throw the yarn and bring it through both sts (fig. 1), dropping them off the left needles. Repeat from * once (fig. 2). Then slip the first st on your right needle over the second st to bind off (fig. 3).

Repeat these steps until you have 1 st left. Break the yarn and pull it through the last loop.

figure 1

figure 2

figure 3

The shoulders of the Musician gansey (left) are joined by the Three-Needle Bind-off with RS held together; the shoulders of Snakes and Ladders (right) are joined with the same bind-off, but with WS together, in addition to a neck gusset.

design variatison

Historically, shoulder straps were often emphasized by a change in patterning, making them an additional design element. If you're adding a design within the strap, it's best to use a smaller version of a body motif to tie the garment together visually—for example, a four-stitch cable rather than an eight-stitch cable. Bold knit/purl patterns, such as zigzags or diamonds, are also effective. If the patterns are too large, subtract some stitches, chart the resulting motifs, juggle them around, and then knit samples to get an idea of the best finished size.

Avoid simple background patterns for the strap—they don't make a strong visual impact. You can achieve a dramatic effect by continuing a perpendicular strap pattern down the sleeve through the sleeve's definition ridge to the cuff.

When planning the pattern for the strap, leave the two edge stitches without any pattern, as they are the joining stitches where the decreases will be worked. To emphasize these stitches, purl the stitches beside them inside the strap. To deemphasize them, knit the stitches next to them.

shoulder-extension straps

The shoulder-extension strap for an unshaped neckline can be constructed in two ways. The first is to knit extensions 2-3" (5-7.5 cm) long on one shoulder of both the garment front and back and then join the straps to the body with Kitchener stitch. (Be sure to work only one extension on each shoulder.)

In the second method, extensions of 2" (5 cm) or more are knitted across the full width of the garment back and across the shoulders of the front so that the front and back are the same length. The garment pieces are joined at the shoulder line using either Kitchener stitch or the Three Needle Bind-off. Extension straps can be worked in a different pattern from the body of the garment, such as Rig 'n' Furrow, Indian Corn stitch, or another of your choice for visual interest.

RIG 'N' FURROW

Rig 'n' Furrow is a decorative pattern you can use for the second style of extension strap. Bands of stockinette stitch and reverse stockinette alternate to create the effect of the ridges and furrows of a plowed field. You can arrange the stockinette and reverse stockinette in any sequence and width you choose—for example, three rows of stockinette followed by two rows of reverse stockinette or two of stockinette and five of reverse stockinette. Experiment!

Rig 'n' Furrow straps can be joined with the Three Needle Bind-off, but the elegant alternative is to join them with Kitchener stitch so that the patterning is not disrupted. Because the stitches on the needle on the front and back each yield a knit row and Kitchener stitch forms a third knit row, your patterning needs to include at least a three-row span of knitting within the sequence. Again, if using Kitchener stitch for a shoulder seam, limit its use to a child's garment or add reinforcement, such as duplicate stitch on the wrong side, to strengthen the seam.

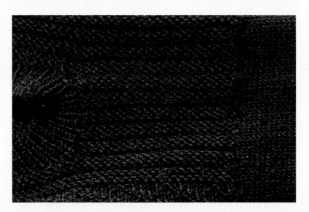

The Rig 'n' Furrow pattern is used in the shoulder area of a gansey and is made from bands of alternating groups of knit and purl rows.

working full-size

Perpendicular shoulder straps look best between 1" (2.5 cm) wide (for child-sized garments) and up to 4" (10 cm) wide (for a large man's garment). For most adult sweaters, I use a strap 2" (5 cm) wide. To determine the number of stitches to cast on, multiply the desired strap width by the stitch gauge.

You can also use the percentage method to calculate how many stitches you'll need. Multiply the total number of body stitches by 5 to 10 percent.

Example: *168 sts × .05 = 8 sts*

At 4 stitches per inch (2.5 cm), the straps are 2" (5 cm) wide.

Of course, the strap pattern also determines the number of stitches to cast on. Let's assume you would like to repeat the eight-stitch

cable that is in the sweater body in the strap, but would like to scale it down to 6 stitches. In a strap 2" (5 cm) wide, you have 8 stitches to work with. The cable should be flanked by a purl stitch on each side to give it more emphasis:

6 sts + 2 sts = 8 sts

Including the knitted edge stitches, you will now need 10 stitches where you only planned 8. That's okay. Let the percentages and measurements guide you, but let the actual patterning determine the final stitch count. (Alternatively, you could scale the cable down to 4 stitches and leave the strap width at 8 stitches.) There's enough flexibility in every garment to account for some variance.

CHAPTER 9

the sleeves

Gansey sleeves are knitted in the round from the armhole to the cuff while, simultaneously, the gusset is decreased away. Some historic examples sported three-quarter-length sleeves, which would have been practical for the fishermen's messy work; however, full-length sleeves were more common.

Like the garment body, the gansey sleeve has patterning, a plain area, and a definition ridge; one starts reading the chart at the bottom right-hand corner. The patterning can be different from or similar to the body patterning. As you can see in the chart on page 85, the sampler sleeve has a cable down the center, which continues from the shoulder strap and is flanked by the same side panels used in the sampler body. The sleeve patterning ends with a definition ridge, followed by a plain area of stockinette stitch and ribbed cuff.

After the first round of the sleeve, the gusset is decreased (the sampler uses paired decreases—ssk and k2tog) at the same frequency as it was increased in the body (see Chapter 6) until nothing is left of the gusset but the seam stitches. When the gusset is completed, the frequency of decreases changes to the rate you determine for shaping the sleeve (see page 88).

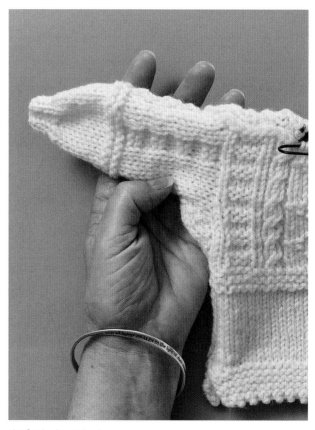

The finished sampler sleeve.

double decreases

SL 2 TOG, K1, PSSO (S2KP)

This RS double decrease has a centered, vertical appearance. Slip 2 tog kwise (fig. 1). Knit 1 (fig. 2). Pass 2 slipped sts over (fig. 3). The finished decrease (fig. 4). I use this decrease for the tip of the underarm gusset's second half.

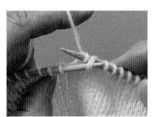

figure 1   figure 2   figure 3   figure 4

SL 1, K2TOG, PSSO (SK2P)

This RS double decrease leans to the left. Slip 1 st kwise (fig. 1). Knit 2 sts tog (fig. 2). Pass the slipped st over (fig. 3). The finished decrease (fig. 4). I use this decrease to give the appearance of closure to a gusset, such as the triangular neck gusset.

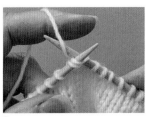

figure 1   figure 2   figure 3   figure 4

the sampler

UPPER BODY AND NECKLINE

Continued from page 75.

With the garment now joined at both shoulders, you are ready to pick up the armhole sts to work the sleeve.

Pick-up round: Slip one gusset and its seam sts (11 sts) off the holder onto US 7 (4.5 mm) dpns. With the RS of the fabric facing you, join the yarn at the right-hand side of the gusset and work the seam and gusset sts.

Insert your right needle into the first st of the armhole edge to the left of the gusset, throw your yarn, and bring it through. (For more strength and stability, pick up both halves of the selvedge loop—the entire st.)

Pick up 11 sleeve sts evenly spaced up the armhole from the last seam st to the shoulder strap (roughly 2 sleeve sts for every 3 armhole rows).

Work across the 6 sts of the shoulder strap in pattern: k1, p1, k2, p1, k1. Then pick up 11 sts down the armhole—39 sts.

Add a marker before the seam sts and the gusset to indicate the beginning of the rnd.

Keeping the sts of the shoulder strap in pattern, work the sleeve, purling the seam sts and dec 2 gusset sts every other round as follows. (The instructions for s2kp are available on page 83.)

Rnd 19: P1, ssk, k5, k2tog, p1, k12, p1, k2, p1, k12—37 sts.

Rnd 20: P1, k7, p1, k6, p3, k3, p1, 1/1RC, p1, k3, p3, k6.

Rnd 21: P1, ssk, k3, k2tog, p1, k6, p3, k3, p1, k2, p1, k3, p3, k6—35 sts.

Rnd 22: P1, k5, p1, k12, p1, k2, p1, k12.

Rnd 23: P1, ssk, k1, k2tog, p1, k12, p1, k2, p1, k12—33 sts.

Rnd 24: P1, k3, p1, k6, p3, k3, p1, 1/1RC, p1, k3, p3, k6.

Rnd 25: P1, s2kp, p1, k6, p3, k3, p1, k2, p1, k3, p3, k6—31 sts.

Rnd 26: P2tog, p1, k12, p1, k2, p1, k12—30 sts.

Rnds 27, 28, and 29: Work even, cabling according to the chart.

Rnd 30: P2, ssk, work patt to last 2 sts of rnd, k2tog—28 sts.

Rnds 31–34: Repeat Rnds 27–30 once, cabling according to the chart—26 sts.

THE DEFINITION RIDGE AND LOWER SLEEVE

Rnds 35–37: On US 5 (3.75 mm) dpns, purl 1 rnd, knit 1 rnd, purl 1 rnd, maintaining seam sts.

Rnd 38: On US 7 (4.5 mm) dpns, p2, ssk, knit to last 2 sts of round, k2tog—24 sts.

Rnds 39–46: Knit even, maintaining seam sts.

THE CUFF

On US 5 (3.75 mm) dpns, dec to 16 sts in the first rnd of 2 × 2 ribbing, as shown on the chart, so that the 2 purl seam sts flow smoothly into the ribbing.

Work 3 more rnds of ribbing. BO in patt.

Work the other sleeve.

The sampler instructions continue on page 94.

The underarm gusset is decreased as the sleeve is knitted, then the rest of the sleeve shaping begins.

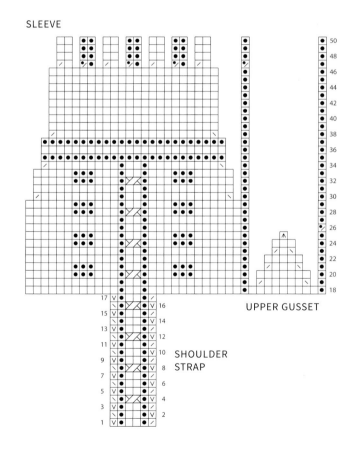

SLEEVE

UPPER GUSSET

SHOULDER
STRAP

KEY

	k on RS, p on WS
•	p on RS, k on WS
/	k2tog on RS, p2tog on WS
\	ssk
•/	p2tog
∧	s2kp
V	sl 1wyb on RS, sl 1 wyf on WS
⧖	1/1 RC

design variations

For the center panel of the sleeve patterning, it's best to choose a bold design motif from the body. You can surround it with background patterns or other motifs from the body. If the motifs seem too large on your chart, subtract stitches until the whole design looks proportional.

Another design option is to continue the center panel all the way to the cuff, ending the rest of the patterning at the definition ridge. If you do this, be certain the center motif is narrow enough to be visible and doesn't wrap around the underside of the sleeve. The placement of the sleeve's definition ridge is arbitrary, but I often align it with the garment's definition ridge.

For the sleeve designs below, I pulled three vertical motifs from the body patterning of the example chart on page 108 (Chapter 11). In option 1, I chose to omit the large center diamond and added a subtle four-stitch cable. In option 2, I scaled down the large center diamond from the body patterning for a bolder look. In both options, the seed-stitch background pattern covers areas that will be decreased during shaping.

BODY PATTERNING

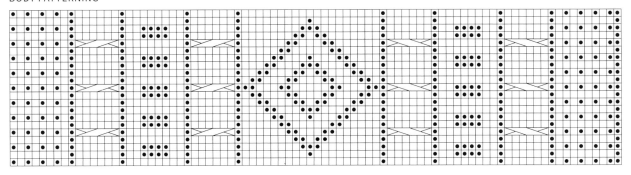

SLEEVE PATTERNING, OPTION 1

KEY

☐	knit
•	purl
⧓	2/2 RC
⧓	2/2 LC
⧓	3/3 RC
⧓	3/3 LC

SLEEVE PATTERNING, OPTION 2

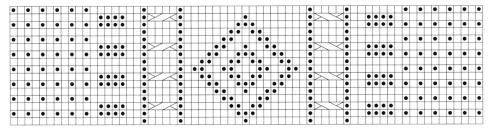

working full-size

DETERMINING THE LENGTH OF THE SLEEVE

Drop-shoulder-sleeve lengths can be difficult to calculate because it is not always clear where the sleeve seam will fall on the arm. One option is to measure the sleeve of a drop-shoulder sweater you already own that fits as you would like your new sweater to fit. Or you can reference the table on page 106 for approximate sleeve lengths for general sizes.

Another way to determine the length of your sleeve is to measure the intended recipient of the sweater from the protruding bone at the back of the neck to the wrist, along the length of a bent arm (so the cuff won't hike up when the elbow bends). It is next to impossible to accurately measure this on yourself, so if you are making this gansey for yourself, have someone help you take this measurement. Subtract 25 percent of the total body stitches in inches from this measurement.

Example: A 42" body circumference garment.

Neck to wrist = 29"

42" × .25 = 10½"

29" – 10½" = 18½" for the sleeve length

PICKING UP STITCHES FOR THE SLEEVE

There are many ways to determine the number of stitches to pick up at the armhole. One is the "pick up and rip out until it looks right" method. You pick up the stitches, count them, and squeeze the pattern into the number of stitches you have. This is not a very disciplined way of doing things, but sometimes this serendipitous approach can add a new dimension to your work.

Another method is to measure the armhole circumference, which includes the garment front and back, but omits the gusset and any live shoulder-strap stitches. (The gusset will be decreased away so it doesn't figure into the final sleeve dimensions.) Multiply the armhole circumference by the stitch gauge to determine the number of stitches you'll need to pick up, adding in any strap stitches for the total sleeve stitch count.

The third method is even more precise: count the number of rows from the last row of gusset stitches all the way around the armhole. If the shoulder seam has been grafted or bound off, you need only count one side of the armhole to the seam and double the number. If the garment has a perpendicular shoulder strap, omit the strap stitches from the calculated total to pick up because they are already available on a holder, but add them to the final total sleeve stitches. Divide the the number of rows in the armhole by your row gauge, then multiply that number by your stitch gauge.

For more on the calculations for picking up armhole stitches, see page 89.

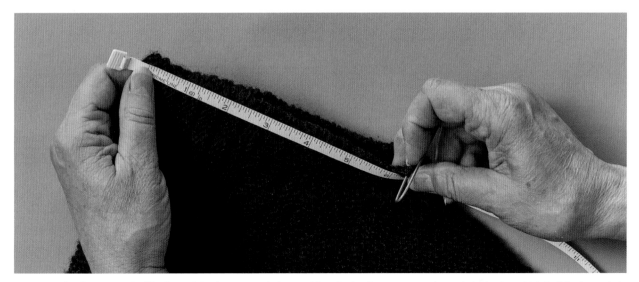

An alternate method for determining how many stitches to pick up for the sleeve: measure the armhole depth, multiply by 2 for the armhole circumference, then multiply that number by your stitch gauge. Do not include gusset and seam stitches in this measurement.

In the example sleeve chart (page 91), you can see that the 9 additional stitches are decreased in the first round of the cuff ribbing.

2. Calculate how many stitches to decrease

To determine how many stitches to decrease overall to shape the sleeve, subtract the lower sleeve circumference from the number of sleeve stitches remaining once the gusset has been decreased.

Number of stitches in sleeve – Number of stitches in lower sleeve width
= Number of stitches to be decreased.

Example: *65 sts – 41 sts = 24 sts*

3. Calculate the number of rounds in which to shape the sleeve

Now, determine the length of the sleeve body, that is, the distance from the end of the gusset to the beginning of the cuff. This is the length within which you will decrease.

Total length of sleeve – [Cuff length + one-half underarm gusset length]
= Length within which to decrease

Example: *18" – [2" + 3"] = 13"*

Multiply the total sleeve-body length by the round gauge to determine the number of rounds within which to decrease.

Area within which to decrease × Round gauge
= Total number of rounds within which to decrease

Example: *13" × 6 rounds/in. = 78 rounds*

Sometimes a few rounds need to be added to the gusset to shape it logically, such as decreasing 2 seam stitches into 1 seam stitch as in the example sleeve chart. The gusset was calculated at 18 rounds, but was drawn over 20 rounds.

4. Calculate how often to decrease

Divide the number of rounds within which to decrease by the number of stitches to be decreased to determine the rate of decreasing.

Number of rounds within which to decrease
÷ Number of stitches to decrease
= Number of rounds to be worked per decrease

Example: 78 rounds ÷ 24 sts = 3.25 rounds per decrease

Round fractions to the nearest whole number, in this case, 3. Work 1 decrease every 3 rounds. To determine the rate of frequency for paired decreases, multiply the rate by 2.

Number of rounds to be worked per decrease × 2
= Number of rounds to be worked per paired decrease

Example: *[1 st every 3 rounds] × 2 = 2 sts decreased every 6 rounds*

THE CUFF

The cuff can vary in its snugness, depending on the rib pattern and your needle size. To calculate the approximate circumference, you will multiply the total body stitches by 20–25 percent and adjust this number to accommodate the ribbing pattern repeat. In the example garment, the cuff calculation is 33.6 stitches and the 2 × 2 ribbing is a 4-stitch repeat, so I rounded the number of cuff stitches to 32, which is evenly divisible by 4. (If the garment ribbing has the same ribbing as the cuff, I double-check my calculations by fitting the body ribbing to my wrist, pinching off the amount of fabric that feels most comfortable, and counting the stitches.)

SHAPING THE SLEEVE

Note: See page 91 for Example Gansey Sleeve Chart.

1. Calculate the number of stitches above the cuff

A sleeve that is full above the cuff offers a looser, more comfortable fit than one that tapers evenly to the cuff. I usually add at least 1–2½" (2.5–6.5 cm) worth of stitches to the cuff measurement, the latter amount yielding a very full sleeve above the cuff. For the example garment, I added 2" (5cm) of stitches:

2" × 4 sts/in. = 8 sts

Add 1 seam stitch for a total of 9 stitches of sleeve ease.

Sleeve ease + Cuff circumference = Lower sleeve circumference

Example: *9 sts + 32 sts = 41 sts*

picking up armhole stitches

FOR A SLEEVE WITHOUT A STRAP

The example on page 108 has a shaped neckline and bound-off shoulders. Both the front and the back of the garment have 48 rows between the last row of the gusset and the shoulder seam. To determine the number of rows in the entire armhole opening, multiply this number by 2:

48 rows × 2 = 96 rows

At a gauge of 6 rows per inch (2.5 cm), each armhole is 8" (20.5 cm) deep. To calculate the number of stitches to pick up for the sleeve, double the armhole depth (to account for each garment half) and multiply this figure by the stitch gauge:

8" × 2 × 4 sts/in. = 64 sts

To calculate the rate of pick-up, divide the number of rows in the armhole by the number of stitches to be picked up:

64 sts/96 rows, or, simplifying the fraction, 2 sts/3 rows

You can pick up one stitch in each of 2 rows, then skip the third row. (If you should end up with an awkward fraction, round up or down to the nearest whole number to make it easier to work with.)

FOR A SLEEVE WITH A STRAP

To pick up the armhole stitches for a sleeve on a sweater with a perpendicular shoulder strap, you need to calculate a little differently. Because the strap stitches are already on a holder, you won't include the strap in the calculations and can work with just one side of the armhole.

In the discussion above, we determined that an armhole 8" (20.5 cm) deep knitted at a gauge of 4 stitches per inch (2.5 cm) requires a total of 64 stitches. Let's assume that the garment has a shoulder strap 2" (5 cm) wide. Calculate the number of stitches in the strap:

2" × 4 sts/in. = 8 sts

Subtract this number from the total number of sleeve stitches needed:

64 sts – 8 sts = 56 sts

This is the total number of stitches to pick up. Half of that is the number of stitches to pick up on each side of the strap:

56 sts ÷ 2 = 28 sts

Now, determine the rate of pick-up. If the strap is 2" (5 cm) wide, the front and back each measure 1" (2.5 cm) shorter (half the strap width) than the desired full length. For a garment the size of the example discussed here, the front and back therefore measure only 7" (18 cm) from the last row of the gusset to the top of the garment. Multiply this length by the row gauge to determine the number of rows on one side:

7" × 6 rows/in. = 42 rows

The rate of pick-up is the ratio of the number of stitches to be picked up on one side of the armhole to the number of rows on one side:

28 sts/42 rows, or, simplifying the fraction, 2 sts/3 rows

You can pick up 1 stitch in each of 2 rows, then skip the third row. (If it's still necessary, round up or down to the nearest whole number.)

charting the sleeve

Although the sleeve is knitted in the round, the entire sleeve is charted to show the shaping more clearly. Because the sleeve is knitted from the armhole to the cuff, it is charted upside down and read starting with the bottom right-hand corner.

The sleeve is charted in the same way as the body (see pages 54-55). First, determine the sleeve and cuff lengths. Measure your body or a favorite sweater along the underarm seam. Even if the sweater has a set-in sleeve, this will give you an accurate measurement for a dropped-shoulder gansey. The example gansey sleeve length is 18" (45.5 cm): 3" (7.5 cm) in which the gusset decreasing occurs, 13" (33 cm) of sleeve body, and 2" (5 cm) of cuff. The sleeve body and gusset total 16" (40.5 cm). Multiply that total by the round gauge and plot it on the chart:

$$16" \times 6 \text{ rounds/in.} = 96 \text{ rounds}$$

Mark the lower sleeve circumference (41 sts) and add the cuff (32 sts wide and 2" [5 cm] long). You don't know the exact number of rounds needed for the cuff at this point because you will be using smaller needles for the ribbing, and the gauge will be tighter than for the body. I estimated 14 rounds on the chart, but I'd measure when knitting to be sure.

For the armhole circumference, multiply the stitch gauge by the total armhole measurement:

$$4 \text{ sts/in.} \times 16" = 64 \text{ sts}$$

Or use the percentage method:

$$168 \text{ sts} \times .40 = 67.2 \text{ sts}$$

Note: I plotted 64 sts for the example sweater, not including the seam stitch, which will be included in the gusset. Because the gansey is a forgiving shape, you can always allow a few stitches of variance. Knitting is not an exact science.

You also need to chart the gusset and its decreases. This should approximate a mirror image of the first half of the gusset. Use the same frequency for decreasing as you used for increasing (see Chapter 6).

EXAMPLE GANSEY SLEEVE CHART

Armhole: 64 sts

Sleeve Body Length: 76 rounds

Bottom Sleeve Width: 41 sts

9 decreases worked in first row of ribbing

Cuff: 32 sts

KEY

☐ k

● p

╱ k2tog

╲ ssk

⋀ s2pp

⊼ s2pp

⤬⤬ 2/2 LC

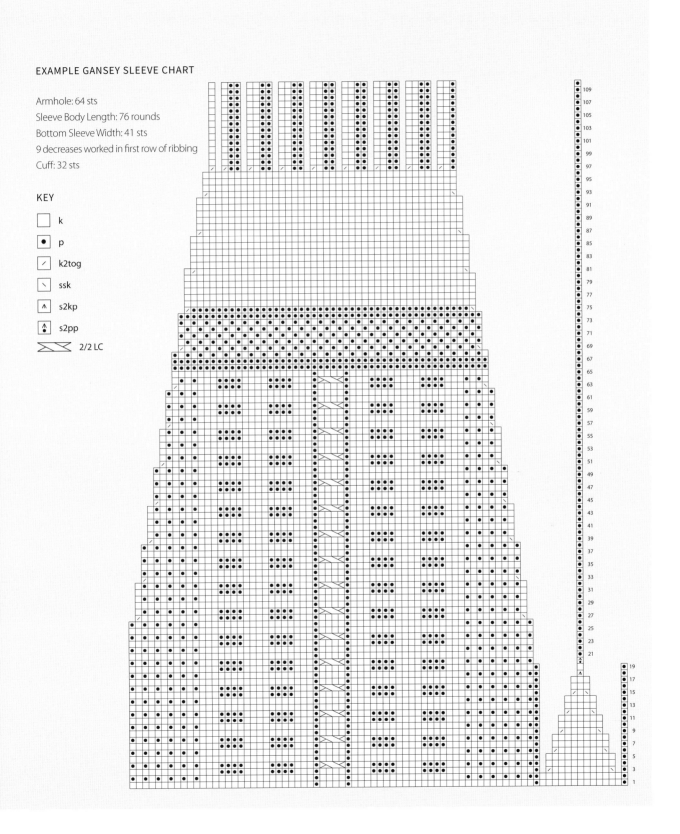

CHAPTER 10

finishing the neckline

Here you are, about to complete the sampler! Next, you'll knit triangular neck gussets and a crew neckband to finish the unshaped neckline.

NECK GUSSETS

Whereas the underarm gusset gives the wearer more freedom of movement, neck gussets contour the fabric around the angles of an unshaped neckline, affording a close, neat fit. Although neck gussets were not always used in traditional ganseys, they are worth knowing about. These tailoring details are examples of ingenious solutions to fit and design problems.

There are three types of neck gussets: triangular, inverted triangular, and the shoulder-strap neck gusset. The type of gusset you select depends on the gansey's shoulder treatment.

The triangular gusset, which is worked within the neckband and can be used with any shoulder treatment, is meant to snug up, or tighten, the neckband. The inverted triangular gusset, worked on the shoulder seam, is used with bound-off shoulder seams. Strap gussets are worked only in conjunction with shoulder straps, and, like the inverted triangular gusset, are worked while joining the shoulder and add width to the neck area.

NECKBANDS

Gansey neckbands come in several styles: rolled, buttoned, folded, and crew. The most straightforward is the crew neckband, knit in either 2 × 2 or 1 × 1 ribbing or stockinette stitch. 2 × 2 ribbing is the most elastic and stockinette stitch is the least. As a design variation, some ganseys feature different rib patterns for the cuffs and neckband. To create the neckband, simply pick up the stitches around the neck, work to the desired length, and bind off loosely in pattern. A neck gusset made up of an odd number of stitches blends well into 1 × 1 ribbing, as does an even number of stitches into 2 × 2 ribbing.

Some gansey knitters worked the neck in 1 × 1 rib for 5" (12.5 cm) or more, but many of these masterpiece sweaters now have sagging necklines, with neckbands that have become misshapen and sloppy with age. To avoid this happening to your gansey over time, make the neckband 2–3" (5–7.5 cm) long.

In *Patterns for Guernseys, Jerseys, and Arans* (1971), Gladys Thompson describes a neat finish for the crew neck. After working the desired length of ribbing or stockinette stitch, knit 1 round, purl 2 rounds, knit 1 more round, then bind off in knit. You'll work a similar finish for the sampler's stockinette stitch neckband: purl 1 round, knit 1 round, bind off in purl.

Examples of five different gansey neckline treatments. From top to bottom: 1 × 1 ribbed crew neckband, folded ribbed neckband in 2 × 2 ribbing, a stand-up collar in cabled ribbing, a ribbed neckband with rolled edge, and a buttoned collar.

the sampler

NECKBAND

Continued from page 84.

The sampler has a stockinette stitch neckband with triangular gussets, worked on the smaller US 5 (3.75 mm) dpns. The triangular gussets are designed to pull in excess fabric around the neck for a neater collar; you will work these on either side at the base of the neck. They use the same decreases as the underarm gussets—ssk and k2tog—and are finished with a double decrease. You have a choice of double decreases: if you want the decrease stitch to continue up the neckband as in ribbing, the s2kp works well (see page 83). To create a closed triangle, as for the sampler, use sk2p (see page 83).

To start, look at your sampler neckline. The front and back are on holders and the cast-on sts for the straps are on waste yarn (fig.1). Working on just one of the strap-stitch areas at a time, pull taut the contrasting yarn that holds the 6 cast-on sts of the right shoulder strap. The sts will pop up, and you can slip them easily onto a dpn. Note that if you used the Invisible Cast-on, every other st will be twisted so that the left, rather than the right, leg of the st is in front (fig. 2). Slip these sts onto a dpn, turning sts as necessary so they are all properly oriented.

Repeat this process for the left shoulder strap st. Fig. 3 shows both groups of 6 strap st on separate dpns, and the front and back (11 sts each) have also been slipped to dpns.

Next, pick up a seventh st from the shoulder-strap edge where the red arrow is pointing in fig. 4, as follows:

As you face the RS of the strap, pick up the running thread in between the second and third sts on the right-hand side of the strap so that there will be 3 sts on either side of the one st coming from the center of the cable. Also pick up one st in the same manner in the other strap. The purpose of this is symmetry: to center the 5-st gusset over 7 sts of the strap—36 sts total on 4 dpns.

Beginning at the right-hand side of the back, work the neckband and neck gussets (which are centered over the shoulder straps) as follows:

Rnd 1: Slip the first st of the back right shoulder, join yarn, p9, p2tog, p5, p2tog, p9, p2tog, p5, ending the round by purling together that first slipped st with the last st of rnd 1. Pm for the beg of the rnd—32 sts.

Rnds 2, 4, 6, and 8: Knit even.

Rnd 3: K10, ssk, k1, k2tog, k11, ssk, k1, k2tog, k1—28 sts.

Rnd 5: K10, sk2p, k11, sk2p, k1—24 sts.

Rnd 7: Purl.

Rnd 9: Bind off in purl. Your sampler is complete!

Neck gussets contour the angular shapes of the neck area. Usually no more than 1½" (3.8 cm) each side on an adult-sized garment, the triangular neck gusset on the miniature sampler consists of five stitches at its greatest width.

NECKBAND

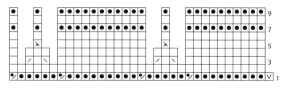

KEY

☐ knit	╱ k2tog	☑ p2tog	⋁ sl 1wyb on RS
● purl	╲ ssk	⅄ sk2p

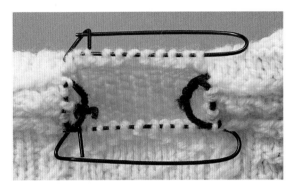

figure 1. The sampler's front and back on holders and the shoulder-strap sts on the contrasting waste yarn.

figure 2. There are 6 sts revealed from the Invisible Cast-on's waste yarn. Note how some are twisted.

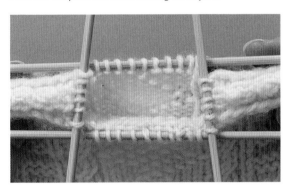

figure 3. All neckband stitches on four needles.

figure 4. The seventh stitch should be picked up between the center cable stitch and the two stitches to its right.

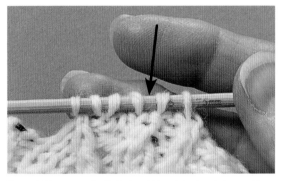

figure 5. The completed crew neckband of the sampler, in stockinette stitch and finished at the edge with garter stitch.

ALTERNATIVE NECKBAND: A ROLLED COLLAR

To knit the sampler neckband as a rolled collar, transfer the 11 sts from each of the holders of the garment front and back to 2 dpns. Transfer the 6 sts from each of the 2 shoulder straps' cast-on sts (on waste yarn) to 2 other dpns–34 sts. Join yarn and knit around the 4 needles with a fifth needle for 1½–2" (3.8–5 cm), then bind off loosely. The collar will curl and will be easier to fit over a toy.

design variations

FOLDED RIBBED NECKBAND

Another way to knit a ribbed neckband is to work the ribbing to twice the desired length. Instead of binding off, fold the ribbing in half to the inside and sew it down, one stitch at a time, directly from the needle, along the ridge of picked-up stitches. This method is extremely elastic and nonbinding and is well suited to children's sweaters.

Sewing down a ribbed neckline along the ridge of picked-up stitches.

THE ROLLED NECKBAND

This collar takes advantage of the tendency for stockinette fabric to roll at the cast-on and bound-off edges of a knitted piece, revealing the reverse stockinette stitch. Pick up stitches around a shaped neckline, or an unshaped neckline with straps or an inverted neck gusset, and work stockinette stitch for 2–4" (5–10 cm). Bind off loosely. I like to use this method with sweaters that have garter welts.

In this example of the classic rolled collar, it is used in conjunction with a wide ribbed neckband, a modern combination.

THE BUTTONED NECKBAND

If you work ribbing, or stockinette stitch, flat rather than in the round, the ends can be overlapped and buttoned. This works best on a neckband from 2–4" (5–10 cm) high.

Pick up the necessary number of neckband stitches, but over one shoulder or shoulder strap, cast on enough extra stitches for an overlap ½–1" (1.3–2.5 cm) wide. I like to work this extension in garter stitch, with an equal amount of extra stitches at each end of the neckband. The extra stitches for the overlap are not secured at the base of the neck. If the neckband stretches out of shape over time, you can tighten it up again by moving the buttons farther from the opening.

In the few historical photos I have seen of this neckband, the buttonholes were worked on the front extension and two to four buttons were sewn on the back. Although I have noted buttoned neckbands in historic photos over either shoulder, this detail typically appeared on the left side of the neck, out of the way of things the men carried on their right shoulders.

A buttoned neckband offered fishermen extra warmth.

inverted triangular neck gusset

This type of gusset will round an unshaped neckline on sweaters with bound-off shoulder seams. The following directions are for a garment whose shoulders have a seam with the ridge on the outside of the garment (the front and back are joined together with wrong sides together).

Put all sts for both sides of one shoulder onto needles—1 needle for the front and 1 for the back, placing markers 7 sts in from where the shoulder sts end and the neck gusset sts will begin. Hold the 2 needles so that the front and back are WS tog.

Beginning at the armhole edge with a third needle, work the Three Needle Bind-off for the front and back of one shoulder (see page 79) up to the markers. Leave the last st of the bind-off on your third needle. Remove the markers.

Row 1: (RS) With the third needle, k1 from your left needle. (There are 2 sts on your third needle.) Turn the work.

Row 2: (WS) Sl 1 pwise (wyf), p1, p1 from your left needle (it was on the right before you turned the work). Discard the third needle. Turn the work.

Row 3: (RS) Sl 1 purlwise (wyb), k2, k1 from shoulder. Turn the work.

Continue to work back and forth in stockinette st, slipping the first st of the row and working a new st at the end of each row.

When the gusset is of the desired width (1–1½" [2.5–3.8 cm] for a child's gansey; 1½–2" [3.8–5 cm] for an adult's) and all the neck gusset sts of the shoulder have been worked, put these sts on a holder and work the other shoulder and gusset to match.

INVERTED TRIANGLE GUSSET   KEY

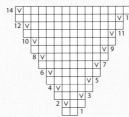

An inverted triangular neck gusset is used with an unshaped neckline and bound-off shoulder seams. The gussets lie on the seam line of the shoulder and serve to widen the neck.

shoulder-strap neck gussets

The first time I knitted strap gussets into one of my ganseys, I was alarmed at the incline they created on the shoulder line. When I put the sweater on, however, I saw that because the shoulders naturally slope upward toward the neck, the fit was quite comfortable.

These gussets (two to each shoulder) round an otherwise boxy neckline caused by the angles formed with a shoulder strap. They are worked in stockinette stitch, at the beginning of the perpendicular shoulder join at the neck edge. Extra stitches are cast on at either end of the foundation (cast-on) row of the strap. I do not recommend using a provisional cast-on here, which could stretch out of shape. A regular cast-on will give needed stability to this edge.

I make each gusset about 1" (2.5 cm) wide at the widest part, although I have seen old photos of strap gussets that were much wider. It is decreased away to nothing, melting into the shoulder strap. For this reason, I would not recommend using this method if your gauge is looser than 6 stitches per inch (2.5 cm). With fewer stitches, there simply isn't enough fabric to make a recognizable gusset, nor enough distance in which to shape it.

Within the gussets, you work two decreases simultaneously. The outermost decrease is the perpendicular joining, while the internal decrease controls the shaping and eventual demise of the gusset itself. You will work both decreases every other row. If you wish, you can place the two decreases side by side to resemble a flanged strap. This effect is strengthened or subdued by the strap's pattern. For example, if both the gusset and strap are in stockinette stitch, the gusset appears to be part of the strap.

Another option is to place one decrease on both the outside and inside edge of each gusset so that the inner decrease delineates the gusset from the strap, regardless of what pattern is used. Keep the outermost stitches of the gussets free from patterning, as they will act as the joining stitches.

Two shoulder-strap neck gussets at each shoulder, worked in stockinette stitch, round an otherwise boxy neckline on a garment with perpendicular shoulder straps. Two decreases are worked simultaneously within the gusset—the outermost decrease is the perpendicular join, and the internal decrease shapes the gusset.

Here is an historical example of very wide strap gussets worked in a ribbing pattern. (Photo courtesy of the Sutcliffe Gallery; 10-08)

PRACTICE STRAP GUSSET

Knit 2 swatches, each 28 sts wide and 1" (2.5 cm) long. These will represent your front and back right shoulder.

Note: The directions that follow are for strap gussets with both decreases worked at the outer edges of the gussets. (There is no patterning in this practice strap—you can add some if you'd like.) These practice strap gussets have 6 sts at the widest part, which would be appropriate for a garment knit at 6 sts per inch (2.5 cm). A strap 2" (5 cm) wide at this gauge requires 12 sts. A 6-st gusset added at each side of the strap adds 12 more sts. Add the strap sts (12) to the gusset sts (12) and you have 24 sts to cast on. You'll be decreasing these 24 sts to 14 within 12 rows, so the practice piece works up very quickly.

Using dpns, CO 24 sts with your working yarn. Knit the first cast-on st onto the right back shoulder needle at one edge, one of the 28 st swatches (on a full-size sweater this would be the neck edge). With your LH needle (the one with the strap and the gusset sts on it), slip the last st of the right back shoulder over the st just knitted (as if you were binding off). Knit across the remaining strap and gusset sts. Knit 1 st from the neck edge of the right front shoulder (the other 28 st swatch), and pull the last strap st over it, again as if binding off. Turn the work.

Continue as follows, slipping pwise wyf for the WS rows and pwise wyb for the RS rows. The shoulder-strap gussets are joined to the front and back by working 2 sts together (one from the strap and one from a shoulder) at the end of every row.

Row 1: (WS) Sl 1 pwise wyf, p5, pm for strap, work strap patt across 12 sts, pm, p5, p2tog. Turn work.

Row 2: (RS) Sl 1 pwise wyb, ssk, k3, sl m, work strap, sl m, k3, k2tog (decreasing the gusset), ssk (perpendicular joining). Turn.

Row 3: Sl 1 wyf, p4, sl m, work strap, sl m, p4 p2tog. Turn.

Row 4: Sl 1 wyb, ssk, k2, sl m, work strap, sl m, k2, k2tog, ssk. Turn.

Row 5: Sl 1 wyf, p3, sl m, work strap, sl m, p3, p2tog. Turn.

Row 6: Sl 1 wyb, ssk, k1, sl m, work strap, sl m, k1, k2tog, ssk. Turn.

Row 7: Sl 1 wyf, p2, sl m, work strap, sl m, p2, p2tog. Turn.

Row 8: Sl 1 wyb, ssk, sl m, work strap, sl m, k2tog, ssk. Turn.

Row 9: Sl 1 wyf, p1, sl m, work strap, sl m, p1, p2tog. Turn.

Row 10: Ssk, remove m, work strap, remove m, s2kp. Turn. (The gussets are finished.)

Row 11: Sl 1, work strap, p2tog. Turn.

Row 12: Sl 1, work strap, ssk. Turn.

Repeat Rows 11 and 12 until all shoulder sts have been used up to complete the perpendicular join.

SHOULDER STRAP GUSSET

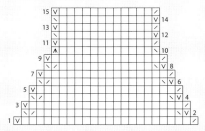

Shoulder strap gussets create a flange when all of the decreases are placed along the outer edges of the strap.

DELINEATED STRAP GUSSET

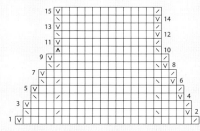

Shoulder strap gussets delineated by moving the decreases away from the edge of the strap.

KEY

☐	k on RS, p on WS
V	sl 1 wyb on RS, sl 1 wyf on WS
╱	k2tog on RS, p2tog on WS
╲	ssk
⋀	s2kp

working full-size

Working a neckband for a full-size garment with shoulder straps is much easier on a 16" (40 cm) circular needle than on double-pointed needles. Join your yarn at the back to conceal the inevitable jog caused by the transition from one round to the next. For necklines without a perpendicular shoulder strap, stitches for the neckband are picked up at each side of the neck.

To calculate how many neckband stitches you'll need to pick up, multiply the total body stitches by 45 percent.

Example: *168 body sts × .45 = 75.6 sts*

Because 2 × 2 ribbing is worked in multiples of 4 stitches, round up to 76 stitches. Be sure to bind off the neckband loosely so the wearer can easily pull on the gansey.

FINISHING THE GARMENT

Once your knitting is off the needles, there is still more to do. Sewing in all those ends is a chore, but once done, you'll be glad that the wrong side looks as good as the right side. Blocking is also essential to finishing the fabric. By washing the garment with a gentle soap made for fine wool, rinsing, and laying it flat to dry, the stitches become more uniform and settle into place. If you have ever ripped out an old sweater, you know how the yarn has kinks in it from being "set" in the knitted fabric. Blocking helps this process. Ganseys, and any textured knitted fabric in particular, benefit so much from this last step.

SEWING IN ENDS

Instead of using rounded-tip tapestry needles (great for Kitchener stitch), I use a sharp tapestry needle so that I can pierce the purl bumps on the wrong side as I sew in my ends. This encourages the natural tendency of the wool fibers to cling to each other; the microscopic scales along the wool fiber will enmesh with others nearby and keep ends securely held more efficiently than if the end was merely run underneath the stitches on the wrong side.

BLOCKING

Properly blocking woolen garments generally requires them to be washed, rinsed, and dried. Afterward, you can touch up with a steam iron if desired. Gansey yarn responds well to blocking, turning what feels like a stiff scratchy fabric into something softer and more supple. I have even ironed gansey yarn fabric with steam (it can take it), something I would not do with other types of yarn.

To block, I start by filling my sink with warm water and adding the recommended amount of good-quality wool soap. I immerse the garment in water and gently squeeze it to allow water and soap to penetrate into the wool. Then I lift it out of the water into another container, supporting all the weight, empty the sink, and refill it with fresh water. I immerse the garment again. I may use two or three sinkfuls of rinse water. Then I put the garment in a pillowcase, close it up, and put it in my washing machine on the spin cycle for a minute. This helps to get a significant quantity of the water out so that the garment can dry faster. Without a wooly board, I lay the garment flat on a towel, turning it over once or twice during the drying process, so the underside of the sweater can dry, too.

For smaller items, I roll up the piece in a towel and press the water out, rather than spinning it in the washing machine. Then I lay it flat to dry on my cookie cooling rack so air can travel beneath it to dry.

CARE OF WOOLENS

Alas, the moth! I do despise plastic bags, but I hate moths and the damage they do even more. When putting away your sweaters for the summer, wash them first. Insects are often attracted to bits of food and such that may be stuck to your prize sweater. When absolutely dry, store your garment in a plastic bag, away from light. I get zippered bags from an online outlet that carries all sorts of bags and boxes for retail businesses. (See Sources and Supplies page 186.)

wooly boards

Wooly boards originated in Shetland and are wonderful tools for blocking drop-shoulder and square-armhole garments. They emulate the shape of a sweater to dry it under tension and "dress" it nicely (as the Shetlanders would say). Many are adjustable and can accommodate several sizes of sweaters with varying armhole depths. You can purchase a manufactured board, but you can also find instructions online to make one yourself.

CHAPTER 11
planning and designing your own

Now that you have knitted the sampler gansey and learned about construction and design options for working full-size ganseys, you are ready to design your own sweaters. This chapter will review the basic strategy and calculations for designing a gansey. When you understand these principles, you can create your own gansey variations, each a wonderfully unique expression of your knitting.

On page 103 you'll find a blank schematic that you can use to record the dimensions of your garment. On page 115 there is a worksheet you can use as a guideline for planning every aspect of your gansey. Finally, you will need graph paper, standard or knitter-specific, to sketch out your garment's size and shape, plot stitch counts, and fill out surface patterns and detail variations. Visit my website at www.knittingtraditions.com/about-knitting-traditions/favorite-links/ for a link to downloadable knitter's graph paper.

This chapter together with the worksheet will provide you with a complete overview of the steps for planning a gansey. (Refer to the chapters on each technique for more in-depth discussion as needed.)

OVERVIEW

There are three steps in designing a gansey: determining the design details, calculating the silhouette, and planning the surface design.

DETERMINING THE DESIGN DETAILS

I start designing at the bottom of the garment and envision all the elements I want to include. For the example garment, I decided on:

- 2 × 2 ribbing
- a single-purl-stitch seam
- a plain area with initial
- a seed-stitch definition ridge
- vertical patterning
- a shaped neckline
- bound-off shoulders
- 2 × 2 ribbing for the neckband and cuffs

To begin, I may write out a list of these details or I might draw a little picture to refer to.

CALCULATING THE SILHOUETTE

Next, I do all the necessary measurements and calculations by multiplying these inches (or centimeters) by my stitch or row gauge to fill in my schematic. Or, I might refer to the Table of Measurements (page 103) to determine the values needed in the schematic. Another option is to take all the measurements needed from a drop-shouldered sweater that fits me well and incorporate these numbers for my new design.

PLANNING THE SURFACE DESIGN

Plotting on the graph paper is the last step. First, I create the outline of the garment, including the gusset, seam stitches, and neckline, and then I fill in the surface design.

creating the schematic

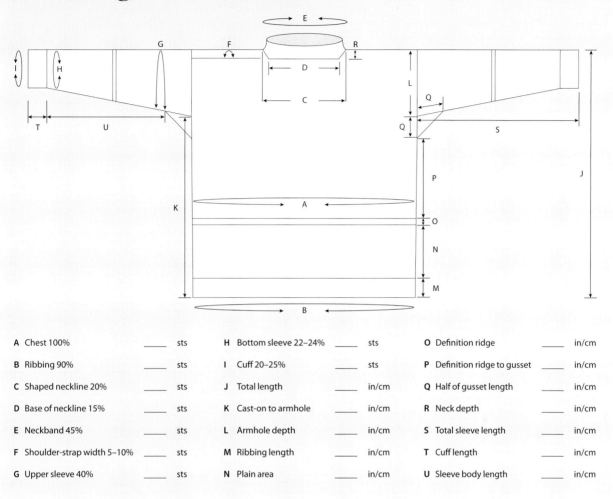

A	Chest 100%	_____ sts	**H**	Bottom sleeve 22–24%	_____ sts	**O**	Definition ridge	_____ in/cm
B	Ribbing 90%	_____ sts	**I**	Cuff 20–25%	_____ sts	**P**	Definition ridge to gusset	_____ in/cm
C	Shaped neckline 20%	_____ sts	**J**	Total length	_____ in/cm	**Q**	Half of gusset length	_____ in/cm
D	Base of neckline 15%	_____ sts	**K**	Cast-on to armhole	_____ in/cm	**R**	Neck depth	_____ in/cm
E	Neckband 45%	_____ sts	**L**	Armhole depth	_____ in/cm	**S**	Total sleeve length	_____ in/cm
F	Shoulder-strap width 5–10%	_____ sts	**M**	Ribbing length	_____ in/cm	**T**	Cuff length	_____ in/cm
G	Upper sleeve 40%	_____ sts	**N**	Plain area	_____ in/cm	**U**	Sleeve body length	_____ in/cm

example gansey values

A	Chest 100%	168 sts	**H**	Bottom sleeve 22–24%	41 sts	**O**	Definition ridge	1" (2.5 cm)
B	Ribbing 90%	151.2 sts	**I**	Cuff 20–25%	33.6 sts	**P**	Definition ridge to gusset	5" (12.5 cm)
C	Shaped neckline 20%	33.6 sts	**J**	Total length	23" (58.5 cm)	**Q**	Half of gusset length	3" (7.5 cm)
D	Base of neckline 15%	25.2 sts	**K**	Cast-on to armhole	15" (38 cm)	**R**	Neck depth	2½" (6.5 cm)
E	Neckband 45%	75.6 sts	**L**	Armhole depth	8" (20.5 cm)	**S**	Total sleeve length	18" (45.5 cm)
F	Shoulder-strap width 5–10%	n/a	**M**	Ribbing length	3" (7.5 cm)	**T**	Cuff length	2" (5 cm)
G	Upper sleeve 40%	67.2 sts	**N**	Plain area	3" (7.5 cm)	**U**	Sleeve body length	13" (33 cm)

THE IN-DEPTH DESIGN PROCESS

First, measure the chest and add 2–4" (5–10 cm) or more of ease. Traditionally, ganseys are close-fitting garments and 2" (5 cm) of ease should suffice. If you like, you may add up to 6" (15 cm) of ease; however, a looser garment does not take advantage of the construction details that make the gansey fit so well.

If you're unsure how much ease you want, pull out your best-fitting sweater and measure the chest circumference. Use that figure as your total chest measurement—the ease is already included. (The table on page 106 lists chest measurements for children's and adults' garments.)

Knit a stockinette-stitch gauge swatch at least 4" × 4" (10 cm × 10 cm). If you don't like the feel and drape of the resulting fabric, try again with a different-size needle. Determine row (round) gauge as well as stitch gauge. For this garment, I used 4 stitches and 6 rounds per inch (2.5 cm), knit with US 9 (5.5 mm) needles and a heavy worsted-weight yarn.

THE SILHOUETTE

WORKING WITH THE PERCENTAGE METHOD

When you've determined the chest measurement of the finished garment (chest measurement + ease), multiply it by your stitch gauge. This gives you the total number of stitches at the chest—that is, 100 percent of the garment's body stitches (Calculation A in the schematic). Round any fractions to the nearest whole number. Ribbing and cuff stitch counts should be adjusted to accommodate the ribbing pattern you've chosen.

Calculation A: Body stitches

[Chest measurement + Ease] × Stitch gauge =
Total number of body stitches

Example: *(40" + 2") × 4 sts per inch = 168 total body stitches*

Using A as 100 percent, fill in the remaining blanks of the schematic as in the examples that follow.

Calculation B: Ribbing stitches

Total body stitches × 90% = Total number of ribbing stitches

Example: *168 sts × .20 = 151.2 sts*

You may need to adjust this figure for the ribbing pattern you've selected. The example sweater has a 2 × 2 ribbing, which is worked in multiples of 4. Therefore, the ribbing stitch count needs to be divisible by 4, so we round up to 152 stitches.

Now, work out the calculations for the neckline, neckband, sleeve, and cuff. Fill these in on the schematic.

Calculation C: Shaped neckline width

Total body stitches × 20% = Total width of shaped neckline

Example: *168 sts × .20 = 33.6 sts*

Calculation D: Base of neckline stitches

Total body stitches × 15%
= Base of neckline stitches (put on holder or bound off)

Example: *168 sts × .15 = 25.2 sts*

Calculation E: Neckband circumference

Total body stitches × 45% = Neckband circumference

Example: *168 sts × .45 = 75.6 sts*

Calculation F: Shoulder strap width

Total body stitches × [5 to 10%] = Shoulder strap width
Example: *No shoulder straps in example garment*

Calculation G: Upper sleeve circumference

Total body stitches × 40% = Upper sleeve circumference

Example: *168 × .40 = 67.2 sts*

Calculation H: Lower sleeve body circumference

Total body stitches × [22 to 24%] = Circumference of lower sleeve body

Example: *168 × .24 = 40.3 sts*

Calculation I: Cuff circumference

Total body stitches × 20% = Cuff circumference

Example: *168 sts × .20 = 33.6 sts*

WORKING WITH THE TABLE

The widths, or horizontal dimensions, of the garment are calculated with the percentage method. Some measurements, however, such as length of ribbing, length to underarm, armhole depth, and sleeve length can be figured in inches (centimeters). You can measure the body to determine what would be most comfortable or use table on page 106. The information in the table is intended only as a guideline, as there is no such thing as an "average" person. In designing the example gansey, I made several departures from the table calculations. For example, most of the measurements for the example garment are based on those for a women's size Large, according to the table. I simply increased the chest measurement from 40–42" (101.5–106.5 cm) to allow for ease. (The proportions of a man's size 42 would have been too large overall for a woman with a 42" [106.5 cm] bust.) The metric equivalents throughout are approximate.

Using body measurements, percentages, and the table, determine the dimensions needed for the following parts of the garment:

Calculation J: Total length

Total length = Personal preference, table measurement,
the sum of K + L, or the sum of L + M + N + O + P + Q

Example: *23"*
(Because I made adjustments in ribbing and the length from cast-on to armhole, this value is ½" [1.3 cm] longer in the table.)

Calculation K: Cast-on to armhole length

Length from cast-on to armhole =
Personal preference or the sum of M + N + O + P + Q

Example: *15"*
(The table indicates 15½" [39.5 cm]. I chose to make it shorter.)

Calculation L: Armhole depth

Armhole depth = Personal preference or table measurement

Example: *8"*

Calculation M: Ribbing length

Ribbing length = Personal preference or table measurement

Example: *3"*
(This ribbing is deeper than that listed in the table. The ½" [1.3 cm] deviation from the table measurement is reflected in the total length.)

Calculation N: Plain area

Plain area = Determined by design layout

Example: *3"*

Calculation O: Definition ridge

Definition ridge = Personal preference or table measurement

Example: *1"*

Calculation P: Definition ridge to gusset

Distance from definition ridge to gusset = Dictated by design layout

Example: *5"*

Calculation Q: Half of gusset length

Half of gusset length = Table measurement ÷ 2

Example: *6" ÷ 2 = 3"*

Calculation R: Neck depth

Neck depth = Table measurement

Example: *2½"*

Calculation S: Total sleeve length

Total sleeve length = Personal preference,
table measurement, or the sum of Q + U + T

Example: *18"*
(I used this figure rather than the 18¾" [47.5 cm], as the table indicates, because my arms are shorter.)

Calculation T: Cuff length

Cuff length = Total sleeve length [S] – [Q + U] or personal preference

Example: *2" = 18" – [3" + 13"]*

Calculation U: Sleeve body length

Sleeve body length = Total Sleeve length [S] – [Q + T]

Example: *13" = 18" – [3" + 2"]*

TABLE OF MEASUREMENTS (IN INCHES)

Sizes	CHILDREN						WOMEN					MEN				
	12 mos.	2/3	4/5	6/7	8/10	12	XS	S	M	L	XL	S	M	L	XL	2XL
Body Chest Measurement (add ease to equal A)	18	22	24	26	28	32	30	34	38	42	46	42	44	46	48	50
Total Length (J)	9¾	11¼	13	14½	17	18½	20½	22¼	22¾	23½	23½	26	26½	27½	28½	29
Length from Cast-on to Start of Gusset (M + N + O + P)	4½	4½	5½	6½	8	9	10	11¾	12¼	12½	12½	12½	12½	12½	12½	13
*Ribbing Length (M)	1	1½	1½	1½	2	2	2	2½	2½	2½	2½	3	3	3	3	3
*Definition Ridge (O)	½	½	½	½	1	1	1	1	1	1	1	1½	1½	1½	1½	1½
Gusset Length (Q x 2)	3	4	4	4	5	5	6	6	6	6	6	6	8	8	8	8
Gusset Width	1½	2	2	2	2½	2½	3	3	3	3	3	3	4	4	4	4
Length from Cast-on to Armhole (K)	6	6½	7½	8½	10½	11½	13	14¾	15¼	15½	15½	16	16	16½	17	17
Armhole Depth (L)	3¾	4¾	5½	6	6½	7	7½	7½	7½	8	8	10	10½	11	11½	12
Neck Depth (R)	1	1	1	1½	1½	1½	2	2	2	2	2	2½	2½	2½	2½	2½
Sleeve Length (Q + U + T)	7½	9½	11	12	13½	15	17	17½	17¾	18	18¼	19½	20	20	20½	20½
*Perpendicular Strap Width (5–10%)	1	1	1	1	1½	1½	1½	1½	1½	2	2	2	2	2½	2½	2½

TABLE OF MEASUREMENTS (IN CENTIMETERS)

Sizes	CHILDREN						WOMEN					MEN				
	12 mos.	2/3	4/5	6/7	8/10	12	XS	S	M	L	XL	S	M	L	XL	2XL
Chest Measurement (+ ease = A)	41.5	56	61	66	71	81.5	76	86.5	91.5	101.5	112	91.5	101.5	117	122	132
Total Length (J)	25	28.5	33	37	43	47	52	56.5	58	59.5	59.5	66	67.5	70	72.5	73.5
Length from Cast-on to Start of Gusset (M + N + O + P)	11.5	11.5	14	16.5	20.5	23	25.5	30	31	31.5	31.5	31.5	31.5	31.5	31.5	33
*Ribbing Length (M)	2.5	3.8	3.8	3.8	5	5	5	6.5	6.5	6.5	6.5	7.5	7.5	7.5	7.5	7.5
*Definition Ridge (O)	1.3	1.3	1.3	1.3	2.5	2.5	2.5	2.5	2.5	2.5	2.5	3.8	3.8	3.8	3.8	3.8
Gusset Length (Q x 2)	7.5	10	10	10	12.5	12.5	15	15	15	15	15	15	20.5	20.5	20.5	20.5
Gusset Width	3.8	5	5	5	6.5	6.5	7.5	7.5	7.5	7.5	7.5	7.5	10	10	10	10
Length from Cast-on to Armhole (K)	15	16.5	19	21.5	26.5	29	33	37.5	38.5	39.5	39.5	40.5	40.5	42	43	43
Armhole Depth (L)	9.5	12	14	15	16.5	18	19	19	19	20.5	20.5	25.5	26.5	28	29	30.5
Neck Depth (R)	2.5	2.5	2.5	3.8	3.8	3.8	5	5	5	5	5	6.5	6.5	6.5	6.5	6.5
Sleeve Length (Q + U + T)	19	24	28	30.5	34.5	38	43	44.5	45	45.5	46.5	49.5	51	51	52	52
*Perpendicular Strap Width (5–10%)	2.5	2.5	2.5	2.5	3.8	3.8	3.8	3.8	3.8	5	5	5	5	6.5	6.5	6.5

The measurements in these tables are approximate and should be used only as general guidelines.
* Subject to personal preference and design layout.

adjusting fit

ACCOMMODATING THE HIPS

If your sweater will fall below your hips, you may want to widen the lower section of the garment. To make the hip area wider, cast on for the garment size with chest measurements that correspond to your hip measurements. Then subtract your needed chest measurement from that of the lower body circumference. This number represents the inches that must be decreased. After calculating the number of stitches to decrease and how often, work the decreases to either side of the seam stitches.

Example:
The gauge is 7 sts and 11 rnds/in. You have a bust/chest of 42" (106.5 cm) but your hips are 46" (117cm). Your calculations for the larger size say to cast on 322 sts, while the 42" (106.5 cm) size requires 294 sts. That is a difference of 28 sts. There are 2 sets of seam sts, and a decrease can be made to either side—4 sts decreased in one row or round.

Work your ribbing or welt in the larger size. Then, decide on the number of inches to work in the decreases. Perhaps you want to work them in gradually, over 10" (25.5 cm), up to the definition ridge.

To decrease away 28 sts at a rate of 4 sts/row:

$$28 \text{ sts} \div 4 \text{ sts per decrease rnd} = 7 \text{ dec rnds}$$

$$10" \times 11 \text{ rnds/in.} = 110 \text{ rnds}$$

$$110 \div 7 = 15.7 \text{ rnds}$$

So work the decrease rnd every 15 to 16 rnds.

MAKING THE BACK LONGER

The plain area in the lower body of a gansey is the perfect place to work short-rows to extend the back of the garment. (See the Eriskay gansey on page 144 and Chapter 4.)

CHARTING THE BODY

A chart records specific information about the garment, stitch by stitch. Use standard or knitters' graph paper (see Resources on page 186) and tape as many copies together as you need to chart the entire garment front (or back). You are knitting in the round, but, as discussed in Chapter 4, because the front and back are the same, the chart only needs to represent one side of the garment.

Note: First, we will discuss a gansey without cables, then one with cables. The approach is slightly different for each variation.

Count out horizontally the number of graph paper squares equal to 50 percent of the sweater's circumference and draw a line to that width. Remember to allow additional space for the gusset and seam stitches to one side of the body. Subtract the seam stitch(es) from the body stitches so that only the area needed for the patterning is calculated.

Calculation A ÷ 2 = Number of stitches across front or back

Number of stitches – seam stitches of one side
= total number of stitches for patterning

Example: *168 sts ÷ 2 = 84 sts for front or back*
84 sts – 1 seam st = 83 sts for patterning

Calculate the length of the sweater (minus the ribbing) and multiply that distance by your row gauge to give you the total number of rows in the sweater body. (The ribbing is not included in this calculation because it's often worked in a different gauge.)

Calculations J – M = Length of sweater minus ribbing

Example: *23" - 3" = 20"*
20" × 6 rows/in. = 120 rounds or rows

Plot the length on the graph paper, leaving room at the bottom for the ribbing. Connect the horizontal and vertical dimensions to create a rectangle. This represents the front (or back) of the gansey. Within this area, you'll design the patterning and details.

To determine the width of the ribbing, use one-half of Calculation B—you are charting only half of the garment:

Calculation B ÷ 2 = Width of the ribbing

Example: *152 sts ÷ 2 = 76 sts*

Because you'll use smaller needles for the ribbing, the gauge will be tighter than that of the body, so unless you swatch the ribbing you won't know exactly how many rounds you'll need. I usually knit my ribbing to the desired length, based on my measurements. For the purposes of the chart, however, draw in at least 10 rows of ribbing for the record, noting on the chart the length (Calculation M) you have selected for the ribbing.

KEY

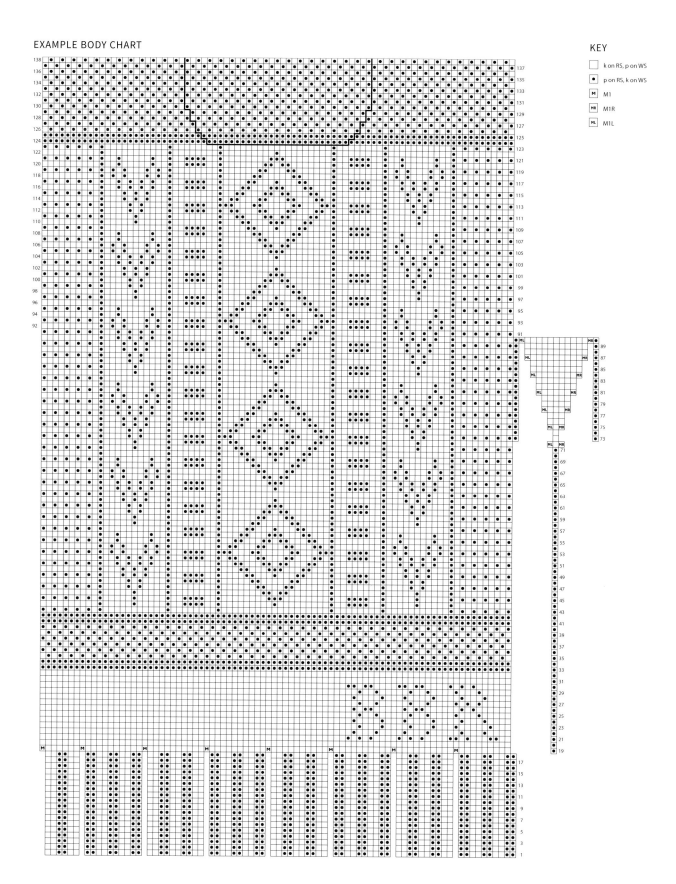

□ k on RS, p on WS

• p on RS, k on WS

M M1

MR M1R

ML M1L

Next, determine number of stitches to increase from ribbing to body.

Example: *168 sts × 10% = 16.8 sts or 16 sts*

Divide the number of stitches to be increased by 2 for half the ribbing you will chart.

Example: *16 ÷ 2 = 8*

Now, determine how often to increase 1 stitch from the ribbing to the body, by dividing the number of stitches to be increased into the body stitches on the chart.

Example: *83 sts ÷ 8 sts = 10 sts*

Draw in the ribbing pattern (k2, p2) below the body in units of 10 sts (more or less, as it rarely comes out exactly even), leaving every 11th column of the chart blank. These spaces represent "no stitch," or spaces where stitches will eventually be, when the increases are made. You can draw in an increase symbol at the top of each of these blank columns.

Next, chart the gussets. Multiply the armhole depth (Calculation L) by the row gauge. Count down that number of rows from the shoulder to determine where the gusset will end in the body (the actual midpoint of the gusset).

Calculation L × Row gauge = Rows from shoulder to gusset midpoint

Example: *8" × 6 rows/in. = 48 rows*

To determine the gusset shaping, calculate the frequency of increases and decreases:

*Round gauge × Calculation Q
= Number of rounds in lower half of gusset [Y]*

Example: *6 rounds/in. × 3" = 18 rounds (I used 19 for visual balance.)*

*Stitch gauge × Gusset width (see table)
= Number of stitches at full width of gusset*

Example: *4 sts/in. × 3" = 12 sts*

Divide your number of stitches at the gusset full width by 2 to determine the number of paired increases or decreases needed to shape the gusset [Z].

Example: *12 sts ÷ 2 = 6 paired increases*

*Number of rounds to work from one increase
(or decrease) round to the next = Y ÷ Z*

Example: *18 rounds ÷ 6 paired increases
= 3 rounds per paired increase*

You have already plotted the armhole depth. The first row below the armhole opening is the last row of the lower half of the gusset. This is where it will be at its widest. Now, count down the length of

half the gusset as calculated (Y.) This row marks the approximate beginning of the gusset. The actual charting may vary by a round or two, to account for the number of rounds in which the seam stitches are increased. In the example, there are 19 rounds in the lower half of the gusset.

In the previous column, we calculated how many stitches the gusset has at this widest point:

Stitch gauge × Gusset width = number of sts at widest part of gusset [Z × 2].

Example: *4 sts/in. × 3" = 12 sts*
Z × 2 = 12 sts

Gussets almost always have an odd number of stitches because they usually begin as a single increase, so you will need to adjust the number of gusset stitches.

Example: *12 sts + 1 st = 13 sts*

Note: Be sure to include the seam stitches on the chart.

The example has a single-stitch seam surrounding each side of the gusset, so I added 2 more stitches to the widest point of the gusset on the chart, for a total of 156 body stitches. I drew a seam stitch next to the body on Row 90 (counting down 48 rows from the shoulder); then I counted over 13 stitches for the gusset and added the other seam stitch in the next square. As this round is the last increase round on the gusset, the next round below the one just plotted will be narrower. (Remember that you are charting downward even though the chart will be read from bottom to top as the gusset is knitted.)

Because the next round has 2 fewer stitches, the gusset shrinks away from the seam stitches by 1 square on each side. There are now 11 gusset stitches across the width. The next 2 rounds are the same width to reflect the rate of increase (every 3 rounds, [Y ÷ Z]). I continued to draw in groups of 3 rounds of stitches, making them 2 stitches narrower every third round, until there was only 1 seam stitch left. That 1 seam stitch continues down to the corresponding chart row of the first round of the body (not the ribbing). The other half of the gusset will be plotted on the sleeve chart.

The neckline shape will determine the patterning of the garment body. Do you want a shaped or unshaped neckline? Will you use shoulder straps? Refer to Chapters 7 and 8, where these decisions and calculations are discussed in depth, then plot your choices on the chart. (Keep intricate patterning such as cables clear of the neckline and armhole areas.)

The example sweater has a shaped neckline. I centered 33 stitches, the total number of neckline stitches (Calculation C), on the horizontal shoulder line of the garment. From this line, I plotted the neck depth (Calculation R). Then I centered the total number of stitches to be bound off or put on a holder (Calculation D) on the neckline opening. I drew in the decreasing steps, 4 on each side, to complete the chart.

INITIAL BODY PATTERNING CHART

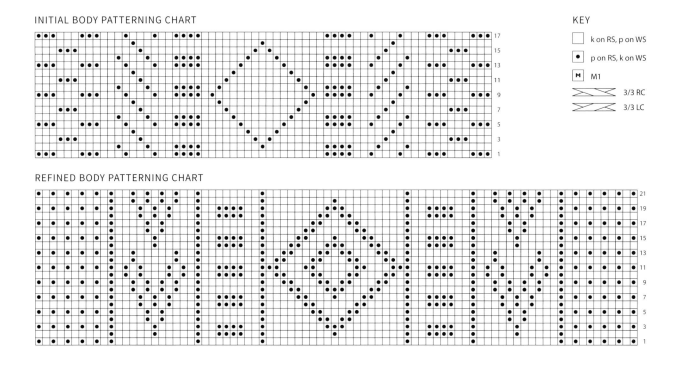

REFINED BODY PATTERNING CHART

KEY

☐	k on RS, p on WS
●	p on RS, k on WS
M	M1
⤬	3/3 RC
⤬	3/3 LC

CHARTING THE BODY PATTERNING

After you've charted the body shape, the next step is to chart the surface patterning. I work from the top down and from the center out. Think about whether you want a vertical or horizontal orientation and which pattern motifs you'll use. Reread the "Working Full-Size" section in Chapter 5 to help you plan an attractive and logical pattern layout. If you want to use an initial in the plain area, include it in the chart, too.

A GANSEY WITHOUT CABLES

For my layout of a gansey without cables, I plotted some ideas on a chart—an initial vision: the 15-stitch diamond is the focal point, with ladders to each side. Beyond those, I mirrored diagonal lines, and the outermost are sections of background patterning.

Then I further refined my ideas, keeping in mind the number of stitches I need to fill (83). The Initial Chart looks quite plain, but by including a variety of motifs that move in different directions from each other (outward, inward, across, up and down) I created a richer-looking layout. I enlarged the diamond and filled it in to make it a stronger focal point. I replaced the straight diagonal lines with a more interesting motif—Vs made of sets of 2 vertical purls. Finally, I chose a different background motif for the edge panels that fit better with the remaining stitches I needed, and I achieved a total of 83 stitches.

A GANSEY WITH CABLES

A gansey with cables requires extra planning because the cables draw in the fabric, changing the size of the garment. In the example gansey without cables, the size of the garment was determined by multiplying the chest measurement by the stitch gauge. This is also a good place to start with a gansey with cables, but it will represent the sweater before the cables are applied. Extra stitches will need to be added to the initial number calculated.

In Chapter 5, I discussed cable splay using an example gansey knitted at 4 stitches/in. with 6-stitch cables that measured 1" (2.5 cm) wide—a difference of 2 stitches for every cable (6 stitches of cable = 1" [2.5 cm], while 4 stitches of stockinette = 1" [2.5 cm]). So, in addition to the total number of stitches (in stockinette) for the body,

2 stitches must be added to the total for every 6-stitch cable included in the design. This keeps the cables from splaying out at the bottom and gives them the extra fabric needed to draw in and puff up.

If we used the model of the first example gansey and stuck in 4 columns of cables without considering cable splay, the final dimension might be 38½" (98 cm), not 42" (106.5 cm), because the cables draw in the fabric.

In the chart below, I substituted 4 cables for the V pattern. I also increased the background patterning at the edges (4 stitches on each side) to maintain the circumference of the garment, by making up for the fabric take-in of the 4 cables, ending with a total of 91 stitches for the front (or back):

83 original sts + (4 cables × 2 extra sts each) = 83 + 8 = 91 total sts

I drew my finished design on the chart, starting at the shoulders, including a 1" (2.5 cm) definition ridge and a plain area for my initials. I drew as many repeats of the central panel as I felt looked good, then placed the definition ridge just below. Next, I filled in the the motifs that flank the central panel, centering them vertically so there were roughly the same number of rows before the first motifs and after the last.

The cables to either side of the diamond would have interfered with the neckline shaping. Rather than redesign the whole pattern, I decided to create a shoulder extension and work a separate motif there. To tie in the design, I used the same background stitch pattern (seed stitch) on the shoulder area as in the definition ridge. For a finishing touch, I mirrored the cables. The cables to the right of the center panel twist one way, and those to the left twist the other.

Once you've charted the body, you can add further refinements to account for cable splay. I added increase symbols to remind myself to increase in the first round of the cables, and I blanked out the stitches below those increases, as they are not there until the increases are worked. I also included decreases at the top of the cables so they won't cause the shoulders to splay out.

Note that the example cabled gansey chart (page 112) has empty spaces in the ribbing that travel all the way up to the base of the cables in the patterning. This is based on the calculations for cable splay and it impacts the ribbing as well.

REFINED CABLED CHART

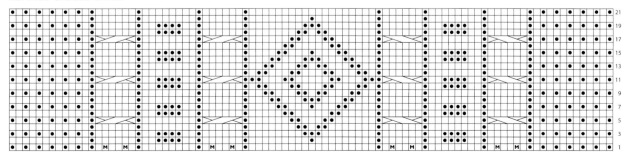

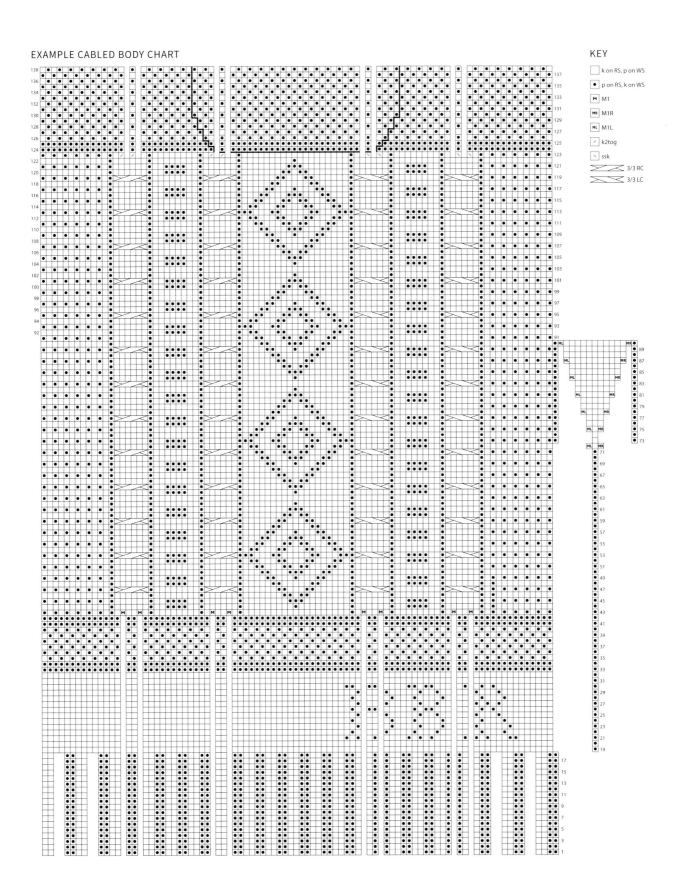

KEY

☐	k on RS, p on WS
•	p on RS, k on WS
M	M1
MR	M1R
ML	M1L
∕	k2tog
∖	ssk
⋙	3/3 RC
⋙	3/3 LC

CHARTING THE SLEEVES

Note: Example gansey sleeve chart is on page 114.

Sometimes I like to plan and chart the sleeves after I have finished knitting the body. That way, I have a clear idea of the interplay of my yarn, gauge, and chosen patterns, which helps me decide on the sleeve design. However, there's no reason why the sleeve can't be worked out before the knitting begins. Read Chapter 9 to work out the silhouette of your sleeve.

The first step is to determine how many stitches to pick up around the armhole. You can do that one of two ways:

1. [Calculation L × 2] × Stitch gauge = Stitches to pick up

Example: *[8″ × 2] × 4 sts/in. = 64 sts*

2. Calculation G = Stitches to pick up

Example: *168 sts × .40 = 67.2 sts (I used 64.)*

Subtract the number of stitches you need for the shoulder straps (Calculation F) if you are including them in your design (see page 81). In the example garment, the shoulders are joined with the Three-Needle Bind-off (page 79).

Sketch out the circumference of the sleeve (Calculation G) at the bottom of the chart. Begin the gusset chart at the block next to the right-hand side of the sleeve chart. You will be drawing the upper half of the gusset along with the seam stitches. (The chart for the lower half of the gusset is with the body chart; its top row shows the gusset's full width.) Draw in the necessary number of rows within that width for the top gusset chart to reflect your rate of decrease.

For the example garment, the full width of the lower half of the gusset is 15 stitches including the seam stitches, and the rate of increase is every 3 rounds. I therefore drew 2 rounds at full width on the bottom of the sleeve gusset, to complete the 3-round increment, before beginning to decrease 2 stitches, one at each end inside the seam stitches, every third round. The top of the gusset should be symmetrical with the bottom and should diminish to a single seam stitch (if that is what you have chosen). There are 2 additional rounds at the top of the sleeve gusset, to accommodate the decreasing frequency. The sides of the sleeve are drawn as straight lines for the length of the gusset, as no decreasing occurs in the sleeve while the gusset is being decreased.

Now, determine the number of rounds for the sleeve minus the cuff:

[Calculation S – Calculation T] × Round gauge = Rounds for sleeve

Example: *[18″ – 2″] × 6 rounds/in. = 96 rounds*

Count up the graph paper the number of rounds for the Sleeve Body (sleeve length – cuff length + upper gusset length) and make a mark there to indicate the bottom of the sleeve and the beginning of the cuff. Before drawing in the sides of the sleeve, however, you need to calculate the rate of decrease for the sleeve body (see page 88).

Sleeve stitches beyond gusset – Calculation H = Stitches to decrease [V]

Example: *65 sts – 41 sts = 24 sts*

Calculation U = Length within which to decrease

Example: *13″*

Round gauge × Length within which to decrease = Total number of rounds within which to decrease [W].

Example: *6 rounds/in. × 13″ = 78 rounds*

Number of rounds within which to decrease ÷ Number of stitches to decrease = Number of rounds to be worked per decrease [W ÷ V]

Example: *78 ÷ 24 = 3.25 rounds*

Round fractions to the nearest whole number, in this case 3.

W ÷ V × 2 = Number of rounds between paired decreases

Example: *3 rounds × 2 = 6 rounds*

Now, draw in the side of the sleeve. As mentioned earlier, the sleeve is drawn straight at each side for the distance of the gusset. At the row where the gusset ends, count out the number of rounds between decreases or paired decreases and indicate the decrease on either side of the chart until you reach the beginning of the cuff.

Count out the number of stitches for the lower sleeve circumference (Calculation H) and draw a connecting line to the sides of the sleeves. Draw the cuff to its circumference (Calculation I, although I reduced this for the ribbing-pattern multiple of the example garment) and to its approximate length (Calculation T).

With the sleeve silhouette now complete, you need only add the patterning. The sleeve motifs should echo those on the body. The main motif is centered on the shoulder seam or strap, and you may add 1 or 2 motifs to either side of it on a vertically patterned sleeve. Or you may work 1 or more of the horizontal patterns from the body on the upper arm, beginning at the top of the sleeve or just after the gusset has ended.

THE NECKLINE

I rarely chart the neckband. For my example, I multiplied the total number of body stitches by 45 percent to determine the number of stitches to pick up for the neckband (Calculation E). This worked out to 75.6 stitches. Because I planned to use 2 × 2 ribbing (worked in multiples of 4), I rounded this number up to 76, which is evenly divisible by 4.

You now have the blueprint for knitting ganseys. As you interpret this information and design on your own, you'll develop a unique gansey that acts as a meaningful expression of your creativity. Enjoy!

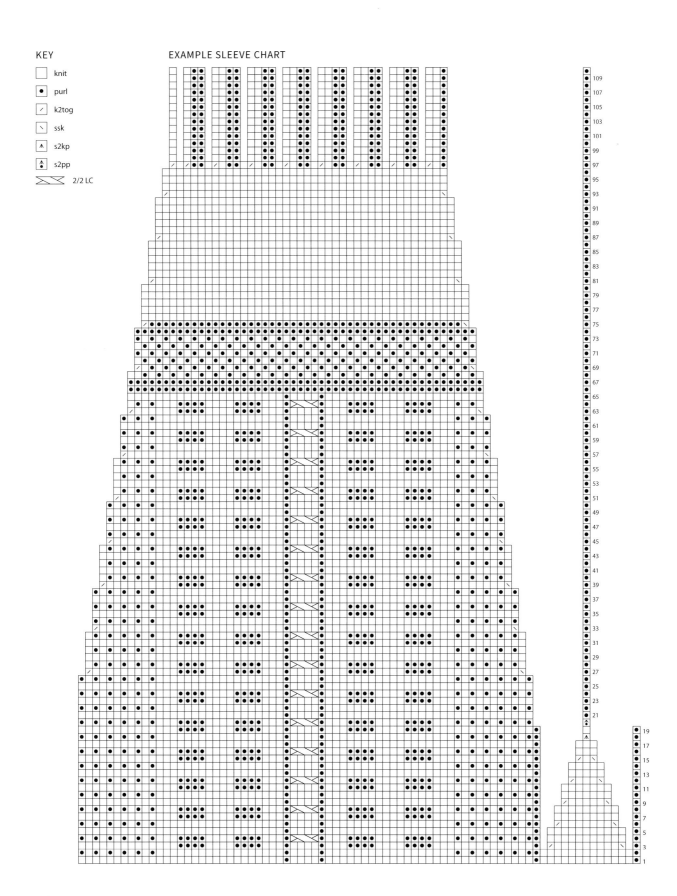

EXAMPLE SLEEVE CHART

KEY

- ☐ knit
- ● purl
- ╱ k2tog
- ╲ ssk
- ⬆ s2kp
- ⬆ s2pp
- ⤬⤬ 2/2 LC

worksheet for designing a gansey

Cast-on method _____

Ribbing/welt style _____

Initials pattern _____

Definition ridge pattern _____

Body patterning _____

Seam stitch(es) _____

Underarm-gusset shaping _____

Shoulder-join method _____

Type of neck gussets _____

Type of neckline _____

Type of neckband _____

Yarn _____

Needles _____

Gauge _____ sts/in. (2.5 cm)

_____ rnds/in. (2.5 cm)

DESIGN PROCESS SUMMARY

1. Knit a swatch in stockinette stitch at least 4" × 4" (10 × 10 cm) to determine gauge.

2. Make calculations and fill out the schematic (page 103).

3. Chart the silhouette: garment body, gussets, and neckline.

4. Plan and chart the body patterning over half the body stitches (the front or the back).

5. Chart the sleeve silhouette; plan and chart the sleeve patterning.

6. Plan the neckband and chart it if desired.

LOWER BODY

Cast on _____ (adjusted Calculation B) stitches onto a size _____ circular needle, two sizes smaller than that to be used for body. Work ribbing for _____ inches/cm (Calculation M). Increase to number of body stitches (Calculation A) in last round of ribbing. Change to larger-size circular needle.

Work stockinette stitch for _____ inches/cm (Calculation N), including seam stitches if desired. Knit initials if you want them, within the plain area. Work _____ inches/cm (Calculation O) in your chosen pattern for definition ridge. Work pattern panels until garment measures _____ inches/cm (Calculation Q) less than length to underarm (Calculation K).

Work gussets for _____ inches/cm (Calculation Q) at side seams, increasing at the rate calculated while continuing in pattern. When lower half of gussets are done, put gussets and seam stitches on holders.

UPPER BODY

For a garment with a shaped neckline, work the front back and forth for _____ inches/cm (Calculation L – Calculation R). Put the _____ neck-opening stitches (Calculation D) on a holder or bind them off. Shape the neckline by decreasing _____ stitches ([Calculation C – Calculation D] ÷ 2) on either side of the neck opening. Work the front to the desired length (Calculation L), then work the back to the desired length (Calculation L), and join the shoulders (see Chapter 8).

For a garment with an unshaped neckline, work front back and forth for _____ inches/cm (Calculation L). Be sure to subtract _____ inches/cm (Calculation F ÷ 2) from the total length of each garment half for the shoulder straps, if necessary. Work back for the desired length (Calculation L), and join shoulders (see Chapter 8).

SLEEVES

Put the gusset stitches on the circular needle and pick up _____ stitches (Calculation G or [Calculation L x Stitch gauge x 2]) around armhole for the sleeve. Calculate the sleeve shaping (see Chapter 9). Decrease the gusset for _____ inches/cm (Calculation Q). Shape the sleeve for _____ inches/cm. (Calculation U), working the patterning, definition ridge, and plain area. When the sleeve measures _____ inches/cm (Calculation Q + Calculation U), decrease any remaining stitches over 20% evenly in next round for a total of _____ stitches (Calculation I). Work cuff to desired length (Calculation T) and bind off loosely in pattern.

NECKLINE

Pick up _____ stitches (Calculation E) around the neck. Work neckline for desired length in desired style (see Chapter 10).

the
patterns

In Mary Wright's book Cornish Guernseys & Knit-Frocks *(1979), there is a photograph of several young boys in ganseys, one of whom is playing a concertina. For this reason, she named the motif on his sweater, which is the same motif I used here, "Musician." This worsted-weight garment features underarm gussets and drop shoulders, just like the ganseys of old. The construction and the patterning are easy for most knitters to knit.*

musician

FINISHED SIZES

Chest circumference:
34½ (38½, 42½, 46½, 50½, 54½)"
(87.5 [98, 108, 118, 128.5, 138.5] cm).

Length:
21¼ (23¼, 24, 24¼, 25¼, 26¼)"
(54 [58, 61, 61.5, 64, 66.5] cm).

Sample shown measures 38½" (98 cm).

YARN

#5 Aran weight.
857 (1047, 1193, 1317, 1492, 1673) yd
(784 [957, 1091, 1204, 1364, 1530] m).

Shown here: Quince & Co. Osprey
(100% American wool; 170 yds [155 m]/
3½ oz [100 g]): Damson, 6 (7, 8, 8, 9, 10) skeins.

NEEDLES

US 7 and 9 (4.5 and 5.5mm): 16" and 32"
(40 and 80 cm) circular (cir) and set of 4 or 5
double-pointed (dpn).

*Adjust needle size if necessary to achieve
the correct gauge.*

NOTIONS

Stitch markers (m); tapestry needle;
stitch holders or waste yarn.

GAUGE

16 sts and 24 rows = 4" (10 cm) in St st
using larger needles.

FEATURED TECHNIQUES

Garter Seam Stitches, Underarm Gussets,
Make 1 Increases, Folded Ribbed Neckband.

NOTES

This pattern was originally sized for women;
for men's sizing, instructions are given to deepen
the armhole. If you make adjustments to the total
length, this must be taken into account in the
placement of the gussets and the amount of yarn
purchased. Check the schematic before making
any changes.

This gansey is knitted in the round from the
cast-on to the armholes and includes underarm
gussets. The body is then split and the back and
front are worked flat. The shoulders are joined
with the Three-Needle Bind-off and the sleeves are
picked up around the armholes and knitted to the
cuff. The neckband is then picked up and knitted.

MUSICIAN BODY CHART

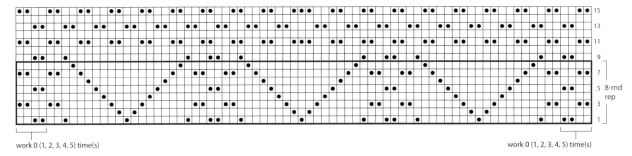

work 0 (1, 2, 3, 4, 5) time(s)   work 0 (1, 2, 3, 4, 5) time(s)

8-rnd rep

RIBBING

With smaller cir needle, CO 120 (136, 148, 164, 180, 192) sts using the Long-Tail Cast-on (see page 21). Place marker (pm) for beg of rnd and join for working in rnds, taking care not to twist sts. Work in 2 × 2 ribbing for 3" (7.5 cm) as follows:

All rnds: *P2, k2; rep from * around.

LOWER BODY

Change to larger cir needle. Working in St st (knit every rnd) for the plain area, inc 18 (18, 22, 22, 22, 26) sts evenly spaced across first rnd—138 (154, 170, 186, 202, 218) sts.

Rnd 1: *K2, pm for seam sts, work 67 (75, 83, 91, 99, 107) sts, pm for midpoint of rnd; rep from *.

Rnd 2: *P2, sm, work 67 (75, 83, 91, 99, 107) sts, sm; rep from *.

Cont in est patt until piece measures 4 (6¼, 7, 7¼, 7½, 7¾)" (10 [16, 18, 18.5, 19, 19.5] cm) from beg.

Note: If you need to adjust the length of the garment, do so in this plain area.

Next rnd: *Work seam sts, beg right edge of chart as marked for your size and work Row 1 of Body Motif Chart across next 67 (75, 83, 91, 99, 107) sts; rep from *.

Cont in est patt until piece measures 11 (12½, 12¾, 11½, 12, 12½)" (28 [31.5, 32.5, 29, 30.5, 31.5] cm) from beg, and seam sts have been worked as purls in last rnd.

UNDERARM GUSSETS

Rnd 1: (gusset inc) *K1, M1L, k1, sm, work in patt to next m, sm; rep from * once more—140 (156, 172, 188, 204, 220) sts, with 3 sts in each gusset.

Rnd 2: *P1, k1, p1, sm, work in patt to next m, sm; rep from * once more.

Rnd 3: (gusset inc) *K1, M1R, k1, M1L, k1, sm, work in patt to next m, sm; rep from * once more—4 sts inc'd.

Cont patt over front and back, work Rows 4–19 (19, 19, 25, 25, 25) of Lower Gusset Chart—164 (180, 196, 220, 236, 252) sts, with 15 (15, 15, 19, 19, 19) sts for each gusset. Place 15 (15, 15, 19, 19, 19) gusset sts on holders, and 67 (75, 83, 91, 99, 107) front sts on holder or waste yarn—67 (75, 83, 91, 99, 107) sts rem for back.

UPPER BODY

BACK

Working back and forth, cont in est patt until armholes measure 6 (6½, 7, 7½, 8, 8½)" (15 [16.5, 18, 19, 20.5, 21.5] cm), or 1" (2.5 cm) less than desired length, ending with Row 8 of chart.

Work Rows 9–13 of Musician Body Chart.

SHAPE NECK

Next row: Working Row 14 of chart, work 19 (21, 25, 27, 29, 32) sts in est patt, BO next 29 (33, 33, 37, 41, 43) sts for neck, then work to end of row—19 (21, 25, 27, 29, 32) sts rem for each shoulder.

Next row: Working Row 15 of chart, work to neck edge, break yarn, and place sts on holder.

Join yarn to other shoulder and work in est patt. Break yarn and place sts on holder.

FRONT

Return 67 (75, 83, 91, 99, 107) held sts for front to larger cir needle. Cont in est patt until front measures 2 (2, 2, 2½, 2½, 2½)" (5 [5, 5, 6.5, 6.5, 6.5] cm) less than back.

SHAPE NECK

Next row: Work 23 (25, 29, 31, 33, 36) sts, join a second ball of yarn and BO 21 (25, 25, 29, 33, 35) sts for neck, then work to end of row—23 (25, 29, 31, 33, 36) sts rem for each shoulder.

Working both sides at the same time with separate balls of yarn, cont in est patt and dec 1 st at each neck edge every RS row 4 times—19 (21, 25, 27, 29, 32) sts rem for each shoulder. *At the same time,* when front is 1" (2.5 cm) less than back, work Rows 9–15 of Musician Body Chart.

JOINING SHOULDERS

Return 19 (21, 25, 27, 29, 32) held sts from one back shoulder to larger dpn. Holding dpn in your LH tog with needle from corresponding front shoulder, and with RS tog (the ridge will be on the inside), join shoulder using Three-Needle Bind-off (see page 79). Rep for other shoulder.

SLEEVES

Return 15 (15, 15, 19, 19, 19) held gusset sts to shorter cir needle.

LOWER GUSSET CHART

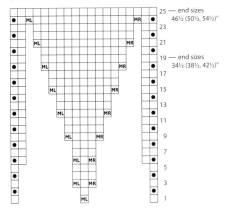

25 — end sizes
46½ (50½, 54½)"

19 — end sizes
34½ (38½, 42½)"

UPPER GUSSET CHART

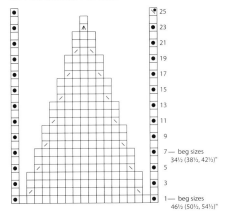

7 — beg sizes
34½ (38½, 42½)"

1— beg sizes
46½ (50½, 54½)"

KEY

☐	knit	╲	ssk	ML	M1L
●	purl	⋀	s2kp	MR	M1R
╱	k2tog	◥	p2tog tbl		

ADJUSTING FOR MEN'S SIZES

You can change the armhole depth for men's sizing to 8 (9, 9½, 10, 10½, 11)" (20.5 [23, 24, 25.5, 26.5, 28] cm), by beginning the gusset when the lower body measures 10 (11, 11¼, 10, 10½, 11)" (25.5 [28, 28.5, 25.5, 26.5, 28] cm) from beg. If you have lengthened the garment, add that difference to the lower body length.

SCHEMATIC

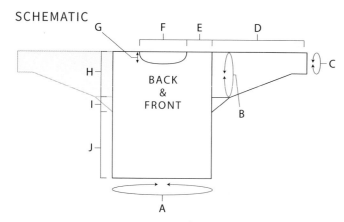

A 34½ (38½, 42½, 46½, 50½, 54½)" (87.5 [98, 108, 118, 128.5, 138.5] cm)

B 14¾ (15¾, 16¾, 17¾, 18¾, 19¾)" (37.5 [40, 42.5, 45, 47.5, 50] cm)

C 7 (7, 8, 8, 9, 10)" (18 [18, 20.5, 20.5, 23, 25.5] cm)

D 17 (17¾, 18, 18¼, 18½, 19)" (43 [45, 45.5, 46.5, 47, 48.5] cm)

E 4¾ (5¼, 6¼, 6¾, 7¼, 8)" (12 [13.5, 16, 17, 18.5, 20.5] cm)

F 7¼ (8¼, 8¼, 9¼, 10¼, 10¾)" (18.5 [21, 21, 23.5, 26, 27.5] cm)

G 2 (2, 2, 2½, 2½, 2½)" (5 [5, 5, 6.5, 6.5, 6.5] cm)

H 7 (7½, 8, 8½, 9, 9½)" (18 [19, 20.5, 21.5, 23, 24] cm)

I 3¼ (3¼, 3¼, 4¼, 4¼, 4¼)" (8.5 [8.5, 8.5, 11, 11, 11] cm)

J 11 (12½, 12¾, 11½, 12, 12½)" (28 [31.5, 32.5, 29, 30.5, 31.5] cm)

MUSICIAN SLEEVE CHART

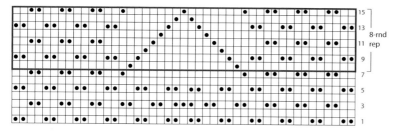

KEY

☐ knit   ⊡ purl   ☐ pattern repeat

Pick-up rnd: Join yarn to beg with a RS row, work Row 7 (7, 7, 1, 1, 1) of Upper Gusset Chart, pm.

FOR WOMEN

Pick up and knit 57 (61, 65, 69, 73, 77) sts evenly around armhole, pm for beg of rnd, and join for working in rnds—72 (76, 80, 88, 92, 96) sts.

Next rnd: Work Row 8 (8, 8, 2, 2, 2) of Upper Gusset Chart to m, sm, k6 (8, 10, 12, 14, 16), pm, work Row 1 of Sleeve Chart over next 45 sts, pm, k6 (8, 10, 12, 14, 16)—2 gusset sts dec'd.

Note: The midpoint of the chevron is aligned with the shoulder seam.

FOR MEN

Pick up and knit 65 (73, 77, 81, 85, 89) sts evenly around armhole, pm for beg of rnd, and join for working in rnds— 80 (88, 92, 100, 104, 108) sts.

Next rnd: Work Row 8 (8, 8, 2, 2, 2) of Upper Gusset Chart to m, sm, k10 (14, 16, 18, 20, 22) sts, pm, work Row 1 of Sleeve Chart over next 45 sts, pm, k10 (14, 16, 18, 20, 22) sts—2 gusset sts dec'd.

Note: The midpoint of the chevron is aligned with the shoulder seam.

ALL SIZES

Working Rows 9 (9, 9, 3, 3, 3)–25 of Upper Gusset Chart, work Rows 2–15 of Sleeve Chart, then rep Rows 8–15 five more times, and cont sts between gusset and motif m in St st— 59 (63, 67, 71, 75, 79) sts rem for Women's, and 67 (75, 79, 83, 87, 91) sts rem for Men's, with 2 seam sts rem between gusset m.

Cont seam sts in est patt, work 4 rnds even.

Dec rnd: Work seam sts, ssk, work to last 2 sts, k2tog—2 sts dec'd.

SLEEVE DECREASES FOR WOMEN

Rep Dec rnd every 5 rnds 10 (6, 6, 0, 0, 0) times more, every 4 rnds 2 (8, 8, 14, 14, 16) times, then every 2 rnds 0 (0, 0, 2, 2, 0) times— 33 (33, 37, 37, 41, 45) sts rem.

Work even until sleeve measures about 14 (14¾, 15, 15¼, 15½, 16)" (35.5 [37.5, 38, 38.5, 39.5, 40.5] cm), or desired length from pick-up.

Change to smaller dpn.

Dec rnd: Knit and dec 5 sts evenly spaced—28 (28, 32, 32, 36, 40) sts rem.

Work in 2 × 2 ribbing for 3" (7.5 cm), making sure the seam sts flow into a purl rib. BO all sts loosely in patt.

SLEEVE DECREASES FOR MEN

Work Dec rnd every 4 rnds 16 (18, 19, 19, 20, 21) times more, then every 2 rnds 0 (0, 1, 1, 0, 1) time(s)—33 (37, 37, 41, 45, 45) sts rem.

Work even until sleeve measures about 15 (16½, 17½, 18½, 19, 19½)" (38 [42, 44.5, 47, 48.5, 49.5] cm), or desired length from pick-up.

Change to smaller dpn.

Dec rnd: Knit and dec 1 (5, 1, 5, 5, 5) st(s) evenly spaced—32 (32, 36, 36, 40, 40) sts rem.

Work in 2 × 2 ribbing for 3" (7.5 cm), making sure the seam sts flow into a purl rib. BO all sts loosely in patt.

NECKBAND

With smaller cir needle or dpn, and RS facing, beg at left shoulder seam and pick up and knit 9 (9, 9, 11, 12, 11) sts along left side of front neck, 21 (25, 25, 29, 31, 35) sts along front neck, 9 (9, 9, 11, 12, 11) sts along right side of front neck, then 29 (33, 33, 37, 41, 43) sts along back neck—68 (76, 76, 88, 96, 100) sts. Pm for beg of rnd, and join for working in rnds.

Work in 2 × 2 ribbing for 3" (7.5 cm). Fold neckband in half to inside and sew it down stitch by stitch to WS (see page 92).

FINISHING

Weave in ends. Block to measurements.

This gansey is reminiscent of many of the old ganseys that featured horizontal panels of simple knit/purl motifs. This type of layout is easy to knit because only one motif is worked at a time, across the front and back, rather than many different motifs worked vertically next to each other. The underarm gusset is unusual in that it is worked in reverse stockinette stitch and has a knitted 6-stitch seam that separates into three parts to surround and bisect the gusset. Although it is knitted in the traditional yarn, this garment has a softer hand, knitted at 6 stitches/inch, rather than 7.

newhaven

FINISHED SIZES

Chest circumference:
34 (38, 42, 46, 50, 54)"
(86.5 [96.5, 106.5, 117, 127, 137] cm).

Length:
22¾ (25, 25¼, 25¼, 26¼, 26¾)"
(52 [58, 59.5, 60.5, 63, 65.5] cm).

Sample shown measures 38" (96.5 cm).

YARN

#2 Sportweight.
1209 (1500, 1718, 1896, 2145, 2409) yd
(1106 [1372, 1571, 1734, 1961, 2203] m).

Shown here: Frangipani 5-ply Guernsey
(100% wool; 240 yds [220 m]/3½ oz [100 g]):
Sea Spray (left) and Pewter (right),
6 (7, 8, 8, 9, 11) balls.

NEEDLES

US 2 (2.75 mm): 16" (40 cm) circular (cir)
and set of 4 or 5 double-pointed (dpn).

US 3 (3.25 mm): 16" and 32" (40 and 80 cm) cir
and set of 4 or 5 dpn.

*Adjust needle size if necessary to achieve
the correct gauge.*

NOTIONS

Stitch holders; stitch markers (m); tapestry needle;
scraps of contrast-color yarn.

GAUGE

24 sts and 36 rows/rnds = 4" (10 cm) in St st
using larger needles.

FEATURED TECHNIQUES

Channel Island Cast-on, Garter-Stitch Welt,
Six-Stitch Seam, Horizontal Pattern Panels,
Bisected Reverse St st Underarm Gussets,
Unshaped Neckline, Three-Needle Bind-off,
Inverted Triangular Neck Gusset, SSK Bind-off.

NOTES

This garment is sized with 2–4" (5–10 cm) of ease.
If you prefer more fullness, knit the next size up.
If you wish the sweater to be shorter or longer,
adjust in the stockinette stitch (St st) area of the
lower body and lower sleeve.

STITCH GUIDE

SSK BIND-OFF

Ssk, *sl 1 kwise, insert LH needle tip through front of 2 sts on RH needle, k2tog tbl; rep from * to end of row.

GARTER-STITCH CONTINUOUS WELT

With longer larger cir needle, CO 204 (228, 252, 276, 300, 324) sts using Channel Island Cast-on (see page 19). Place marker (pm) for beg of rnd, and join to work in rnds, taking care not to twist sts. Work in garter st (purl 1 rnd, knit 1 rnd) for 1¼" (3.2 cm).

LOWER BODY

Work in St st (knit every rnd) for 2¾ (5, 5¼, 5¼, 6¼, 6¾)" (7 [12.5, 13.5, 13.5, 16, 17] cm). If adding initials, work 1" (2.5 cm) in St st after garter welt. Beg initials on 13th st from beg of rnd (lower left side of front) if desired. You can chart your initials using the Blank Initial Chart on page 31 and Alphabet Charts on page 35.

Set-up rnd: Working Row 1 of Motif Chart 1, *work patt over 96 (108, 120, 132, 144, 156) sts, pm for seam sts, k6, pm for seam sts; rep from * to end of rnd. *At the same time,* beg shaping lower gusset when piece measures 12¼ (14½, 14¼, 14, 14, 14)" (31.5 [37, 36, 35.5, 35.5, 35.5] cm) from beg.

FOR ALL SIZES

When Row 61 of Pattern C is reached, inc 1 (5, 1, 5, 1, 5) st(s) evenly across both front and back—97 (113, 121, 137, 145, 161) sts each for front and back.

FOR BOTH THE FRONT AND BACK

The last st in each row worked in Patt C (before the seam sts marker) is worked as the first st of the chart for that row to complete the motif.

UNDERARM GUSSETS

Set-up rnd: *Work in est patt to m, sm, k2, M1P, k2, M1P, k2, sm; rep from * once more— 4 gusset sts inc'd.

Rnds 2 and 3: Work to m, sm, [k2, p1] twice, k2; sm; rep from * once more.

Rnd 4: (inc) *Work to m in est patt, sm, k2, M1P, p1, k2, p1, M1P, k2, sm; rep from * once more—4 gusset sts inc'd.

Cont as est, working Rnds 5–26 (26, 26, 26, 35, 35) of Lower Gusset Chart while *at the same time* working Motif Chart 1 and dec 1 (5, 1, 5, 1, 5) sts in each half when row 89 of Pattern C is reached.

KEY

- ☐ k on RS, p on WS
- ● p on RS, k on WS
- P M1P

LOWER GUSSET CHART

MOTIF CHART 1

MOTIF CHART 2

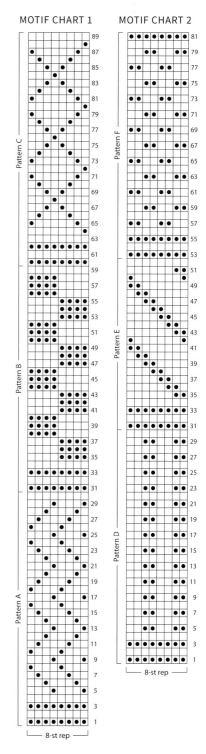

Place 24 (24, 24, 24, 30, 30) sts for each gusset on holders or waste yarn, and 97 (113, 121, 137, 145, 161) sts on another holder or waste yarn for back—97 (113, 121, 137, 145, 161) sts rem for front.

Piece should measure about 15¼ (17½, 17¼, 17, 18, 18)" (38.5 [44.5, 44, 43, 45.5, 45.5] cm) from beg.

UPPER BODY

FRONT

Cont working back and forth until all rows of both motif charts are completed. Place sts on holder.

BACK

Return 97 (113, 121, 137, 145, 161) sts held back sts to longer larger cir needle. Join yarn and work as for front.

SHOULDER JOIN

RIGHT SHOULDER AND GUSSET

Place 32 (36, 40, 44, 48, 52) front sts to one dpn, and 32 (36, 40, 44, 48, 52) back sts to second dpn or on opposite sides of longer larger cir needle with needle tips at armhole.

Holding pieces with RS tog in LH (WS of right front is facing) and dpn in RH, join yarn at armhole and work Three-Needle Bind-off (see page 79) to last 7 sts on both LH needles, with 1 st rem on RH needle. Turn garment RS out.

Holding dpn with single rem st in RH and needle with right back shoulder sts in LH with RS facing, work Neck Gusset Chart as follows:

Row 1: (RS) First st of chart is already on RH needle, k1 from back shoulder, turn.

Row 2: (WS) Sl 1 pwise wyf, p1, discard empty dpn, p1 from front shoulder, turn.

Row 3: Sl 1 kwise wyb, k2, k1 from back shoulder, turn.

Work Rows 4–15 of Neck Gusset Chart as est— 15 neck gusset sts. Place sts on holder.

LEFT SHOULDER AND GUSSET

Repeat as for right shoulder, holding pieces with RS tog in LH (WS of back facing). Join yarn at armhole edge and work Three Needle Bind-Off to last 7 sts on each LH needle. Turn garment RS out.

Holding needle with front left shoulder sts in LH and RS facing, work Neck Gusset Chart. Break yarn.

SCHEMATIC

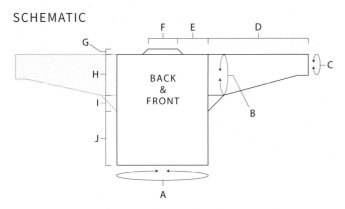

A 34 (38, 42, 46, 50, 54)" (86.5 [96.5, 106.5, 117, 127, 137] cm)

B 16¾ (16¾, 17¾, 18, 18, 19)" (42.5 [42.5, 45, 45.5, 45.5, 48.5] cm)

C 7¾ (8¾, 9¼, 10¼, 11, 11¾)" (19.5 [22, 23.5, 26, 28, 30] cm)

D 19 (19¾, 20¼, 20¼, 20¼, 20¼)" (48.5 [50, 51.5, 51.5, 51.5, 51.5] cm)

E 5¼ (6, 6¾, 7¼, 8, 8¾)" (13.5 [15, 17, 18.5, 20.5, 22] cm)

F 5¼ (6, 6¾, 7¼, 8, 8¾)" (13.5 [15, 17, 18.5, 20.5, 22] cm)

G 1¼" (3.2 cm)

H 7½ (7½, 8, 8¼, 8¼, 8¾)" (19 [19, 20.5, 21, 21, 22] cm)

I 3 (3, 3, 3, 4, 4)" (7.5 [7.5, 7.5, 7.5, 10, 10] cm)

J 12½ (14½, 14¼, 14, 14, 14)" (31.5 [37, 36, 35.5, 35.5, 35.5] cm)

NECKBAND

With smaller cir needle and RS of back facing, join yarn and knit 32 (36, 40, 44, 48, 52) sts from back holder, 15 left neck gusset sts, 32 (36, 40, 44, 48, 52) sts from front holder, 15 right neck gusset sts—94 (102, 110, 118, 126, 134) sts. Pm for beg of rnd and join to work in rnds.

Next rnd: *K1, p1; rep from * around.

Rep last rnd until ribbing measures 1" (2.5 cm) or desired length. BO all sts loosely, using SSK Bind-off (see Stitch Guide).

SLEEVES

With shorter larger cir needle and RS facing, work 24 (24, 24, 24, 30, 30) held gusset sts, pm, then pick up and knit 94 (94, 100, 102, 102, 108) sts evenly around armhole (about 2 sts for every 3 rows)—118 (118, 124, 126, 132, 138) sts.

Pm for beg of rnd, and join for working in rnds.

Next rnd: Work Row 10 (10, 10, 10, 1, 1) of Upper Gusset Chart to m, sm, work Row 53 of Motif Chart 2.

UPPER GUSSET CHART

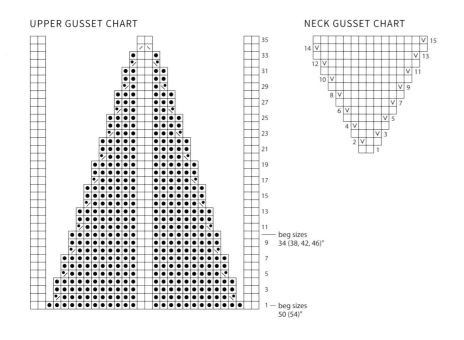

NECK GUSSET CHART

KEY

- k on RS, p on WS
- p on RS, k on WS
- k2tog
- ssk
- p2tog
- ssp
- sl 1 wyb on RS, sl 1 wyf on WS

Cont as est through Row 35 of Upper Gusset Chart, and Rows 54–80 of Motif Chart 2 (Patt F). Then, keeping 6 seam sts in St st, work Rows 31–52 of Motif Chart 2 (Patt E), Rows 31–59 of Motif Chart 1 (Patt B), Rows 1–33 of Motif Chart 1 (Patt A, then first 3 rows of Patt B), then cont in St st. **At the same time,** when Upper Gusset Chart is complete, begin Dec Rnd—100 (100, 106, 108, 108, 114) sts rem, with 94 (94, 100, 102, 102, 106) sts for sleeve and 6 seam sts.

Dec rnd: K6, sm, k2tog, work to last 2 sts, ssk —2 sts dec'd.

Rep Dec rnd every 5 (5, 5, 6, 6, 6) rnds 15 (11, 12, 22, 20, 21) times, then every 4 (5, 5, 0, 0, 0) rnds 11 (12, 12, 0, 0, 0) times—46 (52, 56, 62, 66, 70) sts rem. *Note: Change to larger dpn when too few sts rem to work comfortably on cir needle.*

Work even until sleeve measures 17 (17¾, 18¼, 18¼, 18¼, 18¼)" (43 [45, 46.5, 46.5, 46.5, 46.5] cm), or 2" (5 cm) less than desired length.

CUFF

Change to smaller dpn.

Next rnd: *K1, p1; rep from * around.

Rep last rnd until ribbing measures 2" (5 cm) or desired length. BO all sts loosely in ribbing.

FINISHING

Weave in ends. Block to measurements.

When my eldest son was a little boy, I spun and knit him a sweater. I was new to designing my own garments, and I made the neck too small. Intent on having a family portrait of all of us in sweaters I had made, I wrestled and crammed it on his little head. The poor child's ears were painfully squished, and, in my mind, the trauma of it all led him to a strong aversion to sweaters. I doubt he has ever had a sweater in his closet since, and this is my peace offering to him—a second try on the noble sweater—one that won't pinch his ears. I designed this garment to be a replica of many of the plainer working ganseys: no fussy patterning, but rather a rugged, well-wearing ribbed pattern—a classic.

jorn's gansey

FINISHED SIZES

Chest circumference:
36 (40, 44, 48, 52)"
(91.5 [101.5, 112, 122, 132] cm).

Length:
24¼" (61.5 cm).

Sample shown measures 40" (101.5 cm).

YARN

#2 Sportweight.
1585 (1761, 1938, 2144, 2291) yd
(1449 [1610, 1772, 1960, 2095] m).

Shown here: Wendy Guernsey 5-Ply
(100% wool; 245 yds [224 m]/3½ oz [100 g]):
#520 Navy, 7 (8, 8, 9, 10) balls.

NEEDLES

US 3 (3.25 mm): 16" and 32" (40 and 80 cm)
circular (cir) and set of 4 or 5 double-pointed (dpn).

*Adjust needle size if necessary to achieve
the correct gauge.*

NOTIONS

Stitch markers (m); waste yarn or stitch holders;
tapestry needle.

GAUGE

24 sts and 34 rnds = 4" (10 cm) in St st.

26 sts = 4" (10 cm) in 2 × 2 rib.

FEATURED TECHNIQUES

Multistrand Cast-on, Shoulder Extensions, Three-
Needle Bind-off (seam on RS).

NOTES

The bottom edge is a 2 × 2 ribbing, reinforced by
the Multistrand Cast-on, followed by a generous
plain area with a four-stitch seam. The patterning
and the gusset begin at the same point. The
neckline is unshaped; that is, the front neck
stitches are put on holders, and the shoulders are
knitted longer, then joined to the back shoulders
with the seam on the outside. The neckband is
picked up, worked in ribbing, and finished with
a rolled edge. The sleeves are picked up and knit
down, with the ribbed pattern on the upper arm.
The cuffs, also in ribbing, are finished with a rolled
edge. You can easily adjust the lengths of the body
and sleeves in the plain areas.

STITCH GUIDE

SEAM-STITCH PATTERN

Rnd 1: K3, p1.

Rnd 2: P1, k3.

Rep Rnds 1 and 2 for patt.

2 × 2 RIBBING

CIRCULAR

All rnds: *K2, p2; rep from * around.

FLAT

Row 1: (RS) *K2, p2; rep from * to last 2 sts, k2.

Row 2: (WS) *P2, k2; rep from * to last 2 sts, p2.

Rep Rows 1 and 2 for patt.

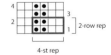

LOWER BODY

RIBBING

Using the Multi-strand Cast-on (see page 22) with the long-tail method (see page 21), cast on as follows: holding together one end from each of 4 balls of yarn, make a slipknot, allowing about a 4" (10 cm) long tail. Using double yarns (2 strands over your thumb and 2 strands over your index finger) and longer cir needle, CO 216 (240, 264, 288, 312) sts. Do not count the slipknot in your stitch count.

Drop 2 of the strands. Remove the slipknot. Pm for beg of rnd and join to work in rnds, taking care not to twist sts. Holding both rem strands of yarn tog, work 6 rnds in 2 × 2 ribbing.

Drop 1 strand. With the rem strand, continue in ribbing until piece measures 3" (7.5 cm) from beg.

PLAIN AREA

Rnd 1: Remove beg-of-rnd m, k3, p1, pm, k104 (116, 128, 140, 152), pm, k3, p1, pm, k104 (116, 128, 140, 152), pm for new beg of rnd.

Rnds 2 and 4: P1, k3, sm, knit to next m, sm, p1, k3, sm, knit to end of rnd.

Rnd 3: *K3, p1, sm, knit to next m, sm; rep from * once more.

If you want to include initials, use the Blank Initial Chart on page 31 to chart out the letters so you can space them well. They should be started on the 10th st from the beg of the rnd and after 1" (2.5 cm) of St st has been worked.

Cont as est until piece measures 12¾ (12¼, 11¾, 11¼, 10¾)" (32.5 [31, 30, 28.5, 27.5] cm) from beg, ending with Rnd 3.

BEGIN GUSSET AND PATTERNING

Rnd 1: *Work Row 1 of Lower Gusset Chart, sm, beg 2 × 2 ribbing and inc 2 sts evenly spaced to next m, sm; rep from * once more—224 (248, 272, 296, 320), with 106 (118, 130, 142, 154) sts each for front and back, and 6 sts for each gusset and seam sts.

LOWER GUSSET CHART

UPPER GUSSET CHART

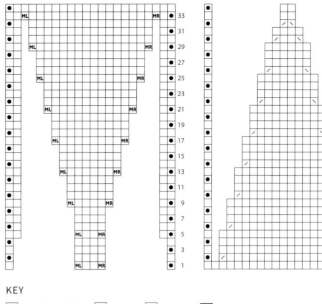

KEY

| | k on RS, p on WS | | ML | M1L | | / | k2tog | | | pattern repeat |
| | p on RS, k on WS | | MR | M1R | | \ | ssk | | | |

Rnd 2: *K5, p1, sm, [k2, p2] to 2 sts before m, k2, sm; rep from * once more.

Rnd 3: *P1, k5, sm, [k2, p2] to 2 sts before m, k2, sm; rep from * once more.

Cont in ribbing patt on front and back as est and work Rows 4–34 of Lower Gusset Chart—256 (280, 304, 328, 352) sts, with 106 (118, 130, 142, 154) sts each for front and back, and 22 sts for each gusset and seam sts.

UPPER BODY

DIVIDE FRONT AND BACK

Place 22 sts between gusset m on holder or waste yarn. Turn and work in patt across back to next m. Place 22 sts between gusset m on holder or waste yarn, then place next 106 (118, 130, 142, 154) sts on waste yarn for front—106 (118, 130, 142, 154) sts rem for back.

BACK

Work in est patt until back measures 24¼" (61.5 cm) from beg. Place sts on waste yarn.

FRONT

Work in est patt until front measures 22¼ (22¼, 21¾, 21¾, 21¾)" (56.5 [56.5, 55, 55, 55] cm) from beg, or 2 (2, 2½, 2½, 2½)" (5 [5, 6.5, 6.5, 6.5] cm) less than back.

Next row: Work 34 (38, 42, 46, 50) sts in est patt, place next 38 (42, 46, 50, 54) sts on waste yarn for neck, join a second ball of yarn and work to end of row—34 (38, 42, 46, 50) sts rem for each shoulder.

Work both sides at the same time with separate balls of yarn until front measures same as back.

JOIN SHOULDERS

Note: Below, the left and right shoulders refer to the garment as you are wearing it.

Be certain to join the shoulders with the RS facing you. Work the left shoulder seam from the armhole to the neck and the right shoulder seam from neck to armhole. This way, the shoulders will appear identical.

Place 34 (38, 42, 46, 50) right front shoulder sts and 34 (38, 42, 46, 50) right back shoulder sts onto 2 dpn. Holding needles with WS tog, join shoulder using Three-Needle Binf-off (see page 79). Rep for left shoulder.

NECKBAND

Place 38 (42, 46, 50, 54) held sts for back neck on shorter cir needle. With RS facing, working sts in est patt, pick up and knit 14 (14, 18, 18, 18) sts along left side of neck, place 38 (42, 46, 50, 54) held front neck sts on left needle tip and work them in est patt, then pick up and knit 14 (14, 18, 18, 18) sts along right side of neck—104 (112, 128, 136, 144) sts. Pm for beg of rnd and join for working in rnds.

Work in 2 × 2 ribbing as est by front and back sts until neckband measures 2" (5 cm), or to desired length.

Rolled Edge

Rnds 1–5: Knit.

BO all sts loosely kwise.

SLEEVES

Return 22 held gusset and seam sts to shorter cir needle.

Rnd 1: With RS facing, p1, k21, pm, pick up and knit 90 (98, 102, 110, 114) sts evenly around armhole to gusset—112 (120, 124, 132, 136) sts. Pm for beg of rnd and join to work in rnds.

Rnd 2: (dec) K1, ssk, knit to 3 sts before m, k2tog, p1, sm, purl to end of rnd—
2 gusset sts dec'd.

Rnds 3 and 5: P1, knit to m, sm, [k2, p2] to last 2 sts, k2.

Rnd 4: Knit to 1 st before m, p1, sm, [k2, p2] to last 2 sts, k2.

Cont as est, work Rows 6–34 of Upper Gusset Chart—94 (102, 106, 114, 118) sts rem, with 90 (98, 102, 110, 114) sleeve sts and 4 seam sts.

SHAPE SLEEVE

Note: Change to dpn when there are too few sts to work comfortably on cir needle.

Dec rnd: Work seam sts, sm, k1, ssk, knit to last 3 sts, k2tog, k1—2 sts dec'd.

Rep dec rnd every 6 rnds 4 (11, 22, 20, 23) times, then every 5 rnds 18 (11, 0, 3, 0) times—48 (56, 60, 66, 70) sts rem. **At the same time,** when sleeve measures 6" (15 cm) from pick-up, keeping seam sts in est patt, change to St st over rem sts. Cont even until sleeve measures 18 (19, 20, 20½, 21)" (45.5 [48.5, 51, 52, 53.5] cm), or 3" (7.5 cm) less than desired length.

CUFF

Rnd 1: (dec) P1, k2, p1, knit to end of rnd and dec 0 (4, 4, 6, 6) sts evenly spaced—48 (52, 56, 60, 64) sts rem.

Rnd 2: P1, k2, [p2, k2] to last st, p1.

Keeping seam sts in est patt, work until ribbing measures 3" (7.5 cm).

Knit 5 rnds. BO all sts loosely kwise.

FINISHING

Weave in ends. Block to measurements.

SCHEMATIC

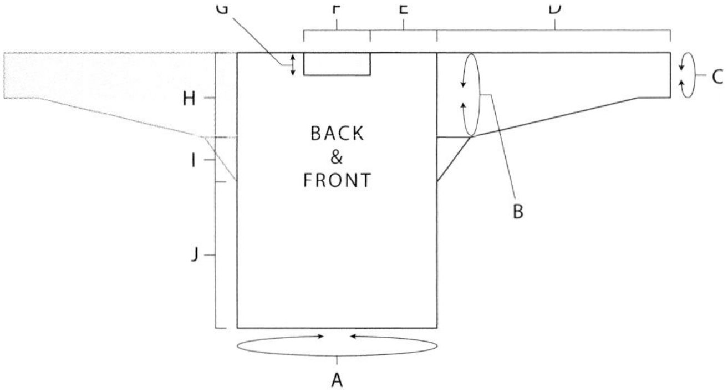

A   36 (40, 44, 48, 52)" (91.5 [101.5, 112, 122, 132] cm)

B   14½ (15¾, 16¼, 17½, 18¼)" (37 [40, 41.5, 44.5, 46.5] cm)

C   8 (9¼, 10, 11, 11¾)" (20.5 [23.5, 25.5, 28, 30] cm)

D   21 (22, 23, 23½, 24)" (53.5 [56, 58.5, 59.5, 61] cm)

E   5¼ (5¾, 6½, 7, 7¾)" (13.5 [14.5, 16.5, 18, 19.5] cm)

F   5¾ (6½, 7, 7¾, 8¼)" (14.5 [16.5, 18, 19.5, 21] cm)

G   2 (2, 2½, 2½, 2½)" (5 [5, 6.5, 6.5, 6.5] cm)

H   7½ (8, 8½, 9, 9½)" (19 [20.5, 21.5, 23, 24] cm)

I   4" (10 cm)

J   12¾ (12¼, 11¾, 11¼, 10¾)" (32.5 [31, 30, 28.5, 27.5] cm)

This heavy worsted-weight drop-shouldered gansey is a loose interpretation of the Scottish Eriskay ganseys. It has a looser fit and is made of vertical patterns in the lower body topped with a horizontal panel of pattern, with another motif on top. The classic gansey construction includes underarm gussets and incorporates traditional gansey motifs.

the big easy

FINISHED SIZES

Chest circumference:
38 (42, 46, 50, 54)"
(96.5 [106.5, 117, 127, 137] cm).

Length:
23¼ (24¾, 25, 26, 26)"
(59 [63, 63.5, 66, 66] cm).

Sample shown measures 38" (96.5 cm).

YARN

#4 Aran weight.
996 (1228, 1298, 1473, 1596) yd
(911 [1123, 1187, 1347, 1459] m).

Shown here: Quince & Co. Osprey
(100% American wool; 170 yds [155 m] /
3½ oz [100 g]): Gingerbread, 6 (8, 8, 9, 10) hanks.

NEEDLES

US 7 (4.5mm): 16" and 32" (40 and 80 cm)
circular (cir) and set of 4 or 5 double-pointed (dpn).

Adjust needle size if necessary to achieve the
correct gauge.

NOTIONS

Stitch markers (m); cable needle (cn);
stitch holders or waste yarn; tapestry needle.

GAUGE

16 sts and 25 rows = 4" (10 cm) in St st.

FEATURED TECHNIQUES

Continuous Garter Welt, Avoiding Cable Splay,
Underarm Gussets, Wide Neck with Rolled Collar.

NOTES

The bottom edge and sleeve cuffs are worked in
garter stitch. The shoulder seams, worked with the
Three-Needle Bind-off, can be worked two ways.
The wide neckline is accentuated with a picked-up
rolled collar. For a longer garment, add additional
rounds of St st in the plain area (above the garter-
stitch welt).

STITCH GUIDE

3/3 LC (3 over 3 left cross)

Sl 3 sts onto cn and hold in front, k3, k3 from cn.

3/3 RC (3 over 3 right cross)

Sl 3 sts onto cn and hold in back, k3, k3 from cn.

4/4 LC (4 over 4 left cross)

Sl 4 sts onto cn and hold in front, k4, k4 from cn.

4/4 RC (4 over 4 right cross)

Sl 4 sts onto cn and hold in back, k4, k4 from cn.

INDIAN CORN STITCH

Yo, k2, pass yo over the 2 sts.

THE CONTINUOUS GARTER WELT

With longer cir needle, CO 140 (156, 172, 188, 204) sts using the long-tail method (see page 21). Place marker (pm) for beg of rnd, and join to work in rnds, taking care not to twist sts. Work in garter st (knit 1 rnd, purl 1 rnd) for 1¼" (3.2 cm).

LOWER BODY

PLAIN AREA

Next (inc) rnd: Knit and inc 12 sts evenly spaced—152 (168, 184, 200, 216) sts.

Work even in St st (knit every rnd) for 1½ (2½, ¾, 1¾, 1¾)" (3.8 [6.5, 2, 4.5, 4.5] cm).

Beg working from Lower Body Chart for your size as follows:

Rnd 1: *Beg at right edge of chart, work first st of Pattern A, work next 2 sts 1 (3, 2, 4, 6) time(s), work next 11 (11, 13, 13, 13) sts, [M1, k1] 3 (3, 4, 4, 4) times, work next 1 (1, 2, 2, 2) st(s), pm, work Pattern B over next 41 (41, 45, 45, 45) sts, pm, working Pattern C, p1 (1, 2, 2, 2), [k1, M1] 3 (3, 4, 4, 4) times, then work next 11 (11, 13, 13, 13) sts, then work 2 sts at left edge of chart 1 (3, 2, 4, 6) time(s), pm for side; rep from * once more—164 (180, 200, 216, 232) sts.

SEAM STITCHES

Note: The first stitch of Pattern A is the "seam stitch" and will continue in pattern up the body, at the beginning and mid-point of the round, changing to a knit stitch that is part of the gusset, then reverting to alternating knits and purls down the sleeve.

Work Rows 2–19 (19, 17, 17, 17) as est 3 (3, 4, 4, 4) times. Piece should measure about 11½ (12½, 12½, 13½, 13½)" (29 [31.5, 31.5, 34.5, 34.5] cm) from beg. *Note: The gusset for size 52" (132 cm) will begin when piece measures 13" (33 cm).*

Next rnd: *Work in est patt to m, sm, k1 (1, 0, 0, 0), work Row 1 of Chart D over next 39 (39, 45, 45, 45) sts, k1 (1, 0, 0, 0), sm, work in est patt to m, sm; rep from * once more.

Cont as est, work Rows 2–58 of Chart D. ***At the same time,*** when piece measures 13 (14, 13, 13½, 13)" (33 [35.5, 33, 34.5, 33] cm) from beg, shape gussets.

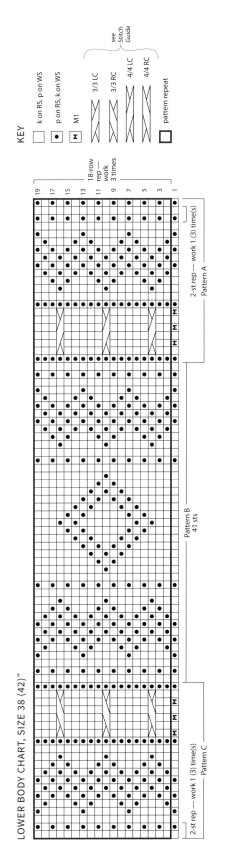

LOWER BODY CHART, SIZE 38 (42)"

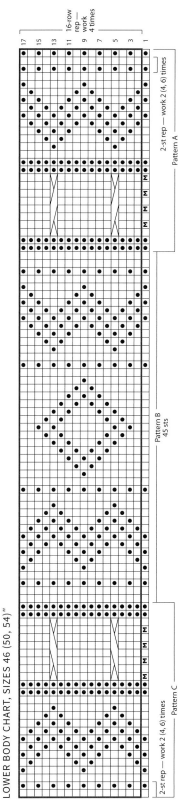

LOWER BODY CHART, SIZES 46 (50, 54)"

KEY

- ☐ k on RS, p on WS
- ● p on RS, k on WS
- ☒ M1
- 3/3 LC
- 3/3 RC
- 4/4 LC (see Stitch Guide)
- 4/4 RC (see Stitch Guide)
- ☐ pattern repeat

UNDERARM GUSSETS

Rnd 1: (set-up) M1RP, k1, MILP, pm for gusset, work 81 (89, 99, 107, 115) sts in est patt, sm, MIRP, k1, M1LP, pm for gusset, work to end of round—168 (184, 204, 220, 236) sts, with 81 (89, 99, 107, 115) sts each for front and back, and 3 sts in each gusset.

Rnd 2: *P1, k1, p1, sm, work in est patt to side m, sm; rep from * once more.

Rnd 3: (inc) *P1, M1R, knit to 1 st before gusset m, M1L, p1, sm, work to side m; rep from * once more—4 gusset sts inc'd.

Work Rows 4–17 (17, 22, 22, 22) of Lower Gusset Chart—188 (204, 232, 248, 264) sts, with 81 (89, 99, 107, 115) sts each for front and back, and 13 (13, 17, 17, 17) sts for each gusset. If necessary, work an extra rnd to end with an odd- (odd-, even-, even-, even-) numbered row of Patterns A and C. Piece should measure 15¾ (16¾, 16½, 17, 16½)" (40 [42.5, 42, 43, 42] cm) from beg.

DIVIDE FRONT AND BACK

Next rnd: Place 13 (13, 17, 17, 17) gusset sts on holder or waste yarn, work 81 (89, 99, 107, 115) front sts, place next 13 (13, 17, 17, 17) gusset sts on waste yarn, and rem 81 (89, 99, 107, 115) back sts on holder or waste yarn—81 (89, 99, 107, 115) sts rem for front.

FRONT

Working back and forth, cont in est patt until Chart D has been finished, ending with a WS row. Piece should measure about 20¾ (21¾, 21¾, 22¾, 22¾)" (52.5 [55, 55, 58, 58] cm) from beg.

SHAPE NECK

Next row: (RS) Work 26 (30, 33, 37, 41) sts in est patt, place next 29 (29, 33, 33, 33) sts onto holder or waste yarn for neck, join a second ball of yarn and work to end of row—26 (30, 33, 37, 41) sts rem for each shoulder.

Working both sides at the same time with separate balls of yarn, dec 1 st at each neck

CHART D

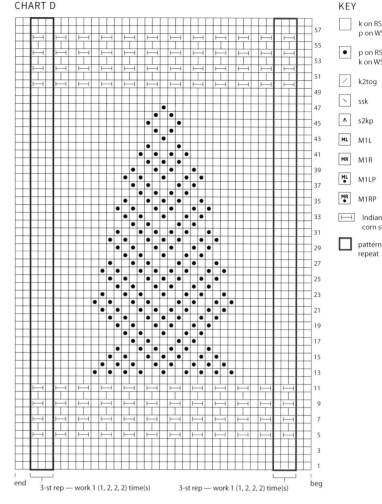

end   3-st rep — work 1 (1, 2, 2, 2) time(s)   3-st rep — work 1 (1, 2, 2, 2) time(s)   beg

KEY

☐	k on RS, p on WS
•	p on RS, k on WS
╱	k2tog
╲	ssk
ᐱ	s2kp
ML	M1L
MR	M1R
ML•	M1LP
MR•	M1RP
⊢⊣	Indian corn st
☐	pattern repeat

edge every RS row 5 times—21 (25, 28, 32, 36) sts rem for each shoulder.

Cont even until armholes measure 7½ (8, 8½, 9, 9½)" (19 [20.5, 21.5, 23, 24] cm). Place rem shoulder sts on holders.

BACK

Return 81 (89, 99, 107, 115) held back sts to longer cir needle. Work back and forth in est patt until Chart D is complete.

Working Charts A and C as est, work St st over center 41 (41, 45, 45, 45) sts until armholes measure 6¼ (6¾, 7¼, 7¾, 8¼)" (16 [17, 18.5, 19.5, 21] cm), ending with a WS row.

SHAPE NECK

Next row: (RS) Work 23 (27, 30, 34, 38) sts in est patt, place next 35 (35, 39, 39, 39) sts onto a holder for neck, join a second ball of yarn and work to end of row—23 (27, 30, 34, 38) sts rem for each shoulder.

Working both sides at the same time with separate balls of yarn, dec 1 st at each neck edge every RS row 2 times—21 (25, 28, 32, 36) sts rem for each shoulder. Cont even until armholes measure 7½ (8, 8½, 9, 9 ½)" (19 [20.5, 21.5, 23, 24] cm).

LOWER GUSSET CHART

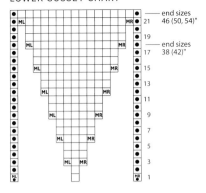

UPPER GUSSET CHART

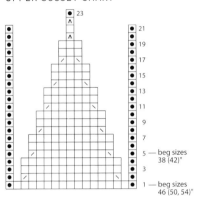

JOINING SHOULDERS

Return held right front shoulder sts onto one dpn and right back shoulder onto second dpn. Holding both dpn with RS tog (WS is facing), join shoulder using Three-Needle Bind-off (see page 79). Rep for left shoulder.

SLEEVES

Return 13 (13, 17, 17, 17) held gusset sts to shorter cir needle. With RS facing, work gusset sts in est patt, pm, then pick up and knit 61 (65, 69, 73, 77) sts evenly around armhole—74 (78, 86, 90, 94) sts. Pm for beg of rnd and join to work in rnds.

Set-up rnd: Work Row 7 (7, 1, 1, 1) of Upper Gusset Chart to m, k11 (13, 14, 16, 18), pm, work Row 1 of Sleeve Motif Chart over next 39 (39, 41, 41, 41) sts, pm, k11 (13, 14, 16, 18).

Cont as est through Row 23 of Upper Gusset Chart, work Sleeve Motif Chart as est—62 (66, 70, 74, 78) sts rem when gusset shaping is complete.

Work 1 rnd even.

Dec rnd: P1, ssk, work in est patt to last 2 sts, k2tog—2 sts dec'd.

Cont Sleeve Motif Chart until Rows 2–19 (19, 17, 17, 17) have been worked 5 (5, 6, 6, 6) times,

and ***at the same time,*** rep dec rnd every 7 rnds 6 (4, 0, 0, 0) times, every 6 rnds 8 (11, 13, 11, 9) times, then every 5 rnds 0 (0, 3, 6, 9) times—32 (34, 36, 38, 40) sts rem. ***At the same time,*** when Sleeve Motif Chart reps have been completed, cont to work first st of every rnd in alternating knit and purl, and cont in St st over rem sts. Work even until sleeve measures 18 (18½, 19, 19½, 20)" (45.5 [47, 48.5, 49.5, 51] cm) from pick-up, or 1" (2.5 cm) less than desired length.

CUFF

Work in garter st for 1" (2.5 cm), ending with a knit rnd. BO all sts loosely pwise.

SCHEMATIC

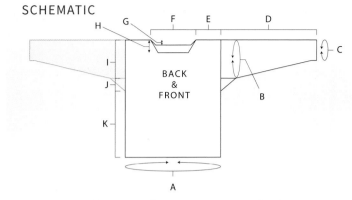

A   38 (42, 46, 50, 54)"(96.5 [106.5, 117, 127, 137] cm)

B   15½ (16½, 17½, 18½, 19½)" (39.5 [42, 44.5, 47, 49.5] cm)

C   8 (8½, 9, 9½, 10)" (20.5 [21.5, 23, 24, 25.5] cm)

D   19 (19½, 20, 20½, 21)" (48.5 [49.5, 51, 52, 53.5] cm)

E   5¼ (6¼, 7, 8, 9)" (13.5 [16, 18, 20.5, 23] cm)

F   9¾ (9¾, 10¾, 10¾, 10¾)" (25 [25, 27.5, 27.5, 27.5] cm)

G   1¼" (3.2 cm)

H   2½ (3, 3¼, 3¼, 3¼)" (6.5 [7.5, 8.5, 8.5, 8.5] cm)

I   7½ (8, 8½, 9, 9½)" (19 [20.5, 21.5, 23, 24] cm)

J   2¾ (2¾, 3½, 3½, 3½)" (7 [7, 9, 9, 9] cm)

K   13 (14, 13, 13½, 13)" (33 [35.5, 33, 34.5, 33] cm)

SLEEVE MOTIF CHART, SIZE 38 (42)"

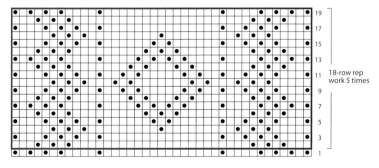

18-row rep
work 5 times

SLEEVE MOTIF CHART, SIZES 46 (50, 54)"

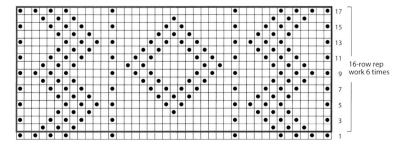

16-row rep
work 6 times

NECKBAND

With shorter cir needle and RS facing, knit 35 (35, 39, 39, 39) held back sts, pick up and knit 12 (14, 14, 14, 14) sts evenly along left neck edge, knit 29 (29, 33, 33, 33) held front sts, then pick up and knit 12 (14, 14, 14, 14) sts evenly along right neck edge—88 (92, 100, 100, 100) sts. Pm for beg of rnd, and join to work in rnds.

Next rnd: *K2, p2; rep from * around.

Rep last rnd until ribbing measures 1" (2.5 cm).

BO all sts loosely in patt.

ROLLED COLLAR

With shorter cir needle and RS facing, fold neckband to outside and pick up and knit 86 (90, 98, 98, 98) sts along base of ribbing. Pm for beg of rnd, and join to work in rnds.

Rnds 1–6: Knit.

Rnd 7: (dec) *K12 (7, 7, 7, 7), k2tog; rep from * 5 (9, 9, 9, 9) more times, k2 (0, 8, 8, 8)—80 (80, 88, 88, 88) sts rem.

Rnds 8–12: Knit.

Rnd 13: (dec) *K8 (8, 10, 10, 10), k2tog; rep from * 7 (7, 6, 6, 6) more times, k0 (0, 4, 4, 4)—72 (72, 81, 81, 81) sts rem.

Rnds 14–18: Knit.

Rnd 19: *K7, k2tog; rep from * around—64 (64, 72, 72, 72) sts rem.

Cont even in St st until rolled collar measures 5½" (14 cm) from pick-up.

BO all sts loosely.

FINISHING

Weave in ends. Block to measurements.

KEY

☐ k on RS, p on WS

▪ p on RS, k on WS

☐ pattern repeat

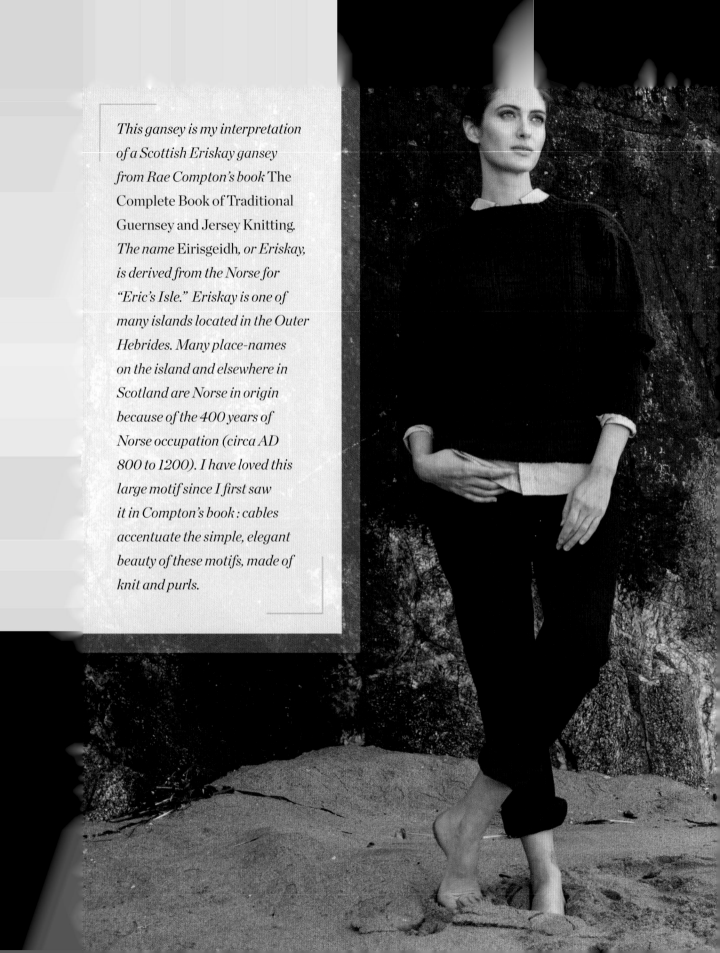

This gansey is my interpretation of a Scottish Eriskay gansey from Rae Compton's book The Complete Book of Traditional Guernsey and Jersey Knitting. *The name* Eirisgeidh, *or Eriskay, is derived from the Norse for "Eric's Isle." Eriskay is one of many islands located in the Outer Hebrides. Many place-names on the island and elsewhere in Scotland are Norse in origin because of the 400 years of Norse occupation (circa AD 800 to 1200). I have loved this large motif since I first saw it in Compton's book : cables accentuate the simple, elegant beauty of these motifs, made of knit and purls.*

eriskay

FINISHED SIZES

Chest circumference:
35¼ (39, 44, 47¾, 52¼)"
(89.5 [99, 112, 121.5, 135.5] cm).

Length:
22½ (23½, 24½, 25½, 26½)"
(57 [59.5, 62, 65, 67.5] cm).

Sample shown measures 39" (99 cm).

YARN

#2 Sportweight.
1538 (1778, 2093, 2366, 2719) yd
(1406 [1626, 1914, 2163, 2486] m).

Shown here: Frangipani 5-ply Guernsey
(100% wool; 240 yds [220 m]/3½ oz [100 g]):
Claret, 7 (8, 9, 10, 12) skeins.

NEEDLES

US 2 (2.75 mm): 16" and 32" (80 cm and 40 cm)
circular (cir) and set of 4 or 5 double-pointed (dpn).

*Adjust needle size if necessary to achieve
the correct gauge.*

NOTIONS

Stitch markers (m); cable needle (cn);
stitch holders or waste yarn; tapestry needle.

GAUGE

27 sts and 40 rnds = 4" (10 cm) in St st.

FEATURED TECHNIQUES

Channel Island Cast-On, Garter-stitch Seam
Stitches, Underarm Gusset, Perpendicular Shoulder
Join, Shoulder-strap Neck Gussets, Optional Short-
row Shaping.

NOTES

This gansey, suitable for men and women, is
knitted in the traditional manner but also includes
some sophisticated construction methods.
Optional short-rows can be worked in the lower
back to diminish any tendencies for the garment
to "ride up." The shoulder straps that join the
shoulders together begin with strap gussets.
These clever devices widen the neck and soften
the angles of an otherwise rectangular neckhole.
Length can be adjusted by knitting more or fewer
rows in the plain area.

STITCH GUIDE

1/1 RC (1 over 1 right cross)

Sl 1 st onto cn and hold to back, k1, k1 from cn.

2/2 RC (2 over 2 right cross)

Sl 2 sts onto cn and hold to back, k2, k2 from cn.

3/3 RC (3 over 3 right cross)

Sl 3 sts onto cn and hold to back, k3, k3 from cn.

4/4 RC (4 over 4 right cross)

Sl 4 sts onto cn and hold to back, k4, k4 from cn.

LOWER BODY

GARTER WELTS (MAKE TWO)

Note: These welts (one for the front and one for the back) are worked flat and then joined to work in the round.

With shorter cir needle, CO 114 (128, 142, 156, 170) sts using Channel Island Cast-on (see page 19). Do not join.

Next row: Knit and inc 1 st at center of row—115 (129, 143, 157, 171) sts.

Knit 16 rows even. Set aside. Rep for second welt, using longer cir needle.

JOINING THE WELTS CIRCULARLY

Note: The RS of each welt has nine purl ridges.

Joining rnd: With longer cir needle and RS of both welts facing, knit to last st of first welt, place marker (pm), k1, k1 from second welt, pm, knit to last st of second welt, pm for beg of rnd, purl last st of second welt and first st of first welt, pm—230 (258, 286, 314, 342) sts.

THE PLAIN AREA

Note: The plain area is where lengthening or shortening of the entire garment is most easily accomplished. It also creates a smooth surface as a background for the intended wearer's initials.

Inc rnd: Knit to next m and inc 6 sts evenly spaced, sm, work Row 1 of Seam Stitch Chart, sm, knit to m and inc 6 sts evenly spaced—242 (270, 298, 326, 354) sts.

Next 2 rnds: *Work next row of Seam Stitch Chart, sm, knit to m, sm; rep from * once more.

KNITTING INITIALS

If desired, chart your initials using the Blank Initial Chart on page 31. Add the initials 9 sts from beg of rnd.

Next 11 rnds: Work seam sts, k7, work Initial Chart, then work in est patt to end of rnd.

Working seam sts as est, cont in St st (knit every rnd) over rem sts until piece measures 3 (4, 5, 6, 7)" (7.5 [10, 12.5, 15, 18] cm) from beg ending with Row 2 of the Seam Stitch Chart.

OPTIONAL SHORT-ROWS FOR BACK

Note: See page 34 for information about wrap and turn (w&t) and for working wraps.

Because ganseys were rectangular in shape, there was no shaping for the back neck, which can cause the bottom edge to "hike up." If you like, you can add a few sets of short-rows in the plain area to offset this, although it is optional.

Short-row 1: (RS) Work to 3 sts before seam sts at end of rnd, w&t.

Short-row 2: (WS) Purl to 3 sts before mid-round seam sts, w&t.

Next row: Work to end of rnd, working wrap tog with the st it wraps. Two extra rows have been added in the back.

You can work the other wrap together with its st when you reach it on the next rnd. This short-row shaping can be worked one or two more times if you desire.

SEAM STITCH CHART

KEY

☐	k on RS, p on WS
⊡	p on RS, k on WS
☐	pattern repeat

DEFINITION RIDGE

Work 10 rnds in garter st as follows.

Rnds 1, 3, 5, 7, and 9: *Work Seam Stitch Chart, sm, purl to m, sm; rep from * once more.

Rnds 2, 4, 6, 8, and 10: *Work Seam Stitch Chart, sm, knit to m, sm; rep from * once more.

PATTERNING

Notes: As you work the cable charts for your size, work the increases shown on Row 1 of the charts. You can substitute any of the baby cables listed in Chapter 6 for Cable 2.

Set-up (inc) rnd: *Work Seam Stitch Chart, work Chart A for your size and inc 1 (1, 0, 0, 0) st(s), Cable 2 (Cable 2, Cable 4, Cable 6, Cable 8), Chart B over 21 sts, Cable 2 (Cable 2, Cable 4, Cable 6, Cable 8), Chart C over 11 sts, Cable 2 (Cable 2, Cable 4, Cable 6, Cable 8), Chart D over 21 sts, Cable 2 (Cable 2, Cable 4, Cable 6, Cable 8), Chart E over 11 sts, Cable 2 (Cable 2, Cable 4, Cable 6, Cable 8), Chart B over 21 sts, Cable 2 (Cable 2, Cable 4, Cable 6, Cable 8), Chart A for your size and inc 1 (1, 0, 0, 0) st(s), sm; rep from * once more—258 (286, 322, 350, 390) sts.

CHART A, SIZE 35¼"

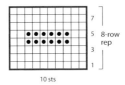

3 sts

CHART A, SIZE 39"

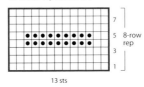

10 sts

CHART A, SIZE 44"

13 sts

CHART A, SIZE 47¾"

14 sts

CHART A, SIZE 53¼"

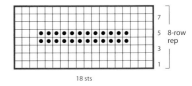

18 sts

KEY

☐ k on RS, p on WS	ML M1L
● p on RS, k on WS	MR M1R
☐ pattern repeat	M M1

⟋⟍ 1/1 RC
⟋⟍ 2/2 RC
⟋⟍ 3/3 RC
⟋⟍ 4/4 RC

see Stitch Guide

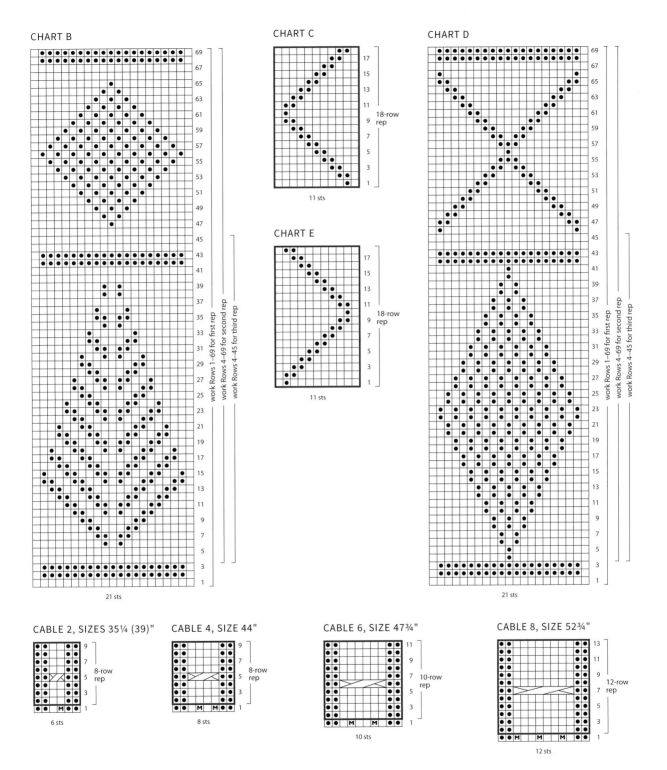

CHART B

CHART C

CHART D

CHART E

work Rows 1–69 for first rep
work Rows 4–69 for second rep
work Rows 4–45 for third rep

21 sts

11 sts

18-row rep

18-row rep

21 sts

CABLE 2, SIZES 35¼ (39)"

6 sts

8-row rep

CABLE 4, SIZE 44"

8 sts

8-row rep

CABLE 6, SIZE 47¾"

10 sts

10-row rep

CABLE 8, SIZE 52¾"

12 sts

12-row rep

LOWER GUSSET CHART

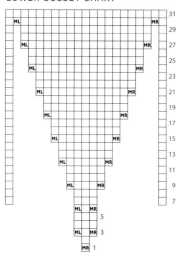

STRAP GUSSET CHART

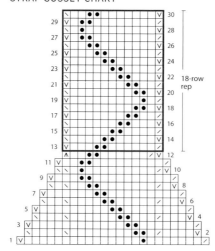

18-row
rep

UPPER GUSSET CHART

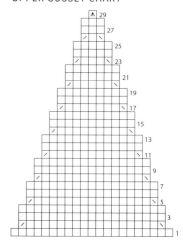

Cont in est patt until piece measures about 10 (10½, 10½, 10½, 11)" (25.5 [26.5, 26.5, 26.5, 28] cm) from beg.

UNDERARM GUSSET

Rnd 1: *Work seam st, M1R (Row 1 of Lower Gusset Chart), work seam st, sm, work in est patt to m, sm; rep from * once more— 2 gusset sts inc'd.

Rnd 2: *Work seam st, work Row 2 of Lower Gusset Chart, work seam st, sm, work in est patt to m, sm; rep from * once more.

Cont in est patt through Row 31 of Lower Gusset Chart—300 (328, 364, 392, 432) sts, with 127 (141, 159, 173, 193) sts each for front and back, and 23 sts for each gusset and seam sts.

DIVIDE FOR FRONT AND BACK

Place 23 sts for each gusset and seam sts on holders or waste yarn, and 127 (141, 159, 173, 193) sts for back on waste yarn—127 (141, 159, 173, 193) sts rem for front.

THE UPPER BODY

Note: The front is worked back and forth to completion before working the back. If you find

that a cable row is to be worked on the WS, you can break the yarn and attach it to the other end of the work so that the cables can be crossed on the RS.

Cont even until 177 rnds/rows have been worked in patt and dec 1 (1, 2, 2, 3) st(s) at top of each cable on last row—121 (135, 147, 161, 175) sts rem. Place sts on waste yarn.

Work back same as front.

SHOULDER STRAPS

With dpn, CO 25 sts using the long-tail method (see page 21).

WORKING SHOULDER STRAP FROM NECK TO SHOULDER

For clarifying which is left and right, pretend you are wearing the gansey. The initials are in the front, so this can help you determine which side to work on first.

RIGHT SHOULDER

Return 37 (44, 48, 51, 55) held sts from right front shoulder to one dpn and 37 (44, 48, 51, 55) sts from right back shoulder to second dpn or opposite ends of longer cir needle with neck edges at needle tips.

With RS facing, hold front shoulder needle in your LH and dpn with strap sts in your RH. K1 from front neck edge, then pass last CO st over, turn.

Row 1: (WS) Sl 1 pwise wyf, p15, k1, p7, purl last strap st tog with 1 st from back neck edge, turn.

Row 2: (RS) Sl 1 pwise wyb, k4, k2tog, k1, p2, k8, ssk, k4, ssk (last strap st tog with next front shoulder st), turn—23 strap sts rem.

Row 3: Sl 1 pwise wyf, p12, k2, p7, p2tog, turn.

Row 4: Sl 1 pwise wyb, k3, k2tog, k3, p2, k6, ssk, k3, ssk, turn—21 strap sts rem.

Row 5: Sl 1 pwise wyf, p9, k2, p8, p2tog, turn.

Row 6: Sl 1 pwise wyb, k2, k2tog, k5, p2, k4, ssk, k2, ssk, turn—19 strap sts rem.

Row 7: Sl 1 pwise wyf, p6, k2, p9, p2tog, turn.

Row 8: Sl 1 pwise wyb, k1, k2tog, k7, p2, k2, ssk, k1, ssk, turn—17 strap sts rem.

Row 9: Sl 1 pwise wyf, p3, k2, p10, p2tog, turn.

Row 10: Sl 1 pwise wyb, k2tog, k9, p1, k1, [ssk] twice, turn—15 strap sts rem.

Row 11: Sl 1 pwise wyf, p2, k2, p9, p2tog, turn.

Row 12: Sl 1 pwise wyb, k2tog, k6, p2, k2, s2kp, turn—13 strap sts rem.

DIAMOND AND X CHART

18-row rep

11 sts

BAR MOTIF CHART

8-row rep

10 sts

KEY

☐	k on RS, p on WS
•	p on RS, k on WS
╱	k2tog on RS, p2tog on WS
╲	ssk
⋀	s2kp
ML	M1L
MR	M1R
V	sl 1 wyb on RS, sl 1 wyf on WS
☐	pattern repeat

Row 13: Sl 1 pwise wyf, p3, k2, p6, p2tog, turn.

Row 14: Sl 1 pwise wyb, k5, p2, k4, ssk, turn.

Row 15: Sl 1 pwise wyf, p5, k2, p4, p2tog, turn.

Cont as est, work Rows 16–30 of Strap Chart, then rep Rows 13–30 until all shoulder sts are used up—13 strap sts rem. Place strap sts on holder.

LEFT SHOULDER

With dpn, CO 25 sts. Return 37 (44, 48, 51, 55) sts from left front shoulder on one dpn and 37 (44, 48, 51, 55) sts from left back shoulder on second dpn or opposite ends of longer cir needle with neck edges at needle tips. Leave rem 47 (47, 51, 59, 65) sts of both front and back on holders or waste yarn for neck. With RS facing, hold back shoulder needle in your LH, and dpn with strap sts in your RH. K1 from back neck edge, then pass last CO st over, turn.

Row 1: (WS) Sl 1 pwise wyf, p15, k1, p7, purl last strap st tog with 1 st from front neck edge, turn.

Row 2: (RS) Sl 1 pwise wyb, k4, k2tog, k1, p2, k8, ssk, k4, ssk (last strap st tog with next back shoulder st), turn—23 strap sts rem.

Cont same as right shoulder—13 strap sts rem. Place strap sts on holder.

SLEEVES

Return 23 held gusset and seam sts to shorter cir needle. With RS facing, join yarn and work seam st, work Row 1 of Upper Gusset Chart, work seam st. Pm, pick up and knit 50 (54, 57, 65, 65) sts evenly along armhole, work 13 held strap sts in patt, then pick up and knit 50 (54, 57, 65, 65) sts along armhole—136 (144, 150, 166, 166) sts. Pm for beg of rnd, and join to work in rnds.

Next rnd: Work seam and gusset sts in est patt, sm, p50 (54, 57, 65, 65), work zigzag patt as est, p50 (54, 57, 65, 65).

SETTING UP THE PATTERN

Set-up rnd: Work seam st, work Row 3 of Upper Gusset Chart, work seam st, sl m, , k14 (18, 18, 20, 17), then work Row 1 of following charts: work Cable 2 (Cable 2, Cable 4, Cable 6, Cable 8), Diamond and X Chart over 11 sts, Cable 2 (Cable 2, Cable 4, Cable 6, Cable 8), Bar Motif Chart over 10 sts, Cable 2 (Cable 2, Cable 4, Cable 6, Cable 8), work zigzag patt as est, Cable 2 (Cable 2, Cable 4, Cable 6, Cable 8), Bar Motif Chart over 10 sts, Cable 2 (Cable 2, Cable 4, Cable 6, Cable 8), Diamond and X Chart over 11 sts, Cable 2 (Cable 2, Cable 4, Cable 6, Cable 8), then k14 (18, 18, 20, 17)—140 (148, 160, 176, 182) sts, with 119 (127, 139, 155, 161) sts for sleeve, and 21 sts for gusset and seam sts.

Cont in est patt through Row 29 of Upper Gusset Chart—122 (130, 142, 158, 164) sts rem, with 119 (127, 139, 155, 161) sts for sleeve, and 3 sts for gusset and seam sts.

Next (dec) rnd: K2tog (or p2tog to maintain patt), work in patt to end of rnd—121 (129, 141, 157, 163) sts rem. Work 1 rnd even.

SHAPING THE SLEEVE

Dec rnd: Work seam sts, ssk, work to last 2 sts, k2tog—2 sts dec'd.

Rep dec rnd every 5 rnds 15 (12, 15, 5, 30) times, then every 4 rnds 12 (17, 16, 30, 2) times. **At the same time,** when Rows 1–18 of Diamond and X Chart have been worked 4 times, work Rows 1–9 once more and dec 1 (1, 2, 2, 3) st(s) over each cable on last rnd. Piece should measure about 8¼" (21 cm) from armhole.

SCHEMATIC

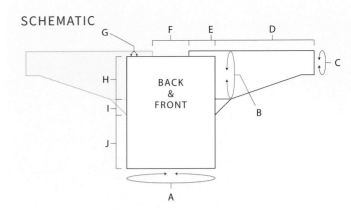

A 35¼ (39, 44, 47¾, 53¼)" (89.5 [99, 112, 121.5, 135.5] cm)

B 16 (17¼, 18¾, 20¾, 21¾)" (40.5 [44, 47.5, 52.5, 55] cm)

C 8¾ (9¼, 9¾, 10¾, 11¾)" (22 [23.5, 25, 27.5, 30] cm)

D 19 (19, 20, 21, 22)" (48.5 [48.5, 51, 53.5, 56] cm)

E 5½ (6½, 7, 7½, 8¼)" (14 [16.5, 18, 19, 21] cm)

F 7 (7, 7½, 8¾, 9¾)" (18 [18, 19, 22, 25] cm)

G 2" (5 cm)

H 8 (8½, 9½, 10½, 11)" (20.5 [21.5, 24, 26.5, 28] cm)

I 3" (7.5 cm)

J 10 (10½, 10½, 10½, 11)" (25.5 [26.5, 26.5, 26.5, 28] cm)

DEFINITION RIDGE

Rnds 1, 3, 5, 7, and 9: Purl, keeping seam sts in est patt and cont sleeve shaping.

Rnds 2, 4, 6, and 8: Knit, keeping seam sts in est patt and cont sleeve shaping.

PLAIN AREA

Keeping seam sts in est patt, work in St st over rem sts—59 (63, 65, 73, 79) sts rem when shaping is complete. Cont even until piece measures 16¼ (16¼, 17¼, 18¼, 19¼)" (41.5 [41.5, 44, 46.5, 49] cm) from pick-up rnd.

CUFF

Dec rnd: [K2, p2] around and dec 7 (7, 5, 5, 7) sts evenly spaced—52 (56, 60, 68, 72) sts rem.

Cont in ribbing as est until cuff measures 2¾" (7 cm), or desired length. BO all sts loosely in patt.

NECKBAND

With shorter cir needle and RS facing, knit 47 (47, 51, 59, 65) held sts from back holder, pick up and knit 25 sts along left shoulder strap, knit 47 (47, 51, 59, 65) held sts from front holder, then pick up and knit 25 sts along right shoulder strap—144 (144, 152, 168, 180) sts. Pm for beg of rnd, and join to work in rnds.

Dec rnd: Purl and dec 24 (24, 24, 28, 28) sts evenly spaced—120 (120, 128, 140, 152) sts rem.

Work 9 rnds in 2 × 2 ribbing. BO all sts loosely in patt.

FINISHING

Weave in ends. Block to measurements.

I was inspired by the crisp stitch definition of Quince & Co.'s Osprey yarn and decided to design a gansey dress with only knits and purls. I love gored skirts, and it made sense to design a flared skirt that narrowed slowly within the panels. Both patterns of the waistband and upper body have elements found in the town of Sheringham— according to Michael Pearson's Traditional Knitting—*I just fleshed them out a bit, as I am sure the gansey knitters might have done, changing motifs to suit their needs and taste.*

alouette

FINISHED SIZES

Chest circumference:
35½ (41, 43½, 48, 50¾)"
(90 [104, 110.5, 122, 129] cm).

Length:
31 (33, 33, 35¼, 35¼)"
(78.5 [84, 84, 89.5, 89.5] cm).

Sample shown measures 35½" (90 cm) chest circumference.

YARN

#4 Aran weight.
1413 (1737, 1843, 2172, 2298) yd
(1292 [1588, 1685, 1986, 2101] m).

Shown here: Quince & Co. Osprey
(100% American wool; 170 yds [155 m] /
3½ oz [100 g]): Delft, 15 (18, 19, 22, 23) skeins.

NEEDLES

US 7 (4.5mm): 16" and 32" (40 and
80 cm) circular (cir) and set of 4 or 5
double-pointed (dpn).

*Adjust needle size if necessary to achieve
the correct gauge.*

NOTIONS

Stitch markers (m); stitch holders
or waste yarn; tapestry needle.

GAUGE

18 sts and 26 rows = 4" (10 cm) in St st.

18 sts and 30 rows = 4" (10 cm) in Chart C patt.

FEATURED TECHNIQUES

Long-tail Cast-on, Split Garter Stitch Welts, Knitted
Cast-on, Underarm Gussets, Three-Needle Bind-off,
Inverted Triangular Neck Gusset.

NOTES

This dress is knitted like a gansey. It begins with a
split garter-stitch welt at the bottom hem, knitted
flat. Once the welts develop into side vents, the
work is joined in the round. The skirt is worked
circularly with gentle decreases to the hip, then
decreased a bit more to the waist. At the waist, the
body is slightly increased and the patterning begins,
including the underarm gussets. The body is split
into halves at the armhole, and the front and back
are knitted flat. The shoulders are joined, then neck
gussets are worked. The three-quarter sleeves are
picked up and knitted to the cuff while decreasing
the underarm gusset away. The neckband is then
picked up and knitted in garter stitch.

This dress is intended to be worn with 2–3"
(5–7.5 cm) positive ease.

LOWER SKIRT

With longer cir needle, CO 109 (121, 127, 139, 145) sts using the long-tail method (see page 21). Do not join.

Work 12 rows in garter st (knit every row).

Set-up row: (WS) K7, place marker (pm), p95 (107, 113, 125, 131), pm, k7.

Next row: (RS) K7, sm, k10 (12, 13, 15, 16), *work Row 2 of Seed Stitch Line Chart over next 3 sts, k15 (17, 18, 20, 21); rep from * 3 more times, work Row 2 of Seed Stitch Line Chart over next 3 sts, k10 (12, 13, 15, 16) sts, sm, k7.

Next row: (WS) K7, sm, p10 (12, 13, 15, 16), *work Row 1 of Seed Stitch Chart, p15 (17, 18, 20, 21); rep from * 3 more times, work Row 1 of Seed Stitch Line Chart, p10 (12, 13, 15, 16), sm, k7.

Rep last 2 rows 12 more times. Piece should measure about 4¾" (12 cm) from beg.

Break yarn and place sts on holder or move aside on needle. Make second welt to match.

JOINING WELTS

Joining rnd: With RS facing, work in est patt across one welt, turn to WS and CO 1 st using Knitted Cast-on (see page 20), turn to RS and work in est patt across second welt, turn to WS and CO 1 st, turn to RS and join to work in the rnd, k1, pm for beg of rnd—220 (244, 256, 280, 292) sts.

Next rnd: Working Row 1 of Vent Top Chart, work last 6 sts of chart, sm, work est patt to m, sm, work Vent Top Chart over next 15 sts to m, sm, work est patt to m, sm, then work first 9 sts of chart.

Cont in est patt, work Rows 2–12 of Vent Top Chart.

Next rnd: *K6, remove m, work in est patt to m, remove m, k6, pm, work Row 2 of Seed Stitch Line Chart over next 3 sts, pm; rep from * once more.

Work 2 rnds in est patt.

Dec rnd: *K1, ssk, work in est patt to 3 sts before m, k2tog, k1, sm, work next row of Seed Stitch Line Chart, sm; rep from * once more—216 (240, 252, 276, 288) sts rem.

Work even until piece measures about 8" (20.5 cm) from beg.

SEED STITCH LINE CHART   **SINGLE SEED CHART**   **VENT TOP CHART**

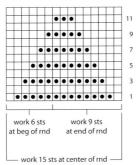

HORIZONTAL BAND CHART

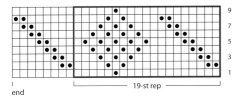

work 6 sts at beg of rnd   work 9 sts at end of rnd

work 15 sts at center of rnd

KEY

☐ k on RS, p on WS   ▪ p on RS, k on WS   ☐ pattern repeat

SHAPE SKIRT

Note: If you wish your dress to be longer, add rounds between decrease rounds.

Dec rnd 1: *K1, ssk, k9 (11, 12, 14, 15), k2tog, k1, work next 3 sts as est, k15 (17, 18, 20, 21), work next 3 sts as est; rep from * 5 more times—204 (228, 240, 264, 276) sts rem.

Next rnd: *K13 (15, 16, 18, 19), work next 3 sts as est, k15 (17, 18, 20, 21), work next 3 sts as est; rep from * 5 more times.

Cont even until piece measures 10" (25 cm) from cast-on edge.

Dec rnd 2: *K13 (15, 16, 18, 19), work next 3 sts as est, k1, ssk, k9 (11, 12, 14, 15), k2tog, k1, work next 3 sts as est; rep from * 5 more times—192 (216, 228, 252, 264) sts rem.

Next rnd: *K13 (15, 16, 18, 19), work next 3 sts as est; rep from * around.

Cont even until piece measures 12 (12½, 12½, 13½, 13½)" (30.5 [31.5, 31.5, 34.5, 34.5] cm) from beg.

Dec rnd 3: *K1, ssk, k7 (9, 10, 12, 13), k2tog, k1, work next 3 sts as est, k13 (15, 16, 18, 19), work next 3 sts as est; rep from * 5 more times—180 (204, 216, 240, 252) sts rem.

Next rnd: *K11 (13, 14, 16, 17), work next 3 sts as est, k13 (15, 16, 18, 19), work next 3 sts as est; rep from * 5 more times.

Cont even until piece measures 13½ (15, 15, 16, 16)" (34.5 [38, 38, 40.5, 40.5] cm) from beg.

Dec rnd 4: *K11 (13, 14, 16, 17), work next 3 sts as est, k1, ssk, k7 (9, 10, 12, 13), k2tog, k1, work next 3 sts as est; rep from * 5 more times—168 (192, 204, 228, 240) sts rem.

Next rnd: *K11 (13, 14, 16, 17), work next 3 sts as est; rep from * around.

Cont even until piece measures 15 (17, 17, 18, 18)" (38 [43, 43, 45.5, 45.5] cm) from beg.

Dec rnd 5: *K1, ssk, k5 (7, 8, 10, 11), k2tog, k1, work next 3 sts as est, k11 (13, 14, 16, 17), work next 3 sts as est; rep from * 5 more times—156 (180, 192, 216, 228) sts rem.

Next rnd: *K9 (11, 12, 14, 15), work next 3 sts as est, k11 (13, 14, 16, 17), work next 3 sts as est; rep from * 5 more times.

Cont even until piece measures 16 (18, 18, 20, 20)" (40.5 [45.5, 45.5, 51, 51] cm) from beg.

UPPER BODY

Set-up rnd: *P1, inc 0 (1, 1, 0, 0), purl to m, sm, work next 3 sts as est, sm; rep from * once more—156 (182, 194, 216, 228) sts.

Next rnd: *Knit to m, sm, work next 3 sts as est, sm; rep from * once more.

Next rnd: *Purl to m, sm, work next 3 sts as est, sm; rep from * once more.

Next rnd: *Knit to m, sm, work next 3 sts as est, sm; rep from * once more.

Next rnd: *K5 (2, 5, 1, 4), work 19-st rep of Row 1 of Horizontal Band Chart 3 (4, 4, 5, 5) times, work last 8 sts of chart, k5 (2, 5, 1, 4), sm, work next 3 sts as est, sm; rep from * once more.

Work Rows 2–9 of Horizontal Band Chart as est.

Next rnd: *Knit to m, sm, work next 3 sts as est, sm; rep from * once more.

Next rnd: *Purl to m, sm, work next 3 sts as est, sm; rep from * once more.

Next rnd: *Knit to m, sm, work next 3 sts as est, sm; rep from * once more.

Next (inc) rnd: *P1, inc 1 (1, 1, 0, 0), p73 (87, 93, 104, 110), inc 1 (0, 0, 0, 0), p1 (0, 0, 0, 0), sm, work next 3 sts as est, sm; rep from * once more—160 (184, 196, 216, 228) sts.

Size 35½" only

Set-up rnd: Working Row 1 of charts, *k2, work Single Seed Chart over next st, Chart A over 9 sts, work Single Seed Chart over next st, Chart C over 51 sts, Single Seed Chart over next st, Chart A over 9 sts, Single Seed Chart over next st, k2, work next 3 sts as est; rep from * once more.

Sizes 41 (43½)" only

Set-up rnd: Working Row 1 of charts, *k2 (5), work Single Seed Chart over next st, Chart B over 15 sts, Single Seed Chart over next st, Chart C over 51 sts, Single Seed Chart over next st, Chart B over 15 sts, Single Seed Chart over next st, k2 (5), work next 3 sts as est; rep from * once more.

Sizes 48 (50¾)" only

Set-up rnd: Working Row 1 of charts, *k0 (3), work Single Seed Chart over next st, Chart A over 9 sts, Single Seed Chart over next st, Chart B over 15 sts, work Single Seed Chart over next st, Chart C over 51 sts, Single Seed Chart over next st, Chart B over 15 sts, Single Seed Chart over next st, Chart A over 9 sts, Single Seed Chart over next st, k0 (3), work next 3 sts as est; rep from * once more.

CHART A

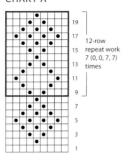

12-row repeat work 7 (0, 0, 7, 7) times

LOWER GUSSET CHART

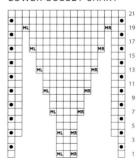

KEY

☐ k on RS, p on WS

▣ p on RS, k on WS

ML M1L

MR M1R

☐ pattern repeat

CHART B

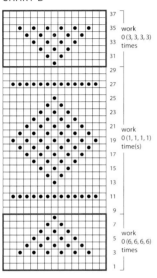

CHART C

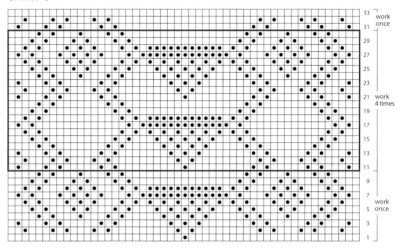

All Sizes

When piece measures 5½ (5, 4½, 4¼, 3¾)" (14 [12.5, 11.5, 11, 9.5] cm) from beg of Horizontal Band, end with Row 2 of Seed Stitch Line Chart and begin underarm gusset. *At the same time,* cont even in est patt as follows: work Chart A Rows 2–20 1 (0, 0, 1, 1) time(s), rep Rows 9–20 six (0, 0, 6, 6) more times, work 1 (0, 0, 3, 3) row(s) in St st over these sts; work Chart B Rows 2–8 zero (1, 1, 1, 1) time(s), rep Rows 1–8 zero (5, 5, 5, 5) more times, work Rows 9–29 zero (1, 1, 1, 1) time(s), work Rows 30–37 zero (3, 3, 3, 3) times, work 0 (0, 1, 2, 2) row(s) in St st over these sts; work Chart C Rows 2–10 once, work Rows 11–30 four times, work Rows 31–33 once, work 0 (0, 1, 2, 2) row(s) in St st over these sts.

UNDERARM GUSSETS

Next (inc) rnd: *Work in est patt to m, sm, k1, M1R, k1, M1L, k1, sm; rep from * once more—4 gusset sts inc'd.

Cont as est, working Rows 2–21 of Lower Gusset Chart—188 (212, 224, 244, 256) sts, with 77 (89, 95, 105, 111) sts each for front and back, and 17 sts for each gusset.

DIVIDE FRONT AND BACK

Note last row worked of each respective chart.

Next rnd: Work in est patt to m, remove m, place next 17 sts onto holder or waste yarn for gusset, next 77 (89, 95, 105, 111) sts onto holder or waste yarn for back, then last 17 sts onto holder or waste yarn for rem gusset—77 (89, 95, 105, 111) sts rem for front.

FRONT

Working back and forth, cont even until all charts have been completed. Place front sts onto holder.

BACK

Join yarn, beg with next chart rows as noted above, and work back same as for front. Place back sts onto holder.

SHOULDER JOIN

LEFT SHOULDER AND GUSSET

Place 26 (32, 35, 40, 43) front shoulder sts onto dpn, and 26 (32, 35, 40, 43) back shoulder sts to second dpn or opposite ends of longer, larger cir needle with needle tips at armhole. Holding pieces with RS tog in LH (WS of left back is facing) and dpn in RH, join yarn at armhole and work Three-Needle Bind-off (see page 79) until 6 sts rem on both LH needles, and 1 st rem on RH dpn. Turn garment to RS.

Holding dpn with single rem st in RH and needle with left front shoulder sts in LH and RS facing, work Neck Gusset Chart as follows:

Row 1: (RS) First st of chart is already on RH needle, k1 from front shoulder, turn.

Row 2: (WS) Sl 1 pwise wyf, p1, discard empty dpn, p1 from back shoulder, turn.

Row 3: Sl 1 kwise wyb, k2, k1 from front shoulder, turn.

Work Rows 4–13 of Neck Gusset Chart as est—13 neck gusset sts. Place sts on holder.

RIGHT SHOULDER AND GUSSET

With WS of front facing and in LH, join yarn at armhole and work Three Needle Bind-off as for left shoulder. Begin the neck gusset by holding the right back shoulder needle in LH.

SLEEVES

Return 17 held gusset sts to shorter cir needle. With RS facing, pick up and knit 67 (72, 76, 81, 85) sts evenly spaced around armhole—84 (89, 93, 98, 102) sts. Pm for beg of rnd, and join to work in rnds.

Rnd 1: Work Row 1 of Upper Gusset Chart, then purl to end.

Rnd 2: (dec) Work Row 2 of Upper Gusset Chart, k5 (8, 10, 12, 14) sts, pm, work Row 2 of Sleeve Chart over 57 sts, pm, k5 (7, 9, 12, 14)—2 gusset sts dec'd.

Cont as est, work Rows 3–21 of Upper Gusset Chart, and work Rows 3–33 of Sleeve Chart once, then work Rows 14–34 once. When the when Upper Gusset Chart is complete—70 (75, 79, 84, 88) sts rem.

Keeping first 3 sts of rnd in Seed St Line, cont as est and work 2 rnds even.

Dec rnd: Work 3 sts as est, k1, ssk, work in patt to last 3 sts, k2tog, k1—2 sts dec'd.

Rep dec rnd every 5 rnds 14 (16, 16, 16, 17) more times—40 (41, 45, 50, 52) sts. *At the same time,* when Sleeve Chart is complete, keep first 3 sts in est patt and work 4 rnds of garter st (knit 1 rnd, purl 1 rnd).

SCHEMATIC

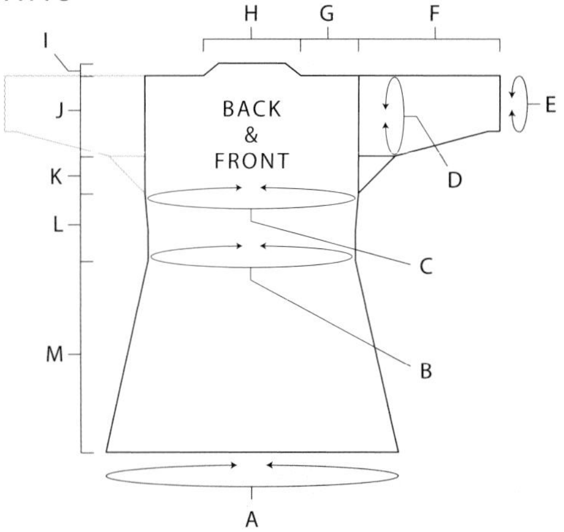

A	49 (54¼, 57, 62¼, 65)" (124.5 [138, 145, 158, 165] cm)
B	34¾ (40, 42½, 48, 50¾)" (88.5 [101.5, 108.5, 122, 129] cm)
C	35½ (41, 43¾, 48, 50¾)" (90 [104, 110.5, 122, 129] cm)
D	15½ (16¾, 17½, 18¾, 19½)" (39.5 [42.5, 44.5, 47.5, 49.5] cm)
E	9 (9, 10, 11, 11½)" (23 [23, 25.5, 28, 29] cm)
F	11½ (12½, 12½, 13, 14)" (29 [31.5, 31.5, 33, 35.5] cm)
G	4½ (5¾, 6½, 7½, 8¼)" (11.5 [14.5, 16.5, 19, 21] cm)
H	8¼" (21 cm)
I	1" (2.5 cm)
J	6½ (7, 7½, 8, 8½)" (16.5 [18, 19, 20.5, 21.5] cm)
K	3" (7.5 cm)
L	5½ (5, 4½, 4¼, 3¾)" (14 [12.5, 11.5, 11, 9.5] cm)
M	16 (18, 18, 20, 20)" (40.5 [45.5, 45.5, 51, 51] cm)

Working first 3 sts in est patt, work St st over rem sts until dec are complete. Cont even until sleeve measures 10½ (11½, 11½, 12, 13)" (26.5 [29, 29, 30.5, 33] cm), or 1" (2.5 cm) less than desired length. Work in garter st for 1" (2.5 cm) over all sts, ending with a purl rnd. BO all sts kwise.

NECKBAND

With RS facing, return 13 held sts for both neck gussets, 25 held front sts, and 25 held back sts to shorter cir—76 sts. With needle tips at back edge of right shoulder, pm for beg of rnd, and join to work in rnds.

Rnd 1: Purl.

Rnd 2: Knit.

Rep Rnds 1 and 2 until neckband measures 1" (2.5 cm), ending with a purl rnd. BO all sts loosely kwise.

FINISHING

Weave in ends. Block to measurements. If needed, turn dress inside out and carefully steam, being certain to avoid touching the iron to the fabric.

UPPER GUSSET CHART

INVERTED TRIANGULAR
NECK GUSSET CHART

SLEEVE CHART

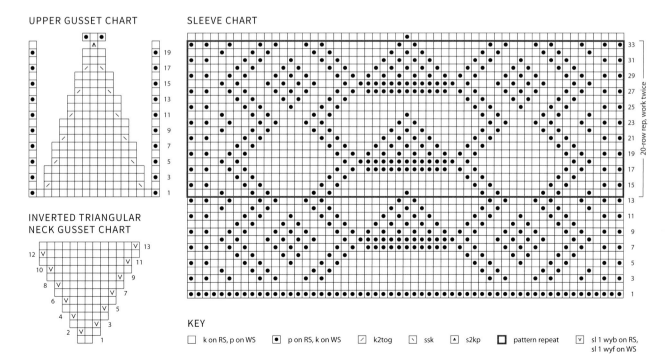

KEY

☐ k on RS, p on WS • ● p on RS, k on WS • ╱ k2tog • ╲ ssk • ▲ s2kp • ☐ pattern repeat • v sl 1 wyb on RS, sl 1 wyf on WS

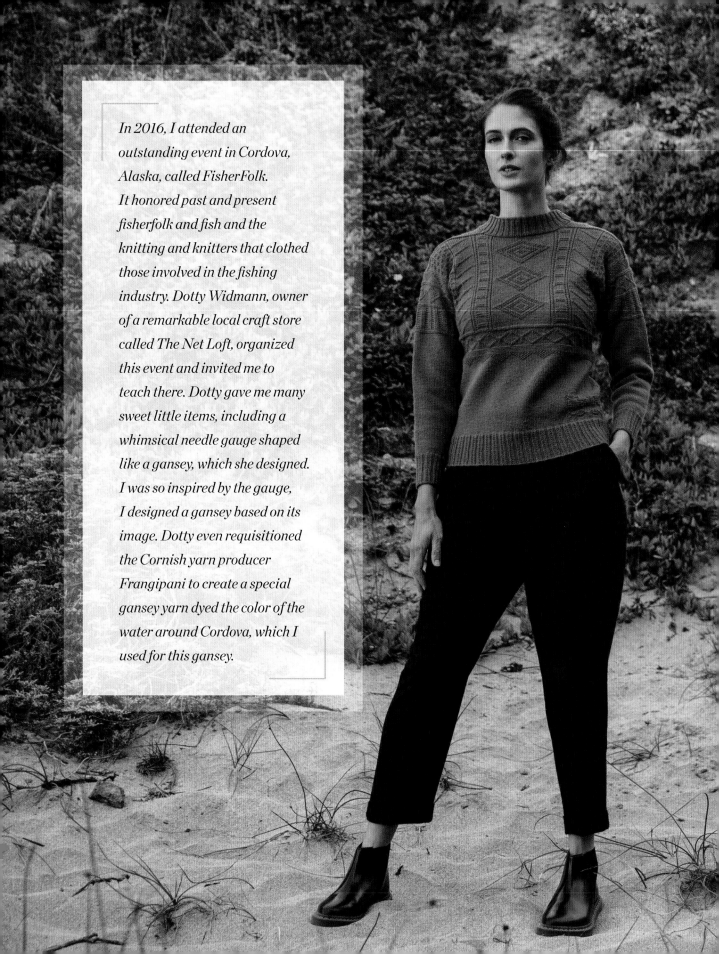

In 2016, I attended an outstanding event in Cordova, Alaska, called FisherFolk. It honored past and present fisherfolk and fish and the knitting and knitters that clothed those involved in the fishing industry. Dotty Widmann, owner of a remarkable local craft store called The Net Loft, organized this event and invited me to teach there. Dotty gave me many sweet little items, including a whimsical needle gauge shaped like a gansey, which she designed. I was so inspired by the gauge, I designed a gansey based on its image. Dotty even requisitioned the Cornish yarn producer Frangipani to create a special gansey yarn dyed the color of the water around Cordova, which I used for this gansey.

cordova

FINISHED SIZES

Chest circumference:
34¾ (38½, 42½, 46¼, 50¼, 54)"
(88.5 [98, 108, 117.5, 127.5, 137] cm).

Length:
22½ (22½, 23½, 23½, 24½, 24½)"
(57 [57, 59.5, 59.5, 62, 62] cm).

Sample shown measures 34¾" (88.5 cm).

YARN

#2 Sportweight.
1500 (1661, 1913, 2083, 2359, 2537) yd
(1372 [1519, 1749, 1905, 2157, 2320] m).

Shown here: Frangipani 5-ply Guernsey
(100% wool; 240 yds [220 m]/3½ oz [100 g]):
Cordova, 7 (7, 8, 9, 10, 11) skeins.

NEEDLES

US 1 (2.5 mm): 16" and 32" (40 and 80 cm)
circular (cir) and set of 4 or 5 double-pointed (dpn).

US 0 (2 mm): 32" (80 cm) cir for garter-stitch section
if desired.

*Adjust needle size if necessary to acheive
the correct gauge.*

NOTIONS

Stitch markers (m); waste yarn or stitch holders;
tapestry needle; three ⅜" (10 mm) buttons;
three ⅜" (10 mm) backing buttons or felt.

GAUGE

29 sts and 42 rnds = 4" (10 cm) in St st
using larger needle.

FEATURED TECHNIQUES

Internally Shaped Underarm Gusset,
Perpendicular Shoulder Join, Buttoned Neckband.

NOTES

This gansey begins with ribbing and has optional
initials. It is knitted in the round up to the armholes
and split so that the upper body can be knitted flat.
The gussets are internally shaped. The shoulders
are joined with shoulder straps patterned in the
Net Motif, and the sleeves are knitted from the
armhole to the cuff. The neckline is slightly shaped.
The neckband is picked up and knitted flat, with
buttonholes. Buttons are used for closures. Rows
are counted in certain parts of this gansey, rather
than taking measurements to assess progress.

The needle gauge that inspired this gansey.

STITCH GUIDE

SSK BIND-OFF

Ssk, *sl 1 kwise, insert LH needle tip through front of 2 sts on RH needle, k2tog tbl; rep from * to end of row.

RIBBING

With longer cir needle, CO 250 (280, 305, 335, 360, 390) sts using the long-tail method (see page 21). Place marker (pm) for beg of rnd and join to work in rnds, being careful not to twist sts.

Work ribbing as follows, or from Ribbing Chart:

Rnd 1: K2, [p2, k3] to last 3 sts, p2, k1.

Rnd 2: P1, k1, [p2, k1, p1, k1] to last 3 sts, p2, k1.

Cont as est until ribbing measures 2¾" (7 cm), ending with Rnd 1 and inc 2 (0, 3, 1, 4, 2) st(s) evenly spaced across last rnd—252 (280, 308, 336, 364, 392) sts.

LOWER BODY

THE PLAIN AREA

Next rnd: *P1, k125 (139, 153, 167, 181, 195); rep from * once more.

Rep last rnd for 1" (2.5 cm).

INITIALS

Cont as est; add initials if desired, with or without the Cordova fish motif, 7 sts from beg of rnd. Fill in and work from Blank Initial Chart (see page 31). (The sample shows the two fish facing each other underneath the initials.)

CORDOVA FISH CHART

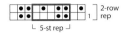

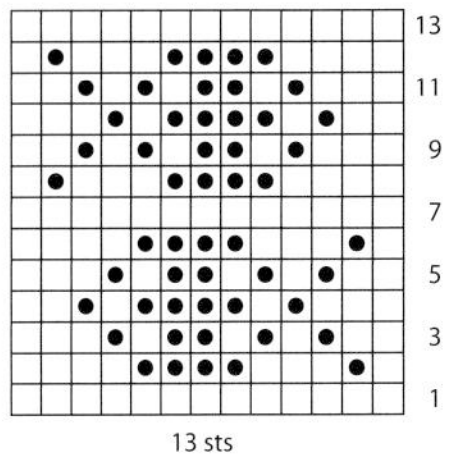

13 sts

KEY

☐	k on RS, p on WS
☐•	p on RS, k on WS
☐	pattern repeat

RIBBING CHART

2-row rep

⌐ 5-st rep ⌐

When the Initial Chart and/or Cordova Fish Chart are complete, cont in St st, maintaining purl st seams, until piece measures 9 (9, 10, 10, 11, 11)" (23 [23, 25.5, 25.5, 28, 28] cm) from beg.

PATTERNING

Definition Ridge of Body and Underarm Gussets

Note: If desired, use cir needle one size smaller than that of the body for the garter-stitch portion of the Definition Ridge.

Read through the next section carefully because the Lower Gusset is begun while the next section of the body patterning is being worked.

Rnds 1–36: *P1, beg at right edge of Definition Ridge Chart and work 14-st rep to 13 sts before seam st, then work last 13 sts at left edge of chart; rep from * once more.

Change back to longer larger cir needle (if smaller needles were used for the garter stitch) and work charts for your chosen size as follows:

Set-up rnd: *P1, k2 (3, 2, 2, 2, 3), work Blocks Motif over 16 (22, 28, 28, 28, 28) sts, Triangle Motif over 0 (0, 0, 7, 12, 18) sts, Left Diagonal Motif over 14 sts, Ladders Motif over 13 (13, 15, 15, 17, 17) sts, Diamond Chart over 35 sts, Ladders Motif over 13 (13, 15, 15, 17, 17) sts, Right Diagonal Motif over 14 sts, Triangle Motif over 0 (0, 0, 7, 12, 18) sts, Blocks Motif over 16 (22, 28, 28, 28, 28) sts, then k2 (3, 2, 2, 2, 3); rep from * once more.

 At the same time, beg Lower Gusset Chart when piece measures 12½ (12, 12½, 11¼, 11¾, 11¼)" (31.5 [30.5, 31.5, 28.5, 30, 28.5] cm) from beg as follows.

Rnd 1: M1RP, p1, M1LP, pm, work in est patt to

next seam st, pm, M1RP, p1, M1LP, pm, work to end of rnd in est patt—4 gusset sts inc'd.

Cont as est, work Rnds 2–33 (33, 33, 41, 41, 41) of Lower Gusset Chart—292 (320, 348, 384, 412, 440) sts, with 125 (139, 153, 167, 181, 195) sts each for front and back, and 21 (21, 21, 25, 25, 25) sts for each gusset.

UPPER BODY

BACK

Place 21 (21, 21, 25, 25, 25) gusset sts on holder or waste yarn, turn and work in est patt to next gusset m, place 21 (21, 21, 25, 25, 25) gusset sts on holder or waste yarn, and rem 125 (139, 153, 167, 181, 195) sts on waste yarn for front—125 (139, 153, 167, 181, 195) sts rem for back.

Working back and forth, cont even in est patt working Diamond Chart a total of 3 times and then cont in St st until back measures 21¾ (21¾, 22¾, 22¾, 23¾, 23¾)" (55 [55, 58, 58, 60.5, 60.5] cm) from beg. Place sts on waste yarn.

FRONT

Return 125 (139, 153, 167, 181, 195) held sts for front to longer cir needle. Working back and forth, cont even in est patt working Diamond Chart a total of 3 times (Rows 1–69, then Rows 36–69, then ending with Rows 70–77) until front measures ½" (1.3 cm) less than back, ending with a WS row.

SHAPING THE NECK

Note: Imagine you are wearing the gansey to identify the right shoulder and left shoulder.

RIGHT SHOULDER

Row 1: (RS) Work 43 (49, 55, 61, 66, 70) sts in est patt and place on holder for left shoulder, BO 39 (41, 43, 45, 49, 55) sts for neck, then work to end of row—43 (49, 55, 61, 66, 70) sts rem for each shoulder.

Row 2: (WS) Work even in est patt.

Row 3: BO 3 sts, work to end of row—40 (46, 52, 58, 63, 67) sts rem.

Row 4: Work even. Place rem sts on holder.

LEFT SHOULDER

Return 43 (49, 55, 61, 66, 70) sts for left

shoulder to shorter cir needle. Join yarn to neck edge for a WS row.

Row 2: (WS) BO 3 sts, work to end of row—40 (46, 52, 58, 63, 67) sts rem.

Row 3: (RS) Work even in est patt.

Row 4: Work even. Place rem sts on holder.

SHOULDER STRAPS

RIGHT SHOULDER

With dpn, CO 13 sts using the Invisible Cast-on (see page 74). Do not remove waste yarn.

Return 40 (46, 52, 58, 63, 67) front right shoulder sts to one dpn, and 40 (46, 52, 58, 63, 67) sts for back right shoulder to second dpn or opposite ends of longer cir needle with tips at neck edge. Drop the back shoulder needle for now.

With RS of front facing and holding that needle in LH, hold needle with shoulder strap sts in RH. K1 from front right neck edge, then pass last strap st over to bind it off, turn.

Row 1: (WS) Working Row 1 of Shoulder Strap Chart, sl 1 pwise wyf, k1, p9, k1, purl tog last st of strap with 1 st from back right neck edge, being careful not to twist your work, turn.

Row 2: (RS) Working Row 2 of Shoulder Strap Chart, sl 1 pwise wyb, p2, k3, p1, k3, p2, ssk last st of strap with 1 st from front. Turn.

Cont as est, work Rows 3–9 of Shoulder Strap Chart, then rep Rows 2–9 until all shoulder sts are used up—13 strap sts rem. Place sts on holder.

LEFT SHOULDER

With dpn, CO 13 sts using Invisible method. Do not remove waste yarn.

Return 40 (46, 52, 58, 63, 67) held front left shoulder sts to one dpn, and 40 (46, 52, 58, 63, 67) sts for back left shoulder to second dpn or to opposite ends of longer cir needle with tips at neck edge.

With RS of back facing, and holding that needle in LH, hold needle with shoulder strap sts in RH. K1 from back left neck edge, then pass last strap st over to bind it off, turn.

Cont as for right shoulder.

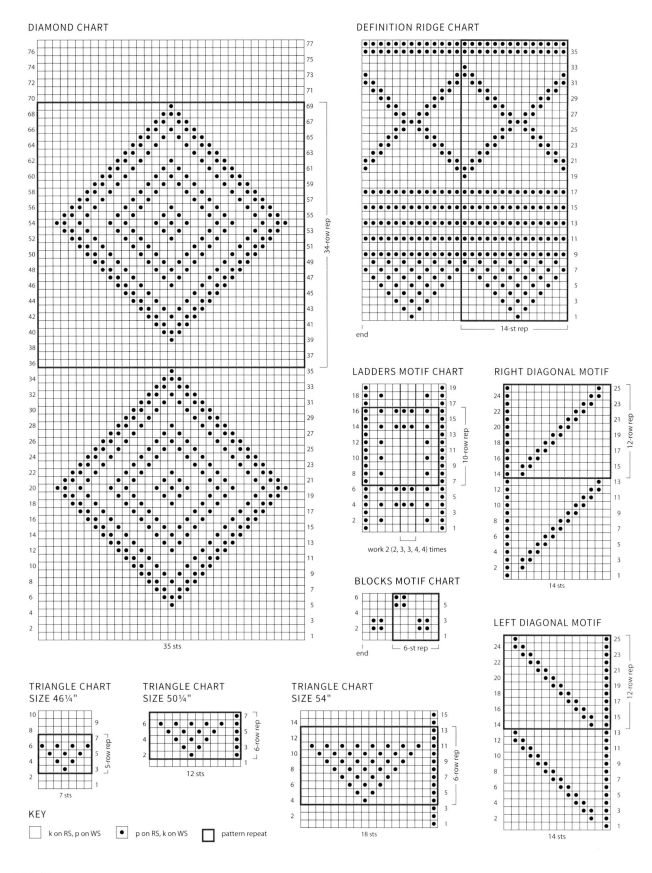

DIAMOND CHART

DEFINITION RIDGE CHART

end

14-st rep

35 sts

LADDERS MOTIF CHART

work 2 (2, 3, 3, 4, 4) times

RIGHT DIAGONAL MOTIF

14 sts

BLOCKS MOTIF CHART

end   6-st rep

LEFT DIAGONAL MOTIF

14 sts

TRIANGLE CHART
SIZE 46¼"

7 sts

TRIANGLE CHART
SIZE 50¼"

12 sts

TRIANGLE CHART
SIZE 54"

18 sts

KEY

☐ k on RS, p on WS   • p on RS, k on WS   ☐ pattern repeat

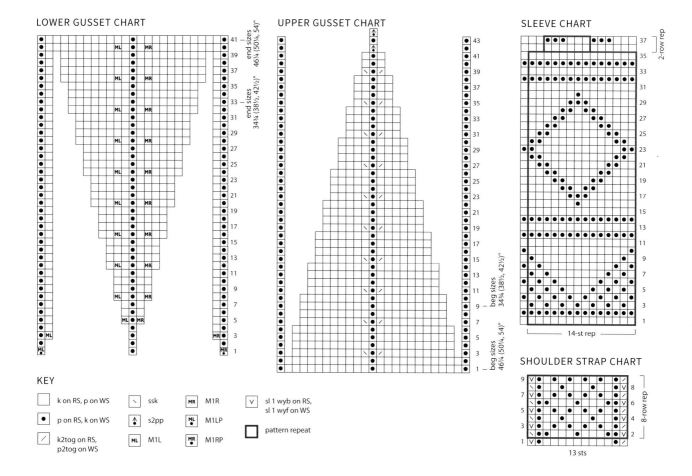

LOWER GUSSET CHART

UPPER GUSSET CHART

SLEEVE CHART

SHOULDER STRAP CHART

KEY

	k on RS, p on WS		ssk		M1R
	p on RS, k on WS		s2pp		M1L
	k2tog on RS, p2tog on WS		M1L		M1RP

sl 1 wyb on RS, sl 1 wyf on WS

pattern repeat

NECKBAND

Note: The neckband is worked back and forth.

Carefully remove waste yarn from the CO of both shoulder straps and place 13 sts for each on separate dpn, making sure all the sts are oriented the same way on the needle.

With shorter cir needle and RS facing, beg at left shoulder strap and sl 8 sts to right needle tip, knit next 5 left shoulder strap sts, pick up and knit 6 sts along sloped left front neck edge, 39 (41, 43, 45, 49, 55) along front BO sts, 6 sts along sloped right front neck, knit 13 right shoulder strap sts, pick up and knit 45 (47, 49, 51, 55, 61) along back BO sts, then knit 8 slipped sts of left shoulder strap—122 (126, 130, 134, 142, 154) sts. Do not join.

Note: The buttonholes should be centered over left shoulder strap, so that the buttons will be centered on the cast-on sts for the tab.

Row 1: (WS) Knit and inc 4 sts evenly spaced, then CO 7 sts—133 (137, 141, 145, 153, 165) sts.

Row 2: (RS) K7, pm, k2, *p2, k2; rep from * to last 4 sts, k4.

Row 3 and all other WS rows: K4, p2, *k2, p2; rep from * to m, k7.

Row 4: (RS) K7, sm, k2, *p2, k2; rep from * to last 4 sts, k4.

Rows 6, 12, and 18 (buttonhole rows): (RS) K3, yo, k2tog, k2, sm, work to end of row in est patt.

Rows 8, 10, 14, and 16: Rep Row 4.

Row 20: BO all sts using SSK Bind-off (See Stitch Guide).

SLEEVES

With shorter cir needle and RS facing, work 21 (21, 21, 25, 25, 25) held gusset and seam sts in est patt (Rnd 9, 9, 9, 1, 1, 1) of Upper Gusset

Chart), pm, pick up and knit 45 (49, 52, 58, 61, 65) sts along armhole to strap sts, work 13 strap sts in est patt, then pick up and knit 45 (49, 52, 58, 61, 65) sts along armhole—124 (132, 138, 154, 160, 168) sts. Pm for beg of rnd, and join to work in rnds.

Next rnd: Work Row 10 (10, 10, 2, 2, 2) of Upper Gusset Chart to m, sm, purl to end of rnd.

Next rnd: Work Row 11 (11, 11, 3, 3, 3) of Upper Gusset Chart to m, k2 (6, 2, 1, 4, 1), beg at right edge of Sleeve Chart and working Row 1, work 14-st rep 7 (7, 8, 9, 9, 10) times, work last st at left edge of chart, k2 (6, 2, 1, 4, 1)—2 gusset sts dec'd.

Cont in est patt, work Rows 12 (12, 12, 4, 4, 4)–45 of Upper Gusset Chart, and work Rows 2–35, then rep Rows 36 and 37 of Sleeve Chart for 2" (5 cm)—104 (112, 118, 130, 136, 144) sts rem. *At the same time,* begin shaping sleeve after Row 45 of Gusset Chart has been completed.

Dec rnd: P1, remove m, ssk, work in est patt to last 2 sts, k2tog—2 sts dec'd.

Work Sleeve Chart, maintaining p1 seam st, and rep dec rnd every 7 rnds 10 (0, 0, 0, 0, 0) times, every 6 rnds 10 (17, 22, 0, 4, 0) times, every 5 rnds 0 (7, 2, 27, 24, 20) times, then every 4 rnds 0 (0, 0, 1, 0, 12) time(s)—62 (62, 68, 72, 78, 78) sts rem.

At the same time, when the Sleeve Chart is complete, work 3 rnds in garter st (purl 1 rnd, knit 1 rnd , purl 1 rnd). Then cont even in St st until the sleeve measures 16 (16½, 17, 17½, 18, 18½)" (40.5 [42, 43, 44.5, 45.5, 47] cm) from pick-up, or 3" (7.5 cm) less than desired length.

CUFF

Dec rnd: P1, knit to end of rnd and dec 7 (7, 8, 7, 8, 8) sts evenly spaced—55 (55, 60, 65, 70, 70) sts rem.

Next rnd: K2, [p2, k3] to last 3 sts, p2, k1.

Cont in est patt of Ribbing Chart until ribbing measures 3" (7.5 cm). BO all sts using the SSK bind-off method.

FINISHING

Weave in ends. Sew buttons to neckband opposite buttonholes. Block to measurements.

SCHEMATIC

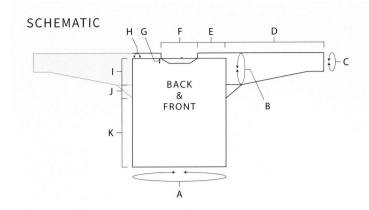

A   34¾ (38½, 42½, 46¼, 50¼, 54)" (88.5 [98, 108, 117.5, 127.5, 137] cm)

B   14¼ (15½, 16¼, 18, 18¾, 19¾)" (36 [39.5, 41.5, 45.5, 47.5, 50] cm)

C   7½ (7½, 8¼, 9, 9¾, 9¾)" (19 [19, 21, 23, 25, 25] cm)

D   19 (19½, 20, 20½, 21, 21½)" (48.5 [49.5, 51, 52, 53.5, 54.5] cm)

E   5½ (6¼, 7¼, 8, 8¾, 9¼)" (14 [16, 18.5, 20.5, 22, 23.5] cm)

F   6¼ (6½, 6¾, 7, 7½, 8½)" (16 [16.5, 17, 18, 19, 21.5] cm)

G   ½" (1.3 cm)

H   1¾" (4.5 cm)

I   6 (6½, 7, 7½, 8, 8½)" (15 [16.5, 18, 19, 20.5, 21.5] cm)

J   3¼ (3¼, 3¼, 4, 4, 4)" (8.5 [8.5, 8.5, 10, 10, 10] cm)

K   12½ (12, 12½, 11¼, 11¾, 11¼)" (31.5 [30.5, 31.5, 28.5, 30, 28.5] cm)

backing buttons

Sewing a button onto a piece of knitting is not always a stable affair. The button pulls on the fabric and eventually tears it with repeated use. Use of backing buttons will reinforce this point of stress and looks more professional. Backing buttons are inexpensive, clear plastic buttons that are unobtrusive on the wrong side of the work. It is helpful to purchase backing buttons the same size or slightly smaller than the regular button as well as matching the number of holes of the 2 buttons. For shank buttons, use backing buttons that have 2 holes.

sewing on buttons

Put 2 T-pins on the button site at right angles to each other, forming an "x". (This step is not necessary if the button has a shank.) As you sew the 2 buttons on (regular button and backing button), matching their holes, the T-pins will act as spacers so the buttons aren't sewn on too tightly.

1. Thread a sewing needle and knot the 2 ends as 1 so that you are working with doubled thread.

2. Put pins in the fabric where you want the button to be.

3. Make a stitch in the back of the work and run the needle between the 2 threads to anchor it to the fabric.

4. Using a clear button for the back and your chosen button for the front, sew the buttons onto the band.

5. To fasten off, bring needle to wrong side of the band, encircle clear button with thread several times, and take needle between the 2 threads and pull. Make another knot, then trim the thread.

In the first edition of Knitting Ganseys, *I designed a child's garment from this wonderful historic motif I saw in Mary Wright's book* Cornish Guernseys & Knit-frocks. *Each year I had the best of intentions to design an adult version, only to put the project on the back burner because of other pressing work. When I discovered the Guernsey yarn made by Sarah Lake of Upton Yarns (a US-made gansey yarn!), I was immediately taken by the beautiful silvery gray 5-ply she had created and knew exactly which gansey it was meant to become.*

snakes
& ladders

FINISHED SIZES

Chest circumference:
35¼ (39¼, 43¼, 47¼, 51¼)"
(89.5 [99.5, 110, 120, 130] cm).

Length:
24 (24, 25, 26, 27)"
61 (61, 63.5, 66, 68.5) cm.

Sample shown measures 35¼" (89 cm).

YARN

#2 Sportweight.
2731 (3043, 3496, 3974, 4469) yd
2497 (2782, 3195, 3634, 4086) m.

Shown here: Upton Yarns Coopworth 5-ply Gansey
(100% wool; 240 yds [219 m]/4¾ oz [140 g]):
Natural Gray, 12 (13, 15, 17, 19) hanks.

NEEDLES

US 1 (2.25 mm): 32" (80 cm) circular (cir) and set
of 4 or 5 double-pointed (dpn) for garter-stitch
definition ridge.

US 2 (2.75 mm): 16" and 32" (40 and 80 cm) cir
and set of dpn.

*Adjust needle size if necessary to achieve
the correct gauge.*

NOTIONS

Cable needle (cn); stitch markers (m);
stitch holder or waste yarn; tapestry needle.

GAUGE

28 sts and 36 rnds = 4" (10 cm) in St st
using larger needles.

36 sts and 42 rows/rnds = 4" (10 cm)
in Snakes and Ladders patt using larger needles.

FEATURED TECHNIQUES

Continuous Garter-stitch Welt, Three-Needle Bind-
off (WS tog), Underarm Gussets, Inverted Triangular
Neck Gussets.

NOTES

This heavily cabled gansey is made of snake cables,
separated by columns of knits and purls that
resemble ladders. I have narrowed the cable a bit
from Mary Wright's chart in her book and decreased
the number of rows between cables to make
them more prominent. This gansey begins with
a Long-tail Cast-on and continuous garter-stitch
welt. The seam sts are made of 5 sts on each side
and help to create a surrounded, and bisected,
underarm gusset. The neck is unshaped, but fits well
with the inverted triangular neck gussets worked on
the shoulder seam. The shoulders are joined with
the Three-Needle Bind-off, with WS held together,
to create a ridge on the RS. The sleeves carry the
design with three cables, and the neckband is
worked in garter stitch. To adjust length, add or
subtract rounds in the plain area of St st.

LOWER BODY

With larger longer cir needle, CO 218 (242, 270, 290, 314) sts using the long-tail method (see page 21). Place marker (pm) for beg of rnd and join to work in rnds, taking care not to twist sts.

GARTER-STITCH WELT

Rnd 1: Purl.

Rnd 2: Knit.

Rep Rnds 1 and 2 until piece measures 1" (2.5 cm), ending with Rnd 1.

PLAIN AREA

Set-up rnd 1: K2, pm, k105 (117, 131, 141, 153), pm, k4, pm, k105 (117, 131, 141, 153), pm for new beg of rnd, 2 sts rem unworked and are now beg of next rnd.

Set-up rnd 2: (inc) P1, M1, p1, k1, p1, sl m, knit to next m and inc 17 (19, 19, 23, 25) sts evenly spaced (about every 6 sts), sl m, p1, k1, p1, M1, p1, sl m, knit to next m and inc 17 (19, 19, 23, 25) sts evenly spaced—254 (282, 310, 338, 366) sts.

LOWER GUSSET CHART

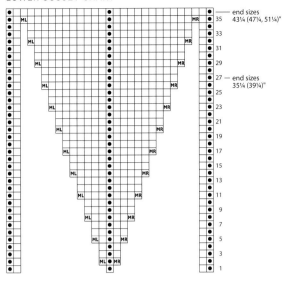

— end sizes 43¼ (47¼, 51¼)"

— end sizes 35¼ (39¼)"

SNAKES BODY CHART

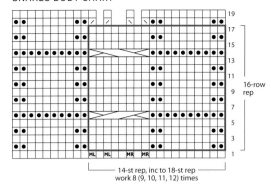

16-row rep

14-st rep, inc to 18-st rep
work 8 (9, 10, 11, 12) times

KEY

	k on RS, p on WS		⟍	ssk				4/4 LC	
•	p on RS, k on WS		ML	M1L				4/4 RC	see Stitch Guide
⟋	k2tog		MR	M1R				pattern repeat	

Rnd 3: *[P1, k1] twice, p1, sl m, k122 (136, 150, 164, 178), sl m; rep from * once more.

Rep Rnd 3 for 1" (2.5 cm). Cont as est, adding initials 7 sts from beg of rnd if desired.

Cont even with St st (knit every rnd) between seam sts until piece measures 5" (12.5 cm) from beg.

DEFINITION RIDGE

Change to smaller longer cir needles.

Rnd 1: Purl.

Rnd 2: Knit.

Rep Rnds 1 and 2 until definition ridge measures 1" (2.5 cm), ending with a purl rnd.

BEGIN PATTERNING

Change to larger longer cir needles.

Rnd 1: *[P1, k1] twice, p1, sl m, [k10, (M1R, k1) twice, (k1, M1L) twice] 8 (9, 10, 11, 12) times, k10, sl m; rep from * once more—318 (354, 390, 426, 462) sts.

Keeping seam sts in est ribbing, work Snakes Body Chart Rows 2–17 over rem sts, then rep

Rows 2–17 until piece measures 14 (13½, 13, 13½, 14)" (35.5 [34.5, 33, 34.5, 35.5] cm) from beg.

BEGIN UNDERARM GUSSET

Rnd 1: *[P1, k1] twice, p1, sl m, work as est to next m, sl m; rep from *.

Rnd 2: (inc) *P1, k1, M1R, p1, M1L, k1, p1, sl m, work as est to next m, sl m; rep from * once more—4 gusset sts inc'd.

Cont in est patt, work Rows 3–27 (27, 36, 36, 36) of Lower Gusset Chart—354 (390, 438, 474, 510) sts, with 154 (172, 190, 208, 226) sts each for front and back, and 23 (23, 29, 29, 29) sts for each gusset. Piece should measure about 16½ (16, 16½, 17, 17½)" (42 [40.5, 42, 43, 44.5] cm) from beg.

DIVIDING FRONT AND BACK

Break yarn and place 23 (23, 29, 29, 29) sts on holder or waste yarn for gusset, join yarn and work 154 (172, 190, 208, 226) front sts in est patt, place next 23 (23, 29, 29, 29) sts on a holder or waste yarn for gusset, then rem 154 (172, 190, 208, 226) back sts on waste yarn—154 (172, 190, 208, 226) sts rem for front.

UPPER BODY

FRONT

Work back and forth in est patt, until front measures about 23¾ (23¾, 24¾ 25¾, 26¾)" (60.5 [60.5, 63, 65.5, 68] cm) from beg, ending with WS row. (If you find you have to cable on the WS, break yarn and rejoin at other end of the front so the cabling occurs on the RS rows.)

Work last 2 rows of Snakes Motif Chart as follows:

Dec row: (RS) *P2, k6, p2, [ssk] twice, [k2tog] twice; rep from * to last 10 sts, p2, k6, p2—122 (136, 150, 164, 178) sts rem.

Next row: (WS) Purl. Place rem sts on waste yarn.

BACK

Return 154 (172, 190, 208, 226) held back sts to longer larger cir needle. Join yarn to beg with a RS row (if you have to cable on the wrong side, just break the yarn and rejoin at the other end of the back so the cabling occurs on RS rows). Work back same as front. Place rem 122 (136, 150, 164, 178) sts on waste yarn.

SHOULDER JOIN

If initials were not worked, you may wish to place a marker on the front to distinguish it from the back.

LEFT SHOULDER AND GUSSET

Place 40 (45, 50, 54, 59) front sts to one dpn, and 40 (45, 50, 54, 59) back sts to second dpn or opposite ends of longer larger cir needle with needle tips at armhole. Holding pieces with WS tog in LH (RS of left front is facing) and dpn in RH, join yarn at armhole and work Three-Needle Bind-off (see page 79) until 7 sts rem on each of shoulder needles, and 1 st on RH dpn.

Turn work so that RS is facing.

Holding dpn with single rem st in RH and cir with left front shoulder sts in LH, work Neck Gusset Chart as follows:

Row 1: (RS) First st of chart is already on RH needle, k1 from front left shoulder, turn.

Row 2: (WS) Sl 1 pwise wyf, p1, discard empty dpn, p1 from back shoulder, turn.

Row 3: Sl 1 kwise wyb, k2, k1 from front shoulder, turn.

Work Rows 4–15 of Neck Gusset Chart as est—15 neck gusset sts. Place sts on holder.

RIGHT SHOULDER AND GUSSET

Place 40 (45, 50, 54, 59) front sts to one dpn, and 40 (45, 50, 54, 59) back sts to second dpn or opposite ends of longer larger cir needle with needle tips at armhole. WIth WS tog and RS of right back shoulder facing and in LH, join yarn at armhole and work Three-Needle Bind-off as for left shoulder.

Begin the neck gusset by holding the right back shoulder needle in LH.

NECKBAND

With shorter larger cir needle and RS facing, purl rem 42 (46, 50, 56, 60) held back sts, p15 neck gusset sts, purl rem 42 (46, 50, 56, 60) held front sts, then p15 neck gusset sts—114 (122, 130, 142, 150) sts. Pm for beg of rnd and join to work in rnds.

Rnd 1: Purl.

Rnd 2: Knit.

Rep Rnds 1 and 2 until neckband measures 1¼" (3.2 cm), end with a purl rnd. BO all sts loosely pwise.

SLEEVES

UPPER GUSSET

Note: When picking up sts along the vertical armhole edges, use the adjacent ladder as a guide, picking up 5 sts between each garter st "rung."

Return 23 (23, 29, 29, 29) held gusset sts to shorter larger cir needle. Join yarn with RS facing.

Next rnd: P1, k10 (10, 13, 13, 13), p1, k10 (10, 13, 13, 13), p1, pm, pick up and knit 106 (112, 120, 126, 134) sts evenly around armhole—129 (135, 149, 155, 163) sts. Pm for beg of rnd and join to work in rnds.

Dec rnd: P1, k1, ssk, k7 (7, 10, 10, 10), p1, k7 (7, 10, 10, 10), k2tog, k1, p1, sl m, p27 (30, 34, 37, 41), pm, p52, pm, p27 (30, 34, 37, 41) sts—2 gusset sts dec'd.

Next rnd: Work Row 12 (12, 3, 3, 3) of Upper Gusset Chart to m, sl m, knit to m, sl m, work Row 1 of Sleeve Chart to m, sl m, knit to end of rnd—139 (145, 159, 165, 173) sts, with 118 (124, 132, 138, 146) sleeve sts and 21 (21, 27, 27, 27) gusset sts.

Note: Sleeve Chart should be centered on the shoulder seam.

Cont in est patt, work Rows 13 (13, 4, 4, 4)–36 of Upper Gusset Chart, work Rows 2–17 of Sleeve Chart 5 times, then work Rows 18 and 19 once. **At the same time,** when Upper Gusset Chart has been completed, and 123 (129, 137, 143, 151) sts rem, begin sleeve shaping.

Dec rnd: [P1, k1] twice, p1, sl m, ssk, work in est patt to last 2 sts, k2tog—2 sts dec'd.

Rep dec rnd every 6 rnds 20 (15, 0, 0, 0) times, every 5 rnds 3 (10, 23, 20, 12) times, then every 4 rnds 0 (0, 5, 10, 21) times. Change to larger dpn when there are too few sts to work comfortably on cir needle. **At the same time,** when Sleeve Chart has been completed, sleeve should measure about 8" (20.5 cm) from pick-up.

SLEEVE DEFINITION RIDGE

Change to smaller dpn and work in garter st over all sts for 1" (2.5 cm) as for body definition ridge and cont dec as est.

LOWER SLEEVE

Change back to larger dpn. Cont in St st with seam sts in rib, cont dec as est—63 (65, 67, 69, 71) sts rem.

Work even until sleeve measures 18 (18½, 19, 19½, 20)" (45.5 [47, 48.5, 49.5, 51] cm) from pick-up.

CUFF

Rnd 1: Knit and dec 4 sts evenly spaced— 59 (61, 63, 65, 67) sts rem.

Work in garter st for 1" (2.5 cm), ending with a purl rnd. BO all sts loosely pwise.

FINISHING

Weave in ends. Block to measurements.

INVERTED TRIANGULAR NECK GUSSET CHART

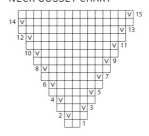

UPPER GUSSET CHART

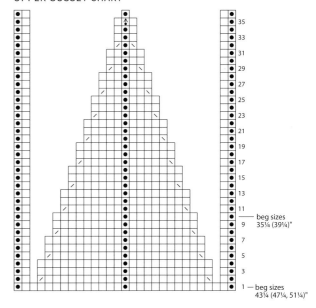

beg sizes 35¼ (39¼)"

beg sizes 43¼ (47¼, 51¼)"

SLEEVE CHART

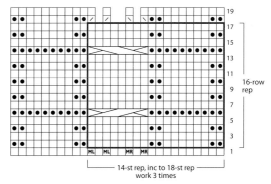

16-row rep

14-st rep, inc to 18-st rep work 3 times

KEY

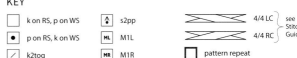

☐ k on RS, p on WS	⬆ s2pp	⤬ 4/4 LC
● p on RS, k on WS	ML M1L	⤬ 4/4 RC
╱ k2tog	MR M1R	☐ pattern repeat
╲ ssk	V sl 1 wyb on RS, sl 1 wyf on WS	

see Stitch Guide

SCHEMATIC

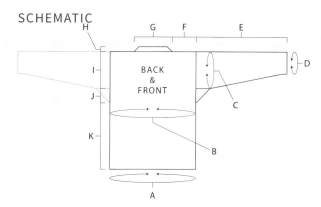

A 36¼ (40¼, 44¼, 48¼, 52¼)" (92 [102, 112.5, 122.5, 132.5] cm)

B 35¼ (39¼, 43¼, 47¼, 51¼)" (89.5 [90.5, 110, 120, 130] cm)

C 13¾ (14¼, 15¼, 16, 16¾)" (35 [36, 38.5, 40.5, 42.5] cm)

D 9 (9¼, 9½, 9¾, 10¼)" (23 [23.5, 24, 25, 26] cm)

E 19 (19½, 20, 20½, 21)" (48.5 [49.5, 51, 52, 53.5] cm)

F 4¾ (5½, 6¼, 6 ¾, 7½)" (12 [14, 16, 17, 19] cm)

G 8 (8½, 9 1/4, 10, 10½)" (20.5 [21.5, 23.5, 25.5, 26.5] cm)

H 1¼" (3.2 cm)

I 7½ (8, 8½, 9, 9½)" (19 [20.5, 21.5, 23, 24] cm)

J 2½ (2½, 3½, 3½, 3½)" (6.5 [6.5, 9, 9, 9] cm)

K 14 (13½, 13, 13½, 14)" (35 [33.5, 33, 34.5, 35.5] cm)

Although ganseys historically have been pullovers, cardigans are eminently practical for modern wear. I designed this garment for the first edition of Knitting Ganseys *to create a sweater that was beautifully patterned without the use of cables. I have added more sizes and neck shaping for this edition of the book.*

grace's cardigan

FINISHED SIZES

Chest circumference, buttoned:
35¾ (40¼, 44¼, 48¼, 52¼, 56¼)"
(91 [102, 112.5, 122.5, 132.5, 143] cm).

Length:
23 (24, 25, 26, 27, 28)"
(58.5 [61, 63.5, 66, 68.5, 71] cm).

Sample shown measures 35¾" (91 cm).

YARN

#2 Sportweight.
1747 (2049, 2337, 2647, 2971, 3312) yd
(1597 [1874, 2137, 2420, 2717, 3028] m).

Shown here: Frangipani 5-ply Guernsey
(100% wool; 240 yds [220 m]/3½ oz [100 g]):
Cedar, 8 (9, 10, 12, 13, 14) skeins.

NEEDLES

US 1 (2.25 mm): 16" and 32" (40 and 80 cm)
circular (cir) and set of 4 or 5 double-pointed (dpn).

Optional: US 0 (2 mm): 16" and 32" (40 and 80 cm)
cir for definition ridges of sleeve and body.

*Adjust needle size if necessary to achieve
the correct gauge.*

NOTIONS

Stitch markers (m); stitch holders or waste yarn;
ten ½" to ⅝" (13 to 16 mm) buttons; ten ½" to ⅝"
(13 to 16 mm) clear backing buttons; tapestry needle.

GAUGE

28 sts and 43 rows/rnds = 4" (10 cm) in St st
using larger needles.

FEATURED TECHNIQUES

Channel Island Cast-on, Split Garter-stitch Welts,
Underarm Gussets, Shaped Neckline, Alternate
Provisional Cast-on, Perpendicular Shoulder Join.

NOTES

Because this is a cardigan, it is worked back and
forth as one piece with a front opening. The back
is joined to the front at the sides from the top of
the welts to the armholes. The buttonband and
buttonhole band are worked as part of the two
front pieces. Once the underarm gussets are knitted
and placed on holders, the back and the two fronts
are knitted separately. The shoulders are joined
with shoulder straps, then the sleeves are picked
up and knitted down to the cuff. The neckband is
the last thing to finish. Due to the placement of the
buttonholes, row counts have been given instead of
measurements for increased accuracy.

READING THE CHARTS

The charts show all sts as they will appear on the RS of the work. Be sure to work the correct number of 2-stitch repeats noted on the Body and Sleeve Charts for your size.

THE CHARTS FOR BACK AND FRONTS

Row 1: (RS) Beg at right edge of Body Chart, work from A to B for right front, work 2 seam sts from Gusset Chart, work Body Chart from C to D for right back, reading same chart row from left to right, work from E to C for left back, work 2 seam sts from Gusset Chart, then work from B to A for left front.

Row 2: (WS) Beg at right edge of Body Chart, work from A to B for left front, work 2 seam sts from Gusset Chart, work Body Chart from C to D for left back, reading same chart row from left to right, work from E to C, work 2 seam sts from Gusset Chart, then work from B to A for right front.

THE SLEEVE CHART

The shoulder strap is shown truncated in the chart. Due to the different sizes, the patterning for your strap may not coincide with the chart after the break in the strap. Once all the shoulder stitches are incorporated into the shoulder strap, sleeve stitches are picked up. The sleeves are worked in the round, beginning from the RH side of the gusset. Work from G to F, then from E to H, working the correct number of 2-stitch repeats for the desired size.

GARTER-STITCH SPLIT WELTS

BACK

With longer larger cir needle, CO 116 (138, 146, 164, 178, 188) sts using Channel Island Cast-on (see page 19). Do not join.

Work in garter st (knit every row) for about 1½" (3.8 cm), or 21 rows. Set aside.

LEFT FRONT

With shorter larger cir needle, CO 64 (68, 76, 80, 84, 92) sts using Channel Island Cast-on. Do not join.

Work in garter st for about 1½" (3.8 cm), or 21 rows. Set aside.

RIGHT FRONT

With shorter larger cir needle, CO 64 (68, 76, 80, 84, 92) sts using the Channel Island Cast-on. Do not join.

Work in garter st for about 1½" (3.8 cm), or 21 rows. Do not break yarn.

Joining (inc) row: (RS) Knit right front sts and inc 3 (3, 5, 5, 7, 7) sts evenly spaced. With same side of back and left front facing (make sure 11 purl ridges are facing), knit back sts and inc 7 (9, 9, 11, 13, 15) sts evenly spaced, then knit left front sts and inc 3 (3, 5, 5, 7, 7) sts evenly spaced—257 (289, 317, 345, 373, 401) sts. Do not join.

LOWER BODY

When beginning each row, slip the first stitch of the buttonbands. On WS rows, slip the stitch purlwise, with the yarn in front. On RS rows, slip the stitch knitwise, with the yarn in back. These slipped sts will give a smooth edge to the buttonbands.

Begin the buttonband pattern on each edge of the garment opening while working St st for the body and seed seam sts at the side seams (located at the bottom of the Gusset Chart). The first buttonhole is worked at the end of this WS row as follows:

Set-up row: (WS) Sl 1 pwise, [p1, k1] 4 times, p57 (61, 71, 75, 81, 89), place marker (pm) for seam sts, p1, k1, pm, p121 (145, 153, 173, 189, 201), pm, p1, k1, pm, p57 (61, 71, 75, 81, 89), [k1, p1] twice, drop yarn, join a second ball of yarn for buttonhole and sl 1 pwise, p1, k1, p2.

Next row: (RS) Sl 1 kwise, k4, drop yarn and pick up yarn from main ball, sl 1 kwise, [knit to m, sl m, k1, p1, sl m] twice, knit to end of row.

Next row: Sl 1 pwise, [p1, k1] 4 times, p57 (61, 71, 75, 81, 89), sl m, p1, k1, sl m, p121 (145, 153, 173, 189, 201), sl m, p1, k1, sl m, p57 (61, 71, 75, 81, 89), [k1, p1] twice, drop yarn, pick up yarn from second ball, sl 1 pwise, p1, k1, p2.

Next row: Work same as last RS row and work initials, beg 6 sts after seam sts m of left front.

Next row: Work in est patt.

Next row: Sl 1 kwise, knit to buttonhole, break yarn from second ball of yarn, and using main ball of yarn, cont in est patt to end of row.

Notes: The 10 buttonholes are grouped in 5 sets of 2. Each buttonhole is worked over 5 rows, with 13 rows after the end of 1 buttonhole and the start of the next buttonhole in that set. Work 26 (29, 31, 34, 37, 39) *rows between the last buttonhole in one set and the start of the first buttonhole in the next set. Buttonholes may not always begin on a WS row.*

Cont in est patt until initials are complete, then work in St st (knit RS rows, purl WS rows) working seam sts as est, until 81 (91, 101, 113, 123, 135) rows have been worked above bottom welts, ending with a RS row. Piece should measure about 9 (10, 11, 12, 13, 14)" (23 [25.5, 28, 30.5, 33, 35.5] cm) from beg.

DEFINITION RIDGE

Change to longer smaller cir needle if desired. Keeping buttonbands and seam sts in est patt, work 11 rows in garter st over rem sts, ending with a WS row.

Change back to longer larger cir needle if necessary.

Keeping seam sts in est patt, work Body Chart for your size until piece measures 12 (12½, 13, 13½, 14, 14½)" (30.5 [31.5, 33, 34.5, 35.5, 37] cm) from beg, ending with a WS row.

UNDERARM GUSSETS

Row 1: (RS) *Work in est patt to seam st m, sl m, work seam st, M1R, work seam st, sl m; rep from * once more, then work to end of row—2 gusset sts inc'd.

Work Rows 2–30 of Lower Gusset Chart as est—299 (331, 359, 387, 415, 443) sts, with 66 (70, 80, 84, 90, 98) sts for each front, 121 (145, 153, 173, 189, 201) sts for back, and 23 sts for each gusset and seam sts. Break yarn. Place sts for both fronts and gussets on separate holders or waste yarn—121 (145, 153, 173, 189, 201) sts rem for back.

UPPER BODY

BACK

Join yarn and cont even in est patt until 5 motifs in the main panels have been worked (Starfish, Diamond, Starfish, Diamond, Starfish), and Row 102 has been worked for the second time. Armholes should measure about 7 (7½, 8, 8½, 9, 9½)" (18 [19, 20.5, 21.5, 23, 24] cm).

LOWER GUSSET CHART

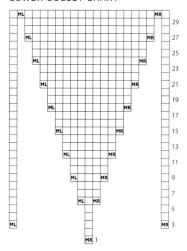

SEAM STITCH CHART

KEY

☐ k on RS, p on WS	MR M1R
● p on RS, k on WS	ML M1L

Next row: Work 41 (45, 51, 54, 60, 65) sts in est patt, join a second ball of yarn and BO 39 (55, 51, 65, 69, 71) sts for neck, then work to end of row—41 (45, 51, 54, 60, 65) sts rem for each shoulder.

Working both sides at the same time with separate balls of yarn, work 1 more row over each shoulder. Break yarns and place sts on holders or waste yarn.

LEFT FRONT

Return 66 (70, 80, 84, 90, 98) held left front sts to shorter larger cir needle. Work in est patt to Row 104, then work Rows 49–93 again.

SHAPE LEFT FRONT NECK

Next Row: (WS) BO 21 (21, 25, 26, 26, 29) sts, then work to end of row—45 (49, 55, 58, 64, 69) sts rem.

Cont in est patt and dec 1 st at neck edge every RS row 4 times—41 (45, 51, 54, 60, 65) sts rem.

Work even to Row 104. Place rem sts on holder.

RIGHT FRONT

Return 66 (70, 84, 90, 98) held right front sts to shorter larger cir needle. Work in est patt to Row 104, then work Rows 49–94 again.

BODY CHART

center of back

D   E   2-st rep—work 3 (4, 5, 7, 8, 9) times

2-st rep—work 3 (4, 5, 7, 8, 9) times   C   B   2-st rep—work 3 (4, 5, 6, 7, 8) times

2-st rep— work 2 (4, 6, 7, 9, 10) times   2-st rep—work 2 (4, 5, 6, 7, 8) times

work seam sts, work gusset

KEY

☐ k on RS, p on WS   ⊡ p on RS, k on WS   ☐ pattern repeat

buttonband
buttonhole band

103
101
99
97
95
93
91
89
87
85
83
81

work 2 times

79
77
75
73
71
69
67
65
63
61
59
57
55
53
51
49
47
45
43
41
39
37
35
33
31
29
27
25
23
21
19
17
15
13

defining ridge

11
9
7
5

2-row rep for lower body

3
1

2-st rep—work 3 (4, 5, 5, 6, 8) times

A

SLEEVE CHART

4-st rep work 8 times

2-st rep work 3 (4, 5, 6, 7, 8) times

2-st rep work 2 (3, 4, 5, 6, 7) times

Upper Gusset

Shoulder Strap

KEY

☐ k on RS, p on WS	⋀ s2kp
● p on RS, k on WS	∨ sl 1 wyb on RS, sl 1 wyf on WS
╱ k2tog on RS, p2tog on WS	☐ pattern repeat
╲ ssk on RS	

SHAPE RIGHT FRONT NECK

Next row: (RS) BO 21 (21, 25, 26, 26, 29) sts, then work to end of row—45 (49, 55, 58, 64, 69) sts rem.

Cont in est patt and dec 1 st at neck edge every WS row 4 times—41 (45, 51, 54, 60, 65) sts rem.

Work even to Row 104. Place rem sts on a holder.

SHOULDER STRAPS

Note: The Shoulder Strap Chart rows are read back and forth. Because the different garment sizes will result in varying lengths of the shoulder strap, your shoulder strap pattern may not correspond to the pattern repeat shown in the chart after the "break," where the sleeve sts will be picked up.

LEFT SHOULDER

With dpn, CO 13 sts using Alternate Provisional Cast-on (see page 74).

Knit 2 rows with contrast yarn. Break off contrast color, turn. Join main color yarn, and knit 1 row. Set aside.

Return 41 (45, 51, 54, 60, 65) held sts for left front to one dpn and 41 (45, 51, 54, 60, 65) held sts for left back to second dpn or opposite ends of longer larger cir needle with needle tips at neck.

With RS of back facing and holding that needle in your LH, hold needle with shoulder strap sts in your RH, k1 from back, then pass last strap st over, turn.

Row 1: (WS) Work Row 1 of Strap Chart to last st of strap, purl tog last st of strap with 1 st from neck edge of front shoulder, turn.

Row 2: (RS) Work Row 2 of Strap Chart to last st of strap, ssk last st of strap with 1 st from back shoulder, turn.

Rep Rows 1 and 2 until all shoulder sts are used up—13 strap sts rem. Place strap sts on holder.

RIGHT SHOULDER

Beg strap for right shoulder same as left shoulder. Return held right front and back sts to needles same as left shoulder.

With RS of front facing and holding that needle in your LH, hold needle with shoulder strap sts in your RH, k1 from front, then pass last strap st over, turn.

Row 1: (WS) Work Row 1 of Strap Chart to last st of strap, purl tog last st of strap with 1 st from neck edge of back shoulder, turn..

Row 2: (RS) Work Row 2 of Strap Chart to last st of strap, ssk last st of strap with 1 st from front shoulder, turn.

Rep Rows 1 and 2 until all shoulder sts are used up—13 strap sts rem. Place strap sts on holder.

NECKBAND

Carefully remove contrast color yarn from Provisional Cast-on of both shoulder straps and place 13 sts of both straps on holders or waste yarn.

With shorter cir needle and RS facing, pick up and knit 21 (21, 25, 26, 26, 29) sts along BO sts of right front neck, 7 sts along sloped edge of right front neck, knit 13 held shoulder strap sts, pick up and knit 38 (54, 50, 64, 68, 70) sts across back neck, knit 13 held shoulder strap sts, pick up and knit 7 sts along sloped edge of left front neck, then pick up and knit 21 (21, 25, 26, 26, 29) sts along BO sts of left front neck—120 (136, 140, 156, 160, 168) sts.

Row 1: (WS) Work 9 sts in est patt for button-band, [k2, p2] to last 11 sts, k2, work 9 sts in est patt for buttonhole band.

Work 3 (3, 3, 2, 2, 2) more rows as est. Work last buttonhole over next 5 rows, then work 3 (3, 3, 4, 4, 4) more rows. BO all sts loosely in patt.

SLEEVES

With shorter larger cir needle and RS facing, knit 23 held gusset and seam sts, pick up and knit 50 (54, 58, 62, 66, 70) sts along armhole to strap sts, work 13 strap sts in est patt, then pick up and knit 50 (54, 58, 62, 66, 70) sts along armhole—136 (144, 152, 160, 168, 176) sts. Pm for beg of rnd and join to work in rnds.

Work Rows 1–30 of Sleeve Chart, decreasing 2 sts of the gusset every third rnd—115 (123, 131, 139, 147, 155) sts rem. Begin sleeve shaping.

Dec rnd: Work 2 seam sts as est, k1, k2tog, work in est patt to last 3 sts, ssk, k1—2 sts dec'd.

Rep dec rnd every 7 rnds 14 (7, 0, 0, 0, 0) times, every 6 rnds 8 (17, 21, 7, 7, 0) times, every 5 rnds 0 (0, 5, 23, 23, 26) times, then every 4 rnds 0 (0, 0, 0, 0, 8) times—69 (73, 77, 77, 85, 85) sts rem. Change to dpn when there are too few sts to work comfortably on cir needle.

At the same time, when sleeve measures about 8" (20.5 cm) from pick-up, work 11 rnds of garter st (purl 1 rnd, knit 1 rnd), keeping seam sts in est patt. *Note: Use shorter smaller cir needle if desired for this section, then change back to shorter larger needle to cont with rest of sleeve.* When definition ridge is complete, cont in St st (knit every rnd), keeping seam sts in est patt.

CUFF

When dec are complete, cont even until sleeve measures 16 (16½, 16½, 17, 17, 17½)" (40.5 [42, 42, 43, 43, 44.5] cm) from pick-up, or 3" (7.5 cm) shorter than desired length.

Next rnd: Knit and dec 1 (5, 5, 5, 9, 9) st(s) evenly spaced—68 (68, 72, 72, 76, 76) sts rem.

Next rnd: [P2, k2] around.

Rep last rnd until ribbing measures 3" (7.5 cm), taking care that seam sts are worked p2.

BO all sts loosely in patt.

FINISHING

Weave in ends. Block to measurements. Sew buttons to buttonband opposite buttonholes (see page 169 for sewing on and backing buttons).

SCHEMATIC

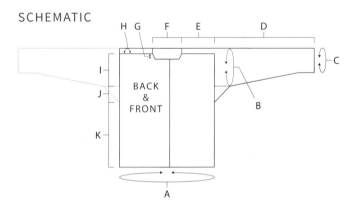

A   36¾ (41¼, 45¼, 49¼, 53¼, 57¼)" (93.5 [105, 115, 125, 135.5, 145.5] cm) including 1" (2.5 cm) overlap

B   16½ (17½, 18¾, 19¾, 21, 22¼)" (42 [44.5, 47.5, 50, 53.5, 56.5] cm)

C   9¾ (10½, 11, 11, 12¼, 12¼)" (25 [26.5, 28, 28, 31, 31] cm)

D   19 (19½, 20, 20½, 21, 21½)" (48.5 [49.5, 51, 52, 53.5, 54.5] cm)

E   5¾ (6½, 7¼, 7¾, 8½, 9¼)" (14.5 [16.5, 18.5, 19.5, 21.5, 23.5] cm)

F   5½ (7¾, 7¼, 9¼, 9¾, 10¼)" (14 [19.5, 18.5, 23.5, 25, 26] cm)

G   1" (2.5 cm)

H   1¾" (4.5 cm)

I   7 (7½, 8, 8½, 9, 9½)" (18 [19, 20.5, 21.5, 23, 24] cm)

J   3" (7.5 cm)

K   12 (12½, 13, 13½, 14, 14½)" (30.5 [31.5, 33, 34.5, 35.5, 37] cm)

sources and supplies

BOOKS

Some of these classic books are out of print, but keep an eye out for secondhand copies available at used and online booksellers.

Compton, Rae. *The Complete Book of Traditional Guernsey and Jersey Knitting.* New York: Arco, 1985.

Domnick, Sabine. *Cables, Diamonds, Herringbone.* Maine: Down East, 2007.

Gibson-Roberts, Priscilla. *Knitting in the Old Way.* Fort Collins, Colorado: Nomad Press, 2004.

Hemingway, Penelope Lister. *River Ganseys.* Lakewood, Ohio: Cooperative Press, 2015.

Hiatt, June Hemmons. *Principles of Knitting.* New York: Touchstone, 2012.

Lovick, Elizabeth. *A Gansey Workbook: Techniques, History, Patterns and More for Beginners and Experts Alike.* Northern Lace Press. 2009, www.northernlace.co.uk.

Michelson, Carmen, and Mary Ann Davis. *The Knitter's Guide to Sweater Design.* Loveland, Colorado: Interweave, 1984.

Pearson, Michael. *Traditional Knitting: Aran, Fair Isle and Fisher Ganseys.* New York: Van Nostrand Reinhold, 1984. Dover, 2015.

Ruhe, Stella. *Dutch Traditional Ganseys: Sweaters from 40 Villages.* Kent, England: Search Press, 2014.

Ruhe, Stella. *More Dutch Traditional Ganseys.* Kent, England: Search Press, 2017.

Rutt, Richard. *A History of Handknitting.* Loveland, Colorado: Interweave, 2003.

Thomas, Mary. *Mary Thomas's Knitting Book.* New York: Dover, 1972.

Thompson, Gladys. *Patterns for Guernseys, Jerseys, and Arans.* New York: Dover, 1979.

van der Klift-Tellegen, Henriette. *Knitting from the Netherlands.* Asheville, North Carolina: Lark Books, 1985.

Walker, Barbara G. *A Treasury of Knitting Patterns.* Pittsville, Wisconsin: Schoolhouse Press, 1998.

Wright, Mary. *Cornish Guernseys & Knit-frocks.* Clifton-upon-Teme, England: Polperro Heritage Press, 2008.

OTHER RESOURCES

BETH'S WEBSITE
www.KnittingTraditions.com

THE CORDOVA GANSEY PROJECT
www.thenetloftak.com/pages/cordova-gansey-project

THE MORAY FIRTH GANSEY PROJECT
Fishing for Ganseys, 2014.
www.gansey-mf.co.uk

LE TRICOTEUR
(machine-made ganseys)
www.guernseyjumpers.com

SCRANN
(national online archive of Moray Firth)
www.scran.ac.uk

TOOLS
Goose-wing knitting sticks, needles, wooly boards, and knitter's graph paper
www.KnittingTraditions.com

KNITTING BELTS (US)
www.principlesofknitting.com

CHARTING PROGRAMS

Stitch Mastery (Mac or Windows):
www.stitchmastery.com

Stitch Painter (Mac or Windows):
www.cochenille.com/stitch-painter

EnvisioKnit (Windows 8/7/Vista/XP):
www.envisioknit.com

Intwined (Mac or Windows):
www.intwinedstudio.com

Knit Visualizer (Mac or Windows):
www.knitfoundry.com/software.html

YARNS

TRADITIONAL GUERNSEY YARNS

BLACKER YARNS, UK
www.blackeryarns.co.uk
enquiries@blackeryarns.co.uk

FRANGIPANI, UK
www.guernseywool.co.uk
jan@guernseywool.co.uk

HANDKNITTING.COM, USA
www.handknitting.com
laurel@handknitting.com

R.E. DICKIE LTD, UK
www.britishwool.com
sales@dickie.co.uk

SCHOOLHOUSE PRESS, USA
www.schoolhousepress.com
info@schoolhousepress.com

UPTON YARNS, USA
www.uptonyarns.com
uptonyarns@gmail.com

OTHER YARNS USED IN THIS BOOK

BROWN SHEEP COMPANY, USA
www.brownsheep.com
Locate a retailer:
www.brownsheep.com/locate-retailer

QUINCE AND CO., USA
www.quinceandco.com
orders@quinceandco.com

abbreviations

beg	begin(s), beginning	psso	pass slipped sts over
BO	bind off	p2tog	purl 2 together
cir	circular	p3tog	purl 3 together
cn	cable needle	pm	place marker
CO	cast on	pwise	purl-wise, as if to purl
cont	continue(s), continuing	rem	remain(s); remaining
dec('d)	decrease(d), decreasing	rep	repeat
dpn	double-pointed needle(s)	RH	right hand
est	established	rnd(s)	round(s)
inc('d)	increase(s), increasing	RS	right side
k	knit	s2kp	sl 2 tog kwise, k1, psso
k2tog	knit 2 together	s2pp	slip 2 tog pwise tbl, p1, pass slipped sts over
k3tog	knit 3 together		
kwise	knit-wise, as if to knit	sk2p	sl1, k2tog, psso
LH	left hand	sl	slip
m	marker(s)	ssk	slip, slip, knit
M1L	Left leaning Make 1 increase	st(s)	stitch(es)
M1LP	Pick up the bar between 2 sts from front to back, purl through back loop.	St st	Stockinette stitch
		tbl	through back loop
		tog	together
M1R	Right leaning Make 1 increase	wyb	with yarn in back
M1RP	Pick up the bar between 2 sts from back to front, purl into front.	wyf	with yarn in front
		WS	wrong side
p	purl	yo	yarnover

metric conversion

To Convert	To	Multiply By
Inches	Centimeters	2.54
Centimeters	Inches	0.4
Feet	Centimeters	30.5
Centimeters	Feet	0.03
Yards	Meters	0.9
Meter	Yards	1.1

DEDICATION

I dedicate this book to all knitters. . .to those who were innovators long ago, to those today who expand this craft through creative explorations of the limits, to my many students, colleagues, and dear friends who have given me so much. I thank you all.

ACKNOWLEDGMENTS

As with the first edition, my humble thanks go to Elizabeth Zimmermann and Priscilla Gibson-Roberts for their contributions to knitting; and for inspiring me to learn, teach, design, and write—all about knitting! Thanks to Dorothea Malsbary for her vision of this book. I owe so very much to Carolyn Vance, my right-hand woman who knits for me, as my own hands become ever more fragile, and who cajoles me gently to keep designing, while editing my hastily written patterns. Nancy Spies generously shared all of her charted medieval alphabets with me so that I could create more interesting alphabets for this book and future ganseys! And, I am indebted to Margaret Klein Wilson and Carolyn Vance, for reading the manuscript and offering extremely helpful suggestions and encouragement as I edited to the final hour.

I must also thank some really awesome knitters: Carolyn Vance, Holly Neiding, David Ritz, Lesli Lanteigne, John G. Crane, and Charles Gandy who knitted many of the garments.

I truly appreciate the generosity of Frangipani, Upton Yarns, and Quince & Co. for the use of their beautiful yarns.

Deep thanks also go to Kathryn Logan of the Moray Firth Gansey Project, the Dales Countryside Museum, the Sutcliffe Gallery, the Wick Society (Johnston Collection), and Norman Kennedy who all generously gave me access to many photographs. I want to thank all the behind-the-scenes people at Interweave who worked on this book and Therese Chynoweth and Maya Elson, in particular, for their patience with me during this process. It's never easy to write a book. Any mistakes left here are all mine.

And, as always, to each of my children, Jorn, Chloë, Terran, and Chelsea…all my love…to infinity and beyond!

about the author

Beth Brown-Reinsel has been teaching historic knitting techniques throughout North America for around three decades. She has also taught extensively in New Zealand and Europe. Encouraging the education and creativity of knitters is her main objective. She has produced three DVDs, more than thirty workshops, and many patterns, which are all created to expand knitters' skills and understanding of their beloved craft. Beth lives in Vermont and loves winter! Learn more about her workshops, patterns, tools, and kits at www.knittingtraditions.com.

index

A
abbreviations 187
alternate provisional cast-on 74
Aran sweaters 41
armhole stitches, picking up 89

B
baby cable 59
bind-offs 79;
    ssk 126, 164;
    three-needle 79
body chart, creating 107–112
body sampler 40
blocking 100
buttoned neckband 96

C
cables 59
cable splay 55
cast-ons 16–17, 19–22, 74;
    Channel Island 17, 18, 19;
    invisible 74;
    knitted 18, 20;
    knotted 17, 20;
    long-tail 20, 21, 22;
    provisional 74;
    alternate provisional 74
cast-on sampler 18
Channel Island cast-on 17, 18, 19
chart, gansey sampler 31
charts, body 107–111;
    motif 42–53;
    reading 32, 66;
    sleeve 90–91
charts:
    alphabet 35;
    anchors 47;
    Betty Martin 39;
    body sampler 40, 108;
    cable 111–112;
    chevrons 44–45;
    diagonal purl lines 44;
    diamond 45–47;
    double moss stitch 42;
    flags 48;
    gansey sampler 31;
    gusset 63;
    hearts 47;

horizontal 52–53;
Humber star 39;
initial (blank) 36;
inverted triangular neck gusset 97;
other background patterns 43;
patterning 86, 110;
moss stitch 42;
neckband 94;
neckline 71;
partial body 58, 68;
seam stitches 60–62;
seed stitch 42;
shoulder strap 76;
shoulder strap gusset 99;
sleeve 85, 91, 114;
 starfish 47;
trees 48;
vertical 49–50;
vertical herringbone 44;
vertical with cables 51–52;
zigzags and marriage lines 43
collar, rolled 95
Complete Book of Traditional Guernsey and Jersey Knitting, The 8
Compton, Rae 8, 10, 38
construction of gansey 14–15
cuffs 15, 88

D
decreases, double 83
definition ridge 15, 29
designing 102–115
design worksheet 115

E
edge, multistrand ribbed 22
ends, sewing in 100

F
finishing 100
fishing industry 37, 41
fit, adjusting 107
folded ribbed neckband 96

G
ganseys,
    form and construction 14–15, 41;
    history of 8–11
gansey knitters 13

Gansey Workbook, A 11
garter stitch 24–26
garter welts 24–26
garter-welt sampler 25
gauge 22, 26, 54–55
Gibson-Roberts, Priscilla 23, 72
graph paper 54
guernseys 8, 10
gussets 15;
    inverted triangular neck 97;
    neck 92;
    shoulder-strap neck 98–99;
    underarm 56, 60–63
gusset sampler 58
gusset shaping 60–63

H
History of Handknitting, A 8

I
initials 29, 34;
    blank chart 36
inverted triangular neck gusset 97
invisible cast-on 74

K
knitted cast-on 18, 20
knitting flat 66–71
knotted cast-on 17, 20

L
long-tail cast-on 20, 21, 22
Lovick, Elizabeth 11
lower-body sampler chart 30, 40

M
make 1 (M1) increase 57
Mary Thomas's Knitting Book 24
measurements,
    design process for 104–105;
    percentage method 23, 104;
    sample for 103;
    table of 106
    metric conversion table 187
mock cable 59
motifs 38–55;
    charts for 42–53;
    creating chart for 54–55
multistrand cast-on 17, 22

explore more knitting techniques in depth

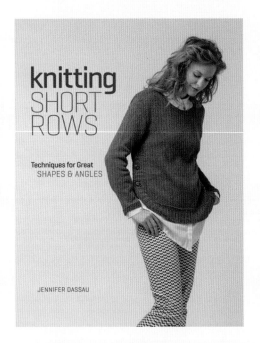

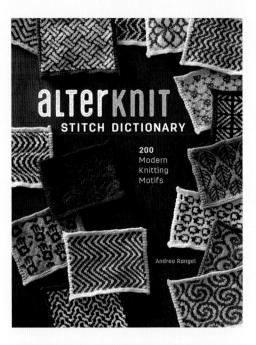

KNITTING SHORT ROWS
TECHNIQUES FOR GREAT SHAPES & ANGLES
by Jennifer Dassau
978-1-63250-258-2
$24.99

ALTERKNIT STITCH DICTIONARY
200 MODERN KNITTING MOTIFS
by Andrea Rangle
978-1-63250-553-8
$26.99

AVAILABLE AT YOUR FAVORITE RETAILER OR INTERWEAVE.COM

 Interweave®